MW01087541

IN THE
MASTER'S
BEDROOM

FINDING DIVINE LOVE
WITH A MODERN-DAY
SPIRITUAL MASTER

BY
MARCUS BOND, PH.D.
WITH JOSEPH GUNNELS

In The Master's Bedroom
Finding Divine Love with a Modern-Day Spiritual Master

By Marcus Bond, Ph.D., with Joseph Gunnels
Limited Edition

Foreword by Darrin Zeer, Best-Selling Author of "Office Yoga" and "Lover's Yoga"
www.darrinzeer.com

This book consists of the recollections, perspectives and viewpoints of its author Marcus Bond regarding his life, experiences and relationship with Kalindi La Gourasana. This book is solely the author's recollection and understanding of Kalindi's teachings and statements to him, including all direct quotes of Kalindi speaking, which is indicated by quote marks. These direct quotes of Kalindi speaking are the author's recollection of what Kalindi said and not necessarily Kalindi's actual words.

This book is not an official publication of Center of The Golden One®, nor does it represent the official position, teachings, quotations, viewpoints or necessarily express the views of Center of The Golden One or of Kalindi La Gourasana's or of her representatives or heirs.

The following are registered trademarks of Center of the Golden One®:
GMP® (Gourasana Meditation Practice®), Path to Ultimate Freedom®, The Intensive®, Miracle of Love®, Center of The Golden One®

ISBN: 978-0-692-52822-8

Library of Congress Control Number: 1-3201104961

Front and back Cover Design by Amundi Sigurdsson

Book Layout and typesetting by Dirk Gräßle

Legal Input provided by J.M. Sandlow, "The Guru Lawyer"
www.thegurulawyer.com

DEDICATION

To Kalindi La Gourasana

I loved you before I met you
You always pointed me towards God and the Highest
You knew my heart better than I
You loved me unconditionally
You showed me the way and continue to illuminate the path
This book is yours. I am yours – eternally.

WHO WAS KALINDI?

Kalindi – born Carol Seidman – started her spiritual journey at the age of 18 when she felt pulled to travel to the Holy Land of Israel. Born into the Jewish faith, Carol was surprised to find herself being deeply moved as she retraced the steps of Jesus along the shore of the Sea of Galilee.

Carol around 1973

On returning to the US, Carol met her first spiritual master, Swami Prabhupada, who introduced her to the path of Bhakti (devotional worship) yoga. During this same time Carol met David Swanson, the man through whom Lord Gourasana would one day make his presence known to the world. Over the next ten years, Carol and David formed a strong spiritual relationship, both searching for God and both wanting to find a way Home to God.

When Gourasana made His presence known to David, Carol knew that she too had found a way Home to God. Soon a group of six disciples formed around Carol and David. Together they were known as The Core. They recognized that the spiritual energy of Gourasana was coming directly from God. While David was opening to the energy of this modern-day Incarnation, the Divine energy of Kalindi was entering Carol. Kalindi's own surrender allowed her to soon become a fully-realized spiritual master, guiding The Core and others toward Union with God.

Kalindi spoke thousands of lectures and meditations to increase the overall consciousness of the planet. Her talks include help and guidance on how to get freer every day from the material illusion, become immersed in the love of God, and return Home to the spiritual realm.

From Kalindi about herself, 1995:

"In my service to God and mankind you can count on a few things from me for certain. First, I am a woman who is in love with God and therefore all of His Creation. My love for all of you is always present and always unconditional; nothing stops my flow of love to you. I love you as I love God and as He loves us – unconditionally."

"Second, I am here to carry His Presence, Love, Energy, Knowledge and Power to assist you in your transformation back to Him. I am here to bring inspiration and faith to those seeking Union, pure Love of God."

Kalindi 1995

"To allow yourself to be open to me and my presence and teachings in your life will connect you directly to the special power and assistance that He is bringing into this world today. It is not necessary to be in my physical presence to allow the link to be made and our relationship to be established. I live in order to be a circuit for you to plug into, for you to connect into the main power house which is God. I am a live socket; if you like, plug in and reap the benefits."

Kalindi left her body on April 18, 2010, having fulfilled her life's purpose. She is succeeded by her first disciple, The Lady, who continues Kalindi's work and now guides the Path to Ultimate Freedom. ♪

CONTENTS

CONTENTS

CONTENTS

CONTENTS

CONTENTS

CONTENTS

CONTENTS

A SPIRITUAL PHENOMENON

Foreword by Darrin Zeer

Best-Selling Author of "Office Yoga" and "Lover's Yoga"

My spiritual path kicked off when I travelled through Southeast Asia for seven years. That's where the idea of enlightenment got planted in me. I was your typical spiritual tourist, seeking answers to an emptiness I felt in my soul. This led me to my ongoing exploration of yoga and meditation during the last quarter century.

In a Tibetan monastery, I learned about breaking the cycle of suffering and moving into Nirvana – meaning true happiness and liberation. In Indian ashrams, I studied the deeper meaning of Yoga, Moksha, and spiritual union.

In Japan, I travelled the Zen road of enlightenment, Satori. I loved hearing from monks and yogis about the Eastern Masters who found their spiritual freedom. I found yoga and meditation to be a spiritual science for self-mastery.

After my return to America, I wrote about yoga and sold over half-a-million books. I became a best-selling author. My desire for spiritual freedom was my guiding light. But I had always felt that enlightenment was not accessible for an ordinary western guy like me. That was until I met Kalindi La Gourasana, a modern-day American Spiritual Master, two decades ago in California.

Kalindi was more of a spiritual phenomenon, than teacher. She burned bright like the fire of the Hindu Goddess, Kali. Being in her presence felt like a sizzling sensation and also a cleansing. She had only one desire – to "break people free from the cycle of birth and death" in this lifetime.

Kalindi had a large following of disciples and seekers. She guided us Westerners into living like modern-day yogis in the marketplace. She lived her own life intensely in the moment. Being around her was not for the faint of heart.

Although she passed away a few years ago, her message strongly echoes inside of me. I feel like her disciples are personal messengers of her unconditional love. She literally pushed me into living life in this moment, and for that I am eternally grateful.

How my friend, Marcus Bond, found this radical path to God is a mystery to me. In America, being a spiritual disciple is a rare life choice. It usually means working pro bono, without much job security. The hours are long and the control over your life is minimal. The main job requirement is to let go and surrender your entire being.

Marcus didn't seem to be that kind of guy. He seemed more like the guy you sat next to in an airport terminal or a bar and have a friendly chat with. He has the gift of being a friend to all. As it turns out, he is a secret weapon for God; you never see him coming, yet he leaves a lasting impact on everyone he meets.

His teaching is free of any tradition, ideology or belief system. He is not airy fairy or preachy. He offers spiritual wisdom like a sports writer from the NY Times. He offers one message – be yourself and live your life in as much freedom and choice as you can muster. He is continually shedding all his concepts of what it means to be free in this lifetime, and that is special and unique.

But then again, Kalindi was no ordinary Master. I had the good fortune to experience Kalindi in all her glory. I also had the honor and pleasure of witnessing Kalindi and Marcus' friendship evolve for over a decade.

Marcus was truly blessed to be a close friend and disciple of Kalindi. And I think Kalindi felt very blessed that a guy like Marcus could be with her, play with her, and meet her in the far out realms in which she existed. I observed that Marcus had the rare gift of being present with Kalindi – moment-by-moment, in all her glory and humanity. He got her, as a woman and as a Master.

Marcus still maintained his reverence and respect for Kalindi. But he also could make her laugh, and just chill with her. He could follow her every mood, which could change dramatically from one moment to the next.

I'll never forget the image over a decade ago of seeing Kalindi and Marcus relaxing side-by-side in Lazy Boy chairs, both laughing ecstatically about the future possibility of thousands of souls finding their way back Home – a very surreal image.

"In the Master's Bedroom" gives a glimpse into a modern-day Master's life from the perspective of her faithful disciple, friend, and companion. As you read this book, you will experience the true love that Kalindi shared so freely.

May this authentic story encourage you on your own path to more peace, love, and freedom. If guys like Marcus and I have a shot at spiritual freedom, then the gates to heaven must be open to all. May you find all that your heart desires.

Peace and Love,
Darrin Zeer

Denver, Colorado
December, 2015

www.darrinzeer.com

Kalindi 1992

INTRODUCTION

"Without love, without truth and light,
life is meaningless and fruitless.
The most important thing a spiritual Master does is
to make the student consciously aware of something vast
and infinite within themselves, which is nothing other
than God Himself"

Sri Chinmoy

Welcome to *In the Master's Bedroom,* the story of my personal relationship with Kalindi La Gourasana, a modern-day, fully realized spiritual Master. I first saw Kalindi at a nine-day spiritual Intensive in San Diego. It was February 1994 and I was one of two hundred people in a large room. At the time, I wasn't looking for a Master. I was there to face my fears, open up emotionally and feel more love.

I received so much more than I'd bargained for. During this Intensive, Kalindi guided me into my first taste of real freedom and a connection to something larger than myself. Yet this was only the beginning. I never expected what was coming next.

I grew up a normal guy from Queens, New York. I was interested in fun, sports, and chasing girls. I enjoyed life. As I went off to college to pursue the American Dream, deep inside I already knew that wasn't what I wanted. I was looking for something else. I didn't know what that was until I met Kalindi.

It was mind-boggling to me that I came to be so close to Kalindi. My background did not lend itself to such associations. I grew up unaware, making fun of spiritual leaders from Gandhi and his austerity to the mystic Bhagwan Rajneesh[1] and all his Rolls Royces. I distrusted organized religion and considered spiritual seekers to be airy-fairy. Bottom line, I had no use for God. Yet, my soul knew 'the dream' was not it for me.

From the instant I saw Kalindi, I was inexorably drawn to her. She demonstrated boundless possibility and spirit in action. She exuded this mixture of beauty, sincerity, authenticity, intense passion, and outright freedom. The way she moved, the way she spoke, had an other-worldly feeling to it, as if she was from another realm. I could not take my eyes off her.

Three years went by during which I meditated when I could, but without any thought of coming closer to Kalindi. I was content to stay in the background. Then one night, while deep in meditative thinking, seeking guidance of where I should live next, I heard a strong and clear voice direct me to move into the house where Kalindi lived.

When I told my girlfriend, she said, "You can't live there, that's where Kalindi lives." I thought the same, yet **the voice was so clear,** I had to act. I sent a message to a person I knew who lived with Kalindi and left it at that. A week later, I was completely astonished when I received a message from Kalindi saying, "Tell him, he can move in if he wants to!" I thought for a moment and said, "Yes," knowing this Yes would change my life forever.

Once there, I quickly found myself out of my comfort zone. The house was like a temple. The depth of connection and seriousness of spiritual life was beyond anything I had known. Those living with and assisting Kalindi were all serious spiritual seekers. I felt like a freshman in high school, monitoring advanced classes.

Even though I felt out of place, I was ecstatic to be there. Inexplicably, a couple of weeks later, I found myself cradling this phenomenal woman in my arms while simultaneously rising into an ocean of unlimited love. This magically sweet and simple moment began my extraordinary journey with Kalindi. I remained close to her until she left her body in April 2010.[2]

Kalindi always reminded me that what I felt when I was with her was not her physically, but rather the energy flowing through her. She called this energy, "God, Father, Lord, Supreme Almighty." I called it Source, Universe, or Spirit.

When I was with Kalindi, I was transported to a higher vibrational level where my mind let go and my soul emerged. I witnessed her power to free people's consciousness and hearts from the shackles of repression and fear, allowing them to feel more of their connection with God. What was equally sensational for me was that, when I was with her, **I loved everyone as well!** In her presence, my own unconditional love flowed.

Kalindi woke up my True Self[3] and guided me through the illusion's[4] traps and minefields. She called herself, "God's travel agent." Without her, I seriously doubted I would have been able to transcend the suffering of my life. I learned to 'let go' fast and call forth light to discern the difference between humility and weakness, surrender and giving in, and blind trust and intelligent faith.

I came to know that the spiritual path is paradoxical. For example, as I found deeper joy and ecstasy, I also faced greater fear and pain. As I ventured further within, I found more light and

---

1   Bhagwan Shree Rajneesh (1931-1990), also known as Osho, was an Indian mystic and outspoken critic of organized religion. His teachings focused on meditation, awareness, love, courage, and humor.

2   Carol Seidman, aka Kalindi La Gourasana, born January 2, 1955, died April 18, 2010. While Kalindi physically left her body in 2010, the energy she carried and the paths she left behind are still available and accessible today.

3   "Finding your True Self is about finding who you are forever and who you always will be. Your True Self is the only part of you that really has access to the big questions, like love, suffering, death, and God. You do not create or manufacture your True Self. It does not develop from upbringing, societal choices or experiences. It is your soul and inmost, essential being. It is who you are before you did anything right or anything wrong, before you had your name, your reputation, your education, your family, and your culture. It is already Home so, when you find your True Self, you return Home again." Robert Rohr, *The Immortal Diamond*, 2013

4   Known in religions and philosophies as the Devil, Maya Devi, and the Veil, the Illusion always works against our highest good. It is an intelligent force that knows our deepest and most vulnerable weaknesses. It will use anything against us, even our most powerful spiritual experiences, to have us suffer and keep us bound to this plane of illusion.

9

awareness but also uncovered dark pits of hatred, anger, and unworthiness.

Kalindi would say, "The path is simple, but not easy." She warned of times when the path becomes unbearable. She was right. It's not easy peeling away and letting go of what feels like endless layers of limiting habits, concepts, and beliefs. At the worst of it, Kalindi said, "If you keep going, you will make it." She added, "Everything is waiting. It is love and ecstasy beyond your comprehension." That promise has been fulfilled.

How Was it to Be with Kalindi?

Kalindi was 42 and I was 37 when we got together in April 1997. For the first couple of years, I knew her as a disciple, lover, devotee and friend. For the next 10 years, I was with her as a disciple, assistant, companion, and confidante. I knew her intimately in every aspect of her life.

Kalindi was present and conscious all the time. Her light always shone. She was a spiritual force of love. Because of this, being with Kalindi was extremely intense. It was wondrous and excruciating at the same time.

Kalindi was constantly changing – newly realizing herself every moment as she continually let go of who she was. I witnessed constant self-realization in action and **it was phenomenal.** Kalindi would say, "God's middle name is 'constant change.'"

There were special times during both large and small gatherings when Kalindi brought in an energy that felt like Home. Her body would sway in slow, flowing waves of angelic motion and her love enveloped everyone. I felt as if transported to Heaven on a delicious wave of ecstasy.

Kalindi was also intense when necessary, wielding what she termed "Break Free Energy" to storm the well-defended, stuck egos of her disciples. When this powerful, eruptive energy came through her, it would shake the walls of my rational cage. I would shy away, quivering with fear in the presence of this power. In the following pages of this book, I will walk you through many of these experiences.

Wherever we were, living with Kalindi had me residing in a temple of truth and reverence with palpable **Presence of God.** It was a peaceful, conscious and immaculate space in which all of my truest spiritual qualities were seduced from the depths of me all the time.

Kalindi loved to talk. I would listen eagerly as she spoke about different spiritual topics. Occasionally, she would ask for my help with something. This surprised me, as my concept was, *"Her consciousness is merged with God. She shouldn't need anything. So, who was I to help her?"* It took a while for me to understand that even a Master needs reminding, love or support sometimes. By the end, she referred to me as her spiritual psychologist.

In all ways Kalindi was thoroughly authentic. Her surrender and humility were always there in plain sight. She had a potent ability to recognize souls ready to make a leap in consciousness. She saw people as souls and True Selves on a journey. To me, it felt like Divine energy itself had come down and filled that sweet little body.

Why I Wrote This Book

Beginning in 2005 and many times thereafter, Kalindi asked me – sometimes sweetly and sometimes emphatically – to write a book about my experiences with her. She would say, "Marcus, you have seen behind the veil. This will be the first time a Master or Guru opens their bedroom door and pulls back the curtain for all to see." Kalindi wanted to be known for who she was – a spiritual Master and fully aware woman who also had bad hair days. She wanted to dispel the concepts people have about spiritual Masters.

When I showed up on Kalindi's doorstep, I existed in a world filled with fear and negative thoughts. My heart was shuttered, and despite my well-polished shell, I felt isolated. I had no purpose. Kalindi pulled me from my suffering and filled me with joy, love, and acceptance for myself and others.

Eventually, I became sufficiently aware to let go of governing self-judgments, connect to my heart and soul, and live my purpose and destiny. For this, I am eternally grateful.

I wrote this book to convey the experiences I had with Kalindi and to testify to her manifestation on this earth. In these pages I record the 'who, what, where, when, and why' of her spiritual teachings in action. Kalindi called forth my deepest desires to serve and give. I feel a sacred duty to share with you and pass on the gifts I received from her and to see the infinite possibilities available to all of us.

With Love and Grace,
Marcus Bond

December 30, 2015
Boulder, Colorado

PART ONE

RISING IN LOVE

CHAPTER 1

LIFE BEFORE KALINDI

He said, "You become. It takes a long time.
That's why it doesn't happen often to people who break easily,
or have sharp edges, or who have to be carefully kept.
Generally, by the time you are Real, most of your hair
has been loved off, and your eyes drop out
and you get loose in the joints and very shabby.
But these things don't matter at all,
because once you are Real you can't be ugly,
except to people who don't understand."

The Velveteen Rabbit

Early Years

To allow you to appreciate the magic of Kalindi as seen through my eyes, and her life as a modern-day spiritual Master, I'll first share how I grew up and the ensuing journey that led me to Kalindi.

I came into this world on December 13, 1959, in Queens, New York, the second of two sons born to Alan Brostoff and Marilyn Bond. My brother Steve was born two-and-a-half years before me. My parents were both college-educated and in their 20's when I was born. My birth name was Mark Elliott Brostoff. In 1998, from Kalindi's suggestion, I changed my name and am now known as Marcus Bond.[1]

For my entire life both my parents have been tremendously supportive of me. I felt loved and encouraged to go for what I wanted. They gave me the encouragement and space I needed, even when my personal desires or spiritual path took me away from them.

During my first years we lived in a little townhouse in Fresh Meadows, Queens – a lower middle-class neighborhood near the Long Island Expressway. My heritage is a mixture of Italian-Catholic and Russian-Jewish. We were not a religious family and practiced what I call **obligatory religious observances.** We celebrated the Jewish holidays as well as Christmas, without feeling pulled to delve into their deeper spiritual meanings.

At four-and-a-half, my life took its first unexpected turn. My parents separated. I don't remember any problems leading up to that morning but when I asked my mom, "Where's Daddy?" she responded, "He went to stay at Grandma's for a little while." My father never lived with us again. He did spend time with Steve and I twice a week and we lived with him one month each summer until he moved to Florida when I was fifteen.

I was a resilient kid, busy having fun, so it seemed that my dad moving out was okay. Steve and I played endless rounds of

---

1   The story of my name change is shared in Chapter 5.

games and sports in the courtyard. There were heaps of neigh-borhood kids, and we had plenty of friends. We would use T-shirts for bases and play rag-tag baseball all afternoon until Mom called us in for dinner.

It was the early 60's and the Beatles had just arrived. By 1965 my brother and I sported mod haircuts and owned pint-sized guitars. We liked joining in on the songs and pretending to play guitar, performing for all who would listen.

Life Turns

All that changed the year I turned seven. That was when my parents' divorce became final and we moved across Queens to Lefrak City. Built by Sam Lefrak, the Donald Trump of his day, Lefrak City is a large apartment complex built alongside the Long Island Expressway. We moved into a two-bedroom apartment on the sixth floor of one of the identical twelve-story, red brick buil-dings. My brother and I shared the large bedroom, and Mom had the small one off the kitchen.

By then, my Dad, a successful CPA and Financial Controller, had remarried and moved into a nice house on Long Island with my new step-mom, Judy. Judy was wonderful and I loved the new setting. The backyard was a pleasant relief from the concrete of the city.

Life was not so easy for my Mom. She was a single, divorced woman in her 30's with two boys to take care of. We lived in Queens, and she held a full-time job in Manhattan working in advertising and sales. She took the subway each morning. It was a 45-minute ride into the city. Rather than being there to pack us off to school, Mom had to leave early and came home long after school let out. Fortunately for us, her dad, Grandpa Joe, was usually there when we came home from school.

Sometimes he couldn't be there and those times were not easy for me. For the first time in my life I learned what it felt like to ache from being home alone. It frightened me and was horribly painful, like a stomach ache that wouldn't go away. There was this one day when I couldn't open a can of tuna fish on my own. I was so hungry. Steve was outside hanging with his friends. I remember standing on the balcony and screaming at my brother for help. He couldn't hear me and I felt so helpless.

On the flip side there were times I wished Steve would disappear. He started picking on me. It's not that he was mean-hearted; it was just his way of having fun. When he rolled me up in a mattress and then jumped off the chair on top of me, he explained that we were just playing. He called it **pretend wrestling and pretend body slams** just like on television. They didn't feel pretend. And it wasn't pretend when he acted out "Three Stooges" gags, poking me or smacking me on the head.

When Grandpa Joe was there, most of the bullying stopped. Grandpa Joe came over from Italy where his name was Joseph Buongiorno. Here in America he was called Joe Bond. Grandpa Joe liked taking us to Little League baseball and model car racing. His famous line when entering our messy room was, "Oy Vey, Earthquake!"

Grandpa Joe became my friend and advisor. I would go to him for help as a boy and as a man. He knew how to explain the inner workings of a camera, how auto insurance worked, and other important things that a teenage boy needs to know. His wife, Grandma Annie, suffered from depression and was on medication that left her passive. I never knew much about her, still I felt her love. When Grandpa Joe died her depression worsened and Annie was put into a nursing home. She became more afraid, mostly sleeping, waking only to scream before falling back into slumber. Her suffering and trauma were unnerving and scary.

Another life-defining moment appeared at first to be quite harmless. I was eight when my Dad took us to the funeral of a relative. Feeling the sadness of the event, I started to cry. My well-intentioned Dad tried to comfort me. He said, *"It's okay, Mark, don't cry.*" So I stopped crying. Unfortunately, I took it to mean that I shouldn't cry – ever. I can recall that moment clearer than I'd like. In retrospect, it was right then and there that I began to shut down my feelings. For the next twenty-five years, until my first Miracle of Love Intensive® in 1994, I never cried again!

I was raised with sports at the center of things. We'd pile around the television to watch all the New York teams. Dad regularly took Steve and I to the ice hockey, football, basketball and baseball games.

My dream growing up was to be a baseball player. I loved playing. My best friend, Dan, and I were on the same team. We both pitched or played shortstop. One year we got all the way to our league championship and many times I was named to the all-star team – heady stuff for a boy of ten.

At this time, my experiences of the world started to change. I was physically small and thin and therefore an easy target. It began with my brother picking on me at home and got exponentially worse at school, where first bullies and then criminals preyed on my frailty.

Entire parts of my day were not safe. Uncertainty and fear began to govern my outlook on places and people. I was regularly harassed by a bully on my way to school. Even the older, larger girls started bullying me in the schoolyard. I became more afraid each time I was targeted.

Then things escalated. At summer camp, I accidentally ran into my first wasps' nest and got stung several times. The very next year at school during a fire drill and in front of my classmates, I ran from a bee all the way down the street. I was afraid of being stung and it was humiliating when the other kids laughed at me. It was nightmarish when a friend's dog attacked me. It bit me on the knee and chest and was going for my throat when my friend's dad grabbed it off.

In grades six through eight I entered Intermediate School 61 in Corona, Queens, and things got worse. Corona was a tough

20

neighborhood. The school was in chaos. The teachers and administration had lost control of a student body that was primarily black and Puerto Rican. As a small white boy, I was utterly intimidated. My classes were filled with older black kids who'd been held back several grades. They ruled over the rest of us.

Losing God

In that same fateful year of 12, my mother enrolled me in Hebrew School to prepare for my Bar Mitzvah. Hebrew School was meaningless to me. I had no connection to the stories and myths of Judaism. What we were taught seemed like empty ritual rather than a rite of passage. The only reason I'd agreed to the whole Bar Mitzvah thing was because my dad promised me a trip to Disney World.

I did not get religion, or rabbis, or any of it. So when the Rabbi threw an eraser at me for talking in class, I threw it back and happily got expelled. After I was thrown out of Hebrew School, my parents hired a tutor. To overcome my disinterest, he phonetically wrote the two prayers I had to speak on the back of baseball cards.

I was all ears when one of my brother's friends convinced me that God could not exist. I had already gotten in trouble at school for refusing to say the Pledge of Allegiance since it referenced, "One nation under God." He argued that no God in his right mind would allow the horrors of this world. I'd just been reading about the Bermuda Triangle. I agreed. He had to be right. Besides, I was growing up without God anyway. It didn't matter if He didn't exist.

During these years, I played a lot of sports, particularly ice and roller hockey, tennis, racquetball, and jai-alai.[1] I liked intensity

---

1   Jai-alai is a ball game originated in Spain's Basque region. It is played in a three-walled court with a hard rubber ball that is caught and thrown with a Cesta, a long, curved wicker scoop strapped to one arm. Jai-alai is known as "the fastest sport in the world" in which a 125 g ball (or pelota) covered with parchment skin travels over 180 mph during games between two players.

and speed. It was a way out of my usual fears and anxieties, a way of being focused and present.

The summer before my sophomore year of high school, Mom decided to move to Manhattan. She said it was better for all of us. She'd be closer to work, and Steve and I would both attend better schools.

I was outraged and frightened. I didn't want to live in Manhattan; I didn't want to leave my friends. I remember saying, "Mom, I'm already getting mugged every day in Queens. What the hell is going to happen in the city?" I'd heard that the public schools in lower Manhattan might be worse. In response, Mom signed me up for an academically competitive high school focused in math and science. I passed the entry exam and was admitted to Peter Stuyvesant High School, which was only seven blocks away from our new home in lower Manhattan.

Stuyvesant had been an all-boys school and only recently started admitting girls. I desperately wanted the girls to like me, but with four times as many boys as girls in the school, the odds were against me. I wanted to be cool, yet I was clueless about how to accomplish that so I opted to join a circle of kids who smoked pot.

At Sixteen

The summer of my 16th year, I was experiencing my first bouts of depression. Feelings of isolation and separateness overtook me. There were times when I couldn't connect to anyone, even my best friends, Dan and Michael. These feelings only grew as I continued on to college and graduate school.

That same year, my Mom's new boyfriend, Harvey, turned me on to whiskey sours and my brother Steve turned me on to music. It was my first foray into drinking and I loved being inebriated. With music, I particularly liked Pink Floyd. Pink Floyd made music I could relate to and when *The Wall*[1] came out it spoke to me personally. Now when I got depressed, I'd make myself a whiskey sour, smoke some pot, and listen to "Dark Side of the Moon" on headphones. This was my way of feeling better. Sometimes, I'd masturbate while drunk, stoned and into the music.

This began an extended period of sex, drugs, and rock and roll experimentation. During this time I toyed with suicide, though never seriously. Basically, I was on the run from everyone and everything. I had no center, no core beliefs. All I knew to do was hide and pretend until I was high or drunk enough to get some relief from feeling so bad.

I was a teenage boy and enslaved to hormones that drove me to hit the XXX movies in Times Square with Dan and Michael. I was wildly open to the idea of sex, and hungry to start. The idea of getting laid became the main goal of my life. Being the first to score would impress my friends and help me feel better. Finally, it happened. I lost my virginity on my 17th birthday. It was after a KISS concert at Madison Square Garden. The girl was 15 years old and I barely liked her, yet she was willing. The experience was pathetic. There was no glory in it but at least it was done.

Party Time

That fall I went off to college at the State University of New York at Albany. From the moment I hit campus, I was free to drink, smoke, chase girls, and do all the drugs I wanted. The only deal I made with myself was to get to the gym, keep playing sports, and make good grades.

During college, I got into LSD. The trips were mostly enjoyable mind-expanding experiences. The parts of me that were anxi-

---

1   The Wall is an album by the English progressive rock group Pink Floyd, released as a double album on November 30, 1979. The Wall is a concept album and deals largely with themes of abandonment and personal isolation. It was first conceived when bassist and lyricist Roger Waters' frustration with the spectators' perceived boorishness became so acute that he imagined building a wall between the performers and audience.

ous and scared would fall away. I'd become playful and curious. The personality of fear that gripped me would lift off, and I'd find myself in an amazing world of colors and imagination. It was like living a dream while awake. Yes, I was high but I was also present in a place that I really liked.

Being out in the world while tripping was hyper real. My buddies and I would drop acid and go see Star Wars. I loved being visually stimulated and experiencing the mind-blowing rush of Acid. LSD turned walking around in the snow into magic. I would feel the sound of the snow crunching under my boots. Disney World took me on a fantasy trip like no other. When we went to Michael Jackson's 3D movie, it was so real I tried to catch what appeared to fly out at us. We would laugh our asses off most of the time. Later on my path, I would have similar but deeper experiences without drugs with my Master Kalindi.

Then I started taking more powerful acid. The first time I took "Window Pane" was the night I went to see Pink Floyd perform "The Wall" at the Nassau Coliseum. "The Wall," seen and heard through "Window Pane," melted the wall they were building on stage and the Coliseum too!

During intermission, I went wandering and had a hard time navigating my way back. I started to freak out. I was alone again. I felt disconnected. I didn't know where my friends were, and I could barely function. It took forever to find our seat, and, when I finally arrived, Roger Waters was singing, "And the worms ate into his brain." I felt he was talking to me. The worms were eating my brain and I couldn't stop it! Now I was melting.

My fears poured out of my dark recesses. I was scared shitless and couldn't say anything about it. I was in a panic for the remainder of the concert. Driving home, I remember thinking, "I don't want to face these fears." The acid had opened closet doors and the skeletons were flying out.

The after-effects from this "bad" trip lingered for months. I was thrown into a deep depression. I felt like I was **trapped**

inside a plate glass window and no one could reach me. I had always used denial to handle what wasn't working in my life and now avoidance was no longer possible. The cold, sunless winters of upstate New York were the perfect backdrop for this black pit of despair. Fortunately, when spring came, the sun shined again and I managed to crawl out of my depression.

During my first two years at college, my girlfriends provided me with some love and a steady avenue for sex. In my junior year, I met a wonderful woman, a senior, one year older than me, beautiful, smart, and sexy. We took the same human sexuality course and enjoyed doing our homework together. She made me feel special.

I count myself lucky to have survived my college years. Partying and social life were my main focus. As a student, I managed a 3.3 grade average. Knowing that a BA in Psychology would most likely lead to working at a tire store, I set my sites on graduate school somewhere in the South.

From here on, my winters had to be warm and sunny. When the Organizational Psychology Doctoral program of the University of South Florida (USF) sent me a letter of acceptance, I chose to go there. The campus was located a few hours away from my Dad, Judy, and my two half-sisters, Stacy and Mindy. Best of all, my wonderful girlfriend agreed to go with me.

USF, located in Tampa on the West coast of Florida, was known as **Coppertone U.** I was 21 years old. My goal was that by 27, I'd have a good job, nice car, and the woman of my dreams. This would be my pinnacle of existence.

That first semester in school, I busted my butt. I knew there was a cut. Of the 20 students accepted only eight would remain when the second semester began. I made it and immediately switched to cruise control. For the rest of my academic life, all I did was just enough to get by which meant that I studied hard enough to maintain a B-minus average and no more. In fact, I was entering a period of life when 'just enough' became my personal motto for many things. My girlfriend and I didn't make it past the first year. I wanted to party and she was ready to settle down.

My fellow students took graduate school quite seriously. They spent extended hours in the library while I wandered in, studied a bit, and then cruised out for the beaches or a bar. Many years later, Kalindi would say to me, "Marcus, you are fine so long as you're having a good time but, when it gets tough, you want to check out, go have a drink, smoke a joint, or pick up a new girl." Her statement really hit me. I had to admit she was right. That's the way it was for most of my twenties and thirties.

Paradise Found and Lost

After completing my Master's Thesis in the spring of 1984, I decided to head for Europe. I'd gone cross-country through the US three years before with my girlfriend so this time I planned a four-week summer trip. It was my first time abroad and I went with my two childhood buddies, Dan and Michael.

We travelled here and there as part of a river of tourists and then stopped when we discovered the idyllic Greek Island of Corfu. Corfu offered cheap beer, beautiful beaches, and topless Scandinavian women. Corfu became Heaven on Earth! We rented a room in a hotel on the top of a hill for $4 a night. A 15-minute walk down to the shore brought us to one of the most beautiful beaches I'd ever seen. The water was crystal clear and aqua blue. The beaches were covered with gorgeous, young, topless Scandinavian women. A taverna on the beach sold 16-ounce Heinekens for 50 cents each! During the day we soaked up the sun, swam in the water, and threw Frisbees with the beautiful, playful girls. We were like bees in a flower garden. At night, we would meet these wonderful women at the town's only disco, The Pink Panther.

Almost every night was another night to remember. We drank Ouzo and danced to the hits of the day. Our hookups went like clockwork. In no time one of the girls would say, "Would you like to come to my room?" This blew my mind. I was used to women in New York and Florida. American women weren't easy to bed. They took serious work so this was a new experience for me, which I embraced wholeheartedly! I thought, "If Scandinavian girls on an island in Greece are so willing and able, what are they like back home?"

I extended my trip for three weeks and traveled to Scandinavia to find out. In Copenhagen, I rented a bike and pedaled over to a park where B.B. King was scheduled to play. Soon after I arrived, I passed this knockout blonde sitting alone on a blanket. Like the girls in Corfu, she was topless.

I was so taken by her that I circled around, studying her from every angle. From the start, she was open and friendly. In no time, things went from saying, "Hi," to sitting together and smoking hash. After half an hour, she called her boyfriend to tell him that she wouldn't be seeing him that night. "Wow," I thought, "this means she is going to stay with me." Her name was Helle. For the rest of that amazing day and into the evening, we got to know one another. It was late when we got back to Helle's apartment. She went off to shower, and I settled onto her couch.

Looking around, I noticed all of these 8.5"x11" black-and-white photos of her topless in a field. I picked out my favorite, put it aside, and when she returned, Helle explained that once each week on page nine of Copenhagen's Monday newspaper some beautiful girl would go topless for the camera. Those selected received 500 Krona or about $90. Helle had entered at the request of the newspaper's resident photographer. They'd done the photo shoot the week before, and these glossies were the result.

Being in bed with Helle was the best part of the day. We fell asleep making love and woke up doing it again. The next day she took me to her school where she was studying nursing. When I walked into the dormitory filled with Danish nursing students, I felt I'd entered a dreamscape. Even here, sex with Helle never stopped. I couldn't believe how she gave blow jobs. It was so incredible. I even asked her if she'd been trained in the art.

Everybody was thrilled when Helle's picture appeared on page nine. They printed my favorite pose. Helle gave me the photograph, which I still have today. Sadly, after a week with Helle, it was time to move on. My summer abroad was nearly over.

Corporate America

By early fall, 1984, I was back in America. I accepted an internship at American Telephone and Telegraph (AT&T) corporate headquarters in New York City. I went from college digs in Tampa to working for one of the largest corporations in the world.

I was hired to conduct research and facilitate training sessions on effective coping skills for managerial women. I developed profiles of highly effective female managers and then created programs designed to bring out that potential in others. I turned this project into the subject of my dissertation. While AT&T spent millions on the project, I got paid a healthy salary to write my doctoral dissertation.

My workday went like this: I plugged away in my cubicle with everyone else and, once the workday ended, stayed put to craft my dissertation. Putting in the hours reflected well on my record with AT&T, so it was win-win for me and for the company. Around 10pm all work would stop. I'd get a call from a friend and it was time to hit the clubs. I would leave the office on 55th Street and Madison Avenue and hook up with the guys. We'd go trolling for girls. I was young. I had stamina. I even had money enough to afford the $25 entrance fee and $8 a pop cost of drinks. Still, it was not easy to get laid in Manhattan. On most nights I went home alone at four in the morning.

While at AT&T, my Grandpa Joe was diagnosed with cancer. He was the first person close to me to get terminally ill. Both Dan and Michael had had a parent die from cancer, now it was my turn. Grandpa Joe had made a difference for me as a child. In my childhood he'd been strong and vital. Now, as the cancer ravaged his body, he shrank into this scared, frail, little man. His terror was like nothing I'd experienced before. He became so utterly needy. I tried to comfort him but had no idea what to do. I felt helpless and sad, distant and numb. When Grandpa Joe died, I felt emotions percolating inside that hadn't been there since childhood.

I stayed at AT&T two and one-half years beyond the internship's original contract. I liked the work, the pay was very good and my performance reviews were excellent. This was a time when corporate life was in constant flux. It was a world of uncertainty and I seemed to thrive in it.

This turned out to be a good and useful talent because AT&T proved to be a forerunner to how my personal life would become. As it was, during the three years I was there, the company went through five distinct reorganizations with eighty-thousand employees (20% of the workforce) 'downsized.'

After the last iteration, my department went from 50 people to eight. Furthermore, our department was moving to New Jersey. I told my boss it was time to go. I'd saved $10,000. I wanted to return to Europe. I was 27 years old and it was the summer of 1987. It was on this trip that I started to awaken. ♪

CHAPTER 2

WAKING UP

*"To know our soul apart from our ego is the first step
toward accomplishing the supreme deliverance.
It is necessary that we know with absolute certainty
that in essence we are spirit.
And we can only arrive at this knowledge
if we render ourselves masters of our ego,
if we rise above all pride,
all appetite, all fear, by knowing that material losses
and the death of the body can never take away the truth
and the greatness of our soul."*

Rabindranath Tagore

Thistime a friend and I headed to Amsterdam as our first stop, with Copenhagen as our second. At first the trip was a repeat performance. We gorged on another round of women and nightlife. We saw Europe on $5 by day and $95 by night!

I'd lost touch with Helle and wanted to look her up. I opened the phone book and called her number. She was home and our love affair began again. This time, I was attracted to more than her physical beauty. Helle had a depth. She was real, open, fun, adventurous, carefree, and honest. She went from sex goddess to fantasy woman and I was in heaven.

Those were the pre-internet days. It took work to hunt down a USA Today to find out how the Mets were doing. Then came the baseball strike. No one was playing ball. That's when I realized that the players didn't care about us. A chunk of my loyal fan-self fell away. I no longer cared so much, though it was years before I finally stopped identifying with sports as a primary force in my life.

As I let go of 'spectator sports,' I started meeting people who knew about the world and America's role in it. I learned about how European societies take care of their people, spreading the wealth among the many rather than concentrating it into the hands of the privileged few. My European counterparts addressed America's militarism and arrogance. Their knowledge made me realize the depth of my own ignorance.

The sports books and spy novels I'd brought with me were left behind. I became quieter and more observant. I let up on entertaining people in order to be liked. I began reading books on philosophy and spirituality. I fell in love with Herman Hesse's, *Journey to the East,*[1] which describes a pilgrimage through mysticism, faith and obedience in search of the Self.

I began to emulate the Europeans and became more real and down-to-earth. I experienced being well-liked without having to

---

1 Hermann Hesse, *Journey to the East*, Picador, Reprint edition, 2003

work at it. As a bonus, I was even more attractive to women. Inside and out, I was changing. My list of metaphysical and philosophical books grew to include: Dante, Heidegger, Kierkegaard,[1] Shirley MacLaine, and Ram Dass. Each author revealed new worlds to me; worlds I'd never dreamed existed. More was possible and more was exactly what I was hungry for.

We headed south. It was mid-summer and Helle and I were scheduled to meet in Athens in a month. She came with her friend, Jens Ole. Jens was a real 'Viking' man. I was pleased to have him along. The four of us took a ferry to the volcanic island of San Torini. We camped on a beautiful black sand beach, bathed in the sea, and lived on a dollar a day. At night, Helle and I split off from the guys. We frequented clubs with no entrance fees, bought drinks for 50 cents each, and danced into the night. By dawn we went off on our own nameless tiny islet where we made love.

I'd never been happier. There was a philosophic underpinning to what we did. We were living 'less is more.' Material existence was no longer our focus. The days became flawless, until it was time to leave Greece and its fantasies behind. Then the fear of loss lifted its ugly head. I couldn't hold the moment. I didn't want to come down from this exquisite trip. Inside I knew, without Helle, without Greece and the ocean, only scared little me would remain.

It wasn't until I read **Be Here Now** by Ram Dass, and the nearly identical experiences he had had as compared to mine, that I realized something else was possible. Like me, Ram Dass thought he'd found liberation through LSD.

Like me, problems arose when, afterwards, he always returned to his predicament. It wasn't until he went to India and met his guru that he became aware of another way.[2] For the first time I wondered if maybe I needed a teacher to find my way, too.

After Greece, we journeyed through France, Portugal, and Spain. I started noticing 'coincidences.' People I met had something to teach me. The most influential of these teachers was Hy Gordon.

Hy was a fascinating 60-year-old man and deep in his own journey when I met him. A successful businessman, Hy dropped acid for the first time on his 55th birthday.

Over the next few hours, he realized there was something more to life than work and decided to travel the world with a back-pack. I met Hy in Pamplona where they run the bulls. I was sitting outside the bullring next to a statue of Hemingway reading "The Sun Also Rises." It was around five in the afternoon when this VW microbus pulled up and the side door opened. Out popped this 60-year-old man who immediately said, "Hello there, young fellow, what are you reading?" We fell into conversation. As we talked, I felt something different about this man.

We wound up spending the next 5 days together. At first, I was excited and chatty and full of questions. Hy had something I wanted. He was so peacefully centered and so quiet. Interestingly, he never really answered a single question. Instead, he gradually helped me to understand that life was more about **being** than talking.

By the end of our time together, I was content to sit in silence with him. When I said we were heading north next, he replied, "Adios amigos, see you when I do." And then he was gone. It sure felt like the Buddha 'appearing when the student is ready.' Within a couple of months, I'd run out of money and it was time to return to America.

---

1 Søren Kierkegaard (1813-1855) Danish Philosopher and Theologian, generally rec-ognized as the first existentialist. His questioning captured my *awakening' experience:* "Where am I? Who am I? How did I come to be here? What is this thing called the world? How did I come into the world? Why was I not consulted? And If I am compelled to take part in it, where is the director? I want to see him."

2 When Ram Dass first went to India, he gave his soon-to-be Master, Neem Karoli Baba (also known as Maharaji), a large dose of LSD. After sitting with him for many hours, nothing happened to Maharaii at all. Ram Dass had found the answer to his question. The LSD did not affect the Master because he was already there. Ram Dass, *Be Here Now,* Lama Foundation, 1978

Austerity

Back in the States, I was a changed man. I returned to Tampa, rented a loft apartment, and furnished it Zen style with little more than a futon and a toaster. I got a job with GTE Telephone (the precursor to Verizon) as a management trainer and facilitator. I stopped watching television (I didn't even have a TV) and let go of spectator sports.

I became more introverted, drawn to the Buddhist practice of a simple life. My friends thought this was a passing phase but it wasn't; it was a beginning. In all ways, I was a changed man. That is except for my seemingly insatiable desire to bed more women, although these experiences often left me feeling empty.

Truth be told, I was in love with Helle. All I really wanted to do was to go back to Denmark and live with her. Over the next couple of years, I saved money at every turn and then I was ready to return.

Copenhagen 1989

From the moment I arrived in Copenhagen, I knew I was in love with everything Danish. I loved Helle, the people, the language, the forests, the pubs, the hash, the sex. It was all I'd dreamed possible.

The Danish are a warm-hearted, down-to-earth people. I jumped into an active five-week course to learn Danish and took a minimum wage job delivering newspapers by bike from 2 to 7am. Correctly, my Dad said I was probably the only Ph.D. delivering newspapers in Copenhagen.

I took advantage of my time in Denmark and traveled extensively. Helle and I rented a car and drove down to the south of Spain. We took a boat over to Morocco and traveled for ten days to Marrakech, Fez, Casablanca, and the Atlas Mountains. Not since a vacation to Jamaica and some trips to Tijuana, Mexico, several years before had I seen such poverty.

The suffering in Jamaica and Tijuana had touched me and scared me because of the crime. Now in Morocco, I witnessed 80% unemployment and many people not knowing if they would have enough bread to eat that day. Still, they seemed to possess this sense of contentment and faith unknown to me. Their faith in God sincerely intrigued me.

In the fall, I traveled into Eastern Europe – Czechoslovakia, Hungary, Poland, and East Germany. This was when Communist regimes were collapsing and the Berlin Wall came down. By chance, I found myself in East Berlin 36 hours after that historic event. Again, I was tou-

Berlin Wall, 1989

ched by the simple, if meager, lifestyle of the East Germans. Things were not as black and white as I had been conditioned to believe.

I traveled to Sweden for a two-week meditation and yoga retreat. I learned to do headstands and to quiet my mind using different meditation and yogic techniques. I loved going deeper into the stillness, and happily fasted in silence for several days before eating food fresh picked from the ashram's garden and fields. A peace came over me that was tangible. I was drawn heart and soul to this simple existence.

When the ashram's Swami addressed us on the final day, I could barely hear what he said. My entire focus was on the bluish green aura that haloed his head. I'd never seen an aura before. That night, I had my first out of body experience in which I flew over a rushing river. My inner life was waking up.

While I was at the retreat, my other grandfather, Stanley Brostoff, died. My family asked me to return home for the funeral. I decided to stay and have my own ceremony. I found a quiet spot to sit alone at the time of the funeral in Florida. I built a fire and threw leaves on it. I meditated next to the fire and sent my farewell message to Grandpa Stanley, whispering, "I loved our times together."

My life was going great until winter set in. As the days grew shorter and the nights grew longer, depression crept back inside of me. Without sunlight, a heavy gloom settled over me. There was little snow and so much rain. By December, I was out of money and the weather had overwhelmed me. I told Helle I had to return to Tampa. I had to get back in the sun. She understood. On parting, we agreed she would come to Florida as soon as she was able.

Betrayal

Back in Tampa, I found an apartment and a roommate but I could not find a job. It took months to find work. My money was all but gone when I landed a job in Organizational Development at GTE (Verizon) Data Services to do Executive Leadership training.

In no time, Helle got a visa and flew over to work as a nurse at Tampa General Hospital. Now both of us had great jobs and once again I was thinking I'd found my absolute reality.

The only problem was Helle now struggled. She didn't understand our culture. I had to train her to be cautious and teach her to fear people and places. I hated doing that. Copenhagen is so much safer than Tampa. Helle couldn't believe it was dangerous to go alone to the Laundromat at two in the morning in shorts and a tank top. Why wasn't it safe to rendezvous with a man she'd just met in a bar on the beach after midnight? Then she started drinking. In no time it got serious. At my brother Steve's wedding, she got so drunk that she passed out on his mother-in-law's couch!

Drinking became part of her everyday life. Helle used liquor to cover up an aching sadness. She missed her family and cozy Danish lifestyle. America was just too jarring. Then she got into trouble at the Hospital. She went to work smelling of booze. It happened more than once. She was in danger of losing her job and her visa. She refused to admit she had a problem. When I asked her to choose between me and the alcohol, she chose to drink and I was crushed and dumbfounded.

We both knew it was time for her to return home. I took her to New York. We stayed for a few days with my Mom. While there, Helle confessed that she'd slept with a friend of mine the previous year in Denmark. This news threw me into a rage. I felt totally betrayed.

Already heartbroken, now I was crushed. It was August 1990. I was devastated. I felt broken. My brilliant Mom gave me a book called *How to Survive the Loss of a Love*[1] and over time I started to heal.[2]

Transformation

Back in Tampa and again living alone, I made my living conditions even more austere. I retreated into my loft apartment and ferociously read a steady diet of books describing spiritual journeys. I was moved by *The Road Less Traveled* and *If You Meet the Buddha on the Road, Kill Him.* My library was filled with Zen classics including *Zen Flesh, Zen Bones* and *Zen Mind, Beginner's Mind.* As a practitioner I was drawn to depth. I was beginning to understand that it came from simplicity and mindfulness. Yet my mind, emotions, and senses were still out of control.

I began exploring the spiritual marketplace with gusto. I went to yoga classes, breath work seminars, and rebirthing workshops. I visited psychics and mediums and learned about channeling. I studied Taoism, the I Ching, and the Enneagram. I bought crystals

---

1 Colgrove, McWilliams & Bloomfield, *How to Survive the Loss of a Love*, Bantam, 1977

2 Within the next year I was able to forgive Helle. Helle and I stayed in touch, speaking occasionally, until her death in 2009 from alcohol and drugs.

and Tibetan gongs and Buddhist and Hindu statues – anything that connected me to eastern philosophy. Judiciously, I practiced several different kinds of Eastern meditation. I even spent a week with a shaman for a river quest and sweat lodges in Oregon.

While I found endeavors helpful and illuminating, my mind was still filled with negative chatter. I was still in a funk that I couldn't shake off. At that point, my stepmother, Judy suggested I participate in something called "The Landmark Forum",[1] as a way to open up to some new possibilities in my life. I was hesitant but with support from my family, I said Yes.

When Werner Erhard's est[2] was happening in the early 70's, my mother, Aunt Francine and her husband Lew had all participated. This was a time when self-help and finding oneself were important themes to people all over the world and est became a kind of Mecca.

Lew Epstein

Lew was a very special man who had gone through a profound transformation when he did est. He developed a way of listening that was so compassionate that it gave people a sense of being heard and understood. People loved Lew.

Lew and Werner had a special relationship together for over ten years. When Werner brought mystics and gurus from the East, like Swami Muktananda from India and The Karmapa[3] from Tibet, these holy men would see auras around Lew and request his counsel. Lew had no interest in being recognized spiritually. His one desire was to help people through listening, forgiveness, compassion, and trusting love. This was his one focus and purpose in life.[4]

During the first years I knew Lew, my brother and I thought he was a kook. We were not interested in transformation or compassion. We would make fun of him, as we did with everyone and everything outside our narrow view of life. My true relationship with Lew began only after I'd attended my first Miracle of Love Intensive in 1994.

The Landmark Forum was an outgrowth of est and was a new kind of transformational work for me. In the Landmark Forum I learned how to "complete my past." I dealt with whatever 'incompletions' (i.e., lack of forgiveness, blame, not taking responsibility, repressed feelings, withheld communications, etc.) that kept my past alive, stopped me from being present, and doomed my future to more of the same. I learned how to create new, previously unimaginable futures. At the end of the day, if not for the opening I had in The Landmark Forum, I doubt I'd have made it to The Intensive® or Kalindi.

---

1 The Landmark Forum (based on the work of Werner Erhard and his *est* seminars from the 70's and 80's) took place over three consecutive days and an evening session. Attendees were urged to be "coachable" and not just be observers during the course. The program was arranged as a discussion where the course leader presented certain ideas and the course participants engaged in voluntary sharing with the course leader to discuss how those ideas applied to their own life. Ideas presented, asserted, and discussed included the following:
  • There is a difference between what happened in a person's life and the meaning or interpretation they made up about it.
  • People pursue an imaginary 'some day' of satisfaction.
  • Human behavior is governed by a need to look good.
  • People created their own meaning to life – none is inherent in the world.
  • People could "transform" by declaring a new way of being instead of changing themselves based on the past.
  • Contacting people you were "incomplete" with to apologize, forgive, and/or take responsibility for your own behavior.

2 *est* stood for Erhard Seminar Training.

3 Swami Muktananda was the founder of the Siddha Yoga spiritual path. Muktananda was a disciple and the successor of Bhagavan Nityananda. He wrote a number of books on the subjects of Kundalini Shakti, Vedanta, and Kashmir Shaivism, including a spiritual autobiography entitled *The Play of Consciousness*.
  The Karmapa (honorific title His Holiness the Gyalwa Karmapa) is the head of the *Karma Kagyu,* the largest sub-school of the Kagyupa, itself one of the four major schools of *Tibetan Buddhism.*

4 Lew passed away peacefully at the age of 84 in 2003.

Between Christmas and New Year's 1991, I met my first wife, Genie, at a Landmark Workshop in San Francisco. She was a beautiful, smart, first generation Japanese-American who lived in Washington, DC. We sat next to each other and hit it off, chatting and flirting the whole time. When we parted, she and I knew we'd see each other again. For the next five months it was all about long-distance dating as one or the other of us traveled back and forth between DC and Tampa. Then Genie came to Tampa, moving in with me in a little two-bedroom house on a lake that I'd recently bought.

Soon we were engaged and planning our wedding for New Year's Eve, 1992. All went smoothly until three months before the wedding when I asked Genie, "Do you think it might be possible to have some kind of open relationship in our marriage?" Her response, "Don't even think about it, and don't ever bring it up again!"

That single question and response created a permanent fault line between us. I was freaked out about monogamy, and monogamy was her safe harbor. Aghast, I said nothing more, depositing those desires underground.

Confronted by conflict and confusion is no way to enter a marriage. I wanted to commit but couldn't believe that having sex with only one woman for the rest of my life would be possible. I felt the whole institution of marriage was outdated.

Feeling shutdown, I was now too afraid to gently or gradually reintroduce the question. On her side, Genie no longer felt safe. We couldn't talk about how we felt so we started to fight. We got married anyway, saying our vows on the beach in St. Petersburg at sunset. Uncle Lew officiated. One hundred of our family and closest friends attended. It was a picture-book wedding.

So was the honeymoon. We took three months to travel through Asia. Starting in Japan, we flew to Thailand for five weeks and then on to Bali, Indonesia, for another five. The experience and memories would have been perfect if only it hadn't been hell between us most of the time. As it was, we managed to fight our way through some of the most beautiful locations on earth. ♪

CHAPTER 3

TOUCHED BY GOD

*"When awareness joins with your ears then listening happens...
when awareness joins with your eyes then seeing happens...
when awareness joins with your hands then touching happens..."*

Osho

*"If you are someone that is searching for the truth, then you
have to start to admit the loneliness that goes on in your heart.
Some of you have been working very hard at awakening or
at attaining freedom – but if you pay attention and go within,
you'll see that there is a longing in your heart that still isn't quite
satisfied. And if you're honest (about it), then there's hope that
you can find the truth that lies within you. In order for you to find
that truth, you have got to face yourself. And it takes a lot of
courage to do this work, and it is the work that you have to do in
order to wake up (all the way). There's no way around it."*

Kalindi

t was 1993. I was 33 years old and newly married. Traditionally, I was entering a time when things settle down, families get started, and career paths stabilize. Instead, I found myself marching to the beat of a different drum. It started with a series of fortunate events that inevitably guided me into my beyond-the-mind future.

Destiny Unfolding

These events began when I received a call from an old friend. Karen dated back to my first year of graduate school in 1981. I hadn't seen or heard from her in more than a decade. She was one of those who didn't make that first semester cut. In my memory, she was a dependent person, requiring help with her studies and a sympathetic ear around her marriage. Now, 12 years later, we met again and fell into an easy rapport. She was now an account executive with an advertising firm in Tampa.

Having recently completed the Landmark Forum, I shared about my experience and how I wanted to introduce this transformative thinking into GTE. Karen replied, "My God, that sounds like what's happening at my company." Karen told me about these consultants from California who were helping them with what they called "Breakthrough Projects." Without having met these guys, we were already on the same page. Karen gave me their names and contact information. I had to call them.

When I spoke to the receptionist at **Expansion Technologies,** I learned that the owners of the company had both been involved in *est* and Landmark. In fact, the company was licensed to use Landmark's technology in business. They even knew my Uncle Lew.

The more I found out, the more I wanted to work for them. Unfortunately, they were in the market for more clients rather than consultants. Long ago I had learned persistence from my Mom. She never gave up, neither would I. When it dawned on them that they were not going to easily be rid of me, they made an offer. If

I could lock down $200,000 worth of new business within the next 6 months, they would need another consultant and they would hire me.

I went to work and in no time I set up sales appointments with executives at GTE and Salomon Brothers, a Wall Street financial firm with a branch in Tampa. I provided the introduction and Dana Carmen, one of the owners led the presentations. It was so much fun! In a single day, we closed $250,000 in three separate deals – two for $50,000 and one for $150,000. Afterwards, Dana said, "I've never quoted a fee of $150,000 to a potential client before!" He was elated! The next year, I learned that annual revenue when I was hired was $500,000. We had increased their income by 50% in a single day. They had no choice but to hire me.

No matter how pleased I was, I wasn't an immediate Yes because, at that same time, a valued position came open at Salomon Brothers and I was recruited to fill it. This was not an easy choice. Both positions included a 50% pay hike. Expansion Technologies offered to set me up with a home office and a good deal of autonomy. Salomon was a corporate, nine to 5+ job with limited time off but solid benefits and security. This was a lifestyle decision for me – pitting freedom and possibility against structure and security. I took the leap and chose Expansion Technologies.

I'd been at my new job for only a short while when Dana shared about an organization called Miracle of Love, based in San Diego, that offered a 9-day spiritual course called The Intensive. I brought Genie in to hear about The Intensive. Although we were interested, it felt like too much. We were significantly involved with Landmark, my new job, and our marriage. Adding something more to the mix didn't make sense.

I heard nothing more about Miracle of Love until November 1993 when the other owner of the company was in Tampa, working with me at Salomon Brothers. One night, as we relaxed in the hot tub at his hotel, he shared about his most recent Intensive experience. Ever since it ended, he'd been waking up at 4 in the morning in a sweat. He described it as being tapped into the energy of God. He said he was shedding layer after layer of betrayal and pain. As he let go of layers of pains, he was filled with love. Tears ran down his face. He was so incredibly open, so nakedly vulnerable. I had never felt love like this before. I was deeply touched.

Genie and I decided to register for the 9-day Intensive. She went first, in January, 1994. Relatives and friends were invited to a celebration on the final day. I flew to San Diego and what a celebration it was! Genie was alive, open, and joyous in a way I'd never seen before. Between staff and participants, there were nearly 200 people in the room, caught up in wave after wave of ecstatic love. Sadly, I wasn't one of them. I was too frightened to join in. I felt too repressed and shutdown.

In five weeks' time it would be my turn. As the weeks passed and my Intensive drew near, I became even more fearful. Somehow, my ego knew it was about to lose complete control. By the time I packed my bags, I was plagued by a sense of dread. It took all my courage just to show up that first day.

The Intensive

What I found at my first nine-day Intensive was not what I expected. I walked into the room thinking I was a fairly open man – what some called a SNAG (Sensitive New Age Guy). Turns out I was emotionally numb and unaware, with no idea of what was going on inside of me. It was hard to grasp how much of me was little more than pretense covering an empty hole. My Landmark improvements were ego polishing. I had no real depth or authenticity. Quite a blow to my self-image!

It was like being introduced to my unadorned self. The format used included small-group sharing, followed by active meditations designed to open the emotional body and release feelings. It took a while for me to realize I didn't know how to share. While others exposed scars from life's traumas, I explained that my life was fine, and it had always been fine. When asked to say more, I elaborated, explaining that everybody goes through hard times and, sure, sometimes we hang on to survive but hard times always end and otherwise life is actually okay.

Slowly, after two-and-a-half days of holding this position, what I saw was happening to others shifted my vantage point. Something opened up in me. During one meditation I suddenly felt a deep sadness. I considered pushing it away and then decided to see what happened if I let myself feel it. What came was a lot of heartbreak. Flashes of memory poured in. I recalled attending that funeral when I was eight and how my Dad told me there was no need to cry. Twenty-five years later I hadn't cried. I came to see that I rationalized sadness, denying or avoiding emotions, literally schooling myself on how not to feel.

I was sufficiently conscious to know that being emotionally numb was unhealthy. I was aghast to discover how much I lived in my mind and not my heart. After breaking open in this meditation, a morass of sadness, upsets and disappointments poured forth. As the memories came back, I worked purposely to feel everything. I cried for the scared little boy and mourned the breakup of my first three romantic relationships. I went back into the fear of being bullied in school and gratefully took the help and support of the group. Every time I let some sorrow go, it felt as though I stepped into a new reality. My tears became a mixture of sadness and joy. It was surprisingly liberating to release in this way.

As The Intensive progressed, a huge weight started to come off. I got glimpses of a different kind of awareness. It felt like something popped inside my head and my perception changed. The music sounded different. I felt lighter and clearer, more connected to what was happening around me, instead of an observer. At one point, it appeared that everyone was moving in slow-motion. The only thing I could relate this heightened awareness to were my LSD experiences, only now I was having it without drugs!

The penultimate moment of The Intensive was a very long meditation, during which we were guided to go within, deep enough to connect to Spirit. To do this, I had to go through my fears and pains, one by one, feel them, release them, and let them go. This left me in a deeper place and ready to handle the next one. For hours I worked at it. How could I not? The room was alive with the sound and emotion of nearly 100 people going inward. I remembered painful events, felt the underlying hurt, and faced down denial and repressed anger. I was becoming aware that these old feelings were pockets of stuck energy that needed to be released, not something to be afraid of and avoided at all cost.

Still, I couldn't break through. I had too little trust and too much fear. How could I let go of what I knew when I did not trust the unknown? At that point, I seemed to give up. Nothing mattered. No one could help. I kept my eyes shut and no longer endeavored. Others were breaking through, I was not. I was the last participant still going.

I didn't know that Kalindi was in the room until she sat next to me on the floor. For the next two hours she stayed at my side while the entire staff and all the participants prayed I could let go. Kalindi held and caressed me. She spoke ever so gently, "You can let go, Mark. You don't have to let your fearstop you, not this time."

I opened my eyes. Kalindi gazed right at me. A stream of light energy flickered from her eyes into mine. I felt it all the way to my soul. Somehow I knew I could trust her. She whispered, "Are you ready to take a leap of faith?"

With her holding me, I felt I could face the unknown. I didn't have to hold back.

Kalindi said, "Take my hand; we'll jump together." When I touched her, I leapt into a space of total uninhibited freedom. Before I knew it, I was dancing alone in a circle made up of everyone else in the room. It was the greatest feeling of my life.

Then Kalindi was with me again. She said, "This is nothing, wait till tomorrow. Then I'll really take you flying." Before I could respond, she was gone, swirling away out of my line of vision. I couldn't imagine what she meant. Something even more amazing was going to happen? How could that be? This was the most amazing experience of my life.

Sure enough, the next day, I danced my way into a connection with something greater than myself.[1] I called it Source, Spirit or Universe, since I still was not okay with God. Whatever it was, I was part of it and felt at one with it. Best of all, I was not alone in this ecstasy. The entire room pulsed with it. Truly, this was a glorious opening.

Love Finds a Way

After The Intensive, I flew to San Francisco to see Uncle Lew. Finally, I could fathom what he'd been saying for so many years. When I told him I could now feel the love, Lew laughed, saying, "Yes, isn't it wonderful, knowing and trusting you are loved?"

One month later my Aunt Francine participated in her first Intensive. After her experience, she and Lew attended an evening with Kalindi in San Francisco. After Kalindi spoke, Lew introduced himself to her. Lew thanked her for letting people love her and she thanked him for being who he was. Later he told me just being in her presence felt like a tremendous gift.

After San Francisco I returned to Florida, gratefully aware of this new found sense of love and freedom. I'd tapped into a different kind of strength and openness. It came from deep within.

I remember being so thankful when it stayed with me rather than fading away like most other 'seminar highs.'

The crowning gift came when I realized I would never again let fear stop me. That one commitment opened me up to a slew of feelings. The more I felt, the less I was in my head, and the more I dropped into my heart.

This was particularly helpful with Genie when she was upset. First off, upset people upset me and I didn't like it. Secondly, from my minds view, her feelings were irrational. She made no sense, and making sense was important to my way of thinking. Now, I could feel her feelings for what they were, not what they weren't. Sometimes I could even understand why she felt that way.

Most importantly, I started to open up and feel love in a way I'd always wanted. Sometimes I overflowed with love and emotion. I'd see a movie or read a book and feel an amazing range of emotions, not the least being relief to feel anything at all. A larger power took hold of me in my life.

Even if I couldn't use the word, God, I now knew that something more existed. As long as I meditated, I maintained my connection and my opening to love. If I stopped meditating, I would shut down and lose my connection. It was as simple as that.

Best of all, was the meditation's focus on opening and releasing feelings and emotions. I had been shut down for so many years, it took a lot for me to open and even more to stay open. Once open and calm, I was able to think and access my higher intelligence. The answers and solutions I got from this place were often outside the box of my usual thinking, as well as being clearer and easier to act on.

During this time, my business horizons were brightening. Expansion Technologies was growing. I successfully sold and deli-

---

1 "Because if you meditatively dance then the ego disappears, the dancer disappears. The dancer becomes thoughtless, silent. The Dance continues and the dancer disappears. This is what I call the divine quality: now it is as if God is dancing through you, you are no more there." Osho, I Am That, Jaico, 2009

vered our consulting and coaching work to many companies and became a Master Coach.[1]

Some incredible people joined the company as contract consultants. One man had been a Landmark Forum leader for twenty years. During my time at Landmark, I had looked up to those leaders. They seemed so all-knowing and all-caring.

For me to work with him was quite a treat. Like me, he had recently shifted away from Landmark after participating in the Miracle of Love Intensive. He said the transformation he'd experienced during The Intensive was greater than anything in his lifetime. His back pain of twenty years had disappeared. He attributed this to the emotional release work he'd done in The Intensive.

An Incarnation of God?

It was this man who alerted me to the upcoming event at the Miracle of Love Center in San Diego called, "The Gourasana Event." He told me Gourasana[2] was Kalindi's spiritual teacher and that He was dying. He said, "This may be the last chance to ever see Him."

I'd been touched by Gourasana when I saw His book "Breaking the Cycle of Birth and Death"[3] in Dana's House in Marin. After reading a few passages, I felt something stir deep within me and I knew I wanted to be in San Diego for this event. I spoke with Genie and she agreed we would both go.

It was October 1994. The event began on a Saturday morning. From the outset I had a difficult time. Kalindi and other members of what they called the 'Core' shared stories about Gourasana, also known as "The Golden One."[4]

They went into detail about how He came into the world. In no time I was overwhelmed. What was being described was so difficult for my rational mind to handle.

Here is what I was hearing: Before manifesting Kalindi, her name was Carol Seidman, and Carol was married to David

Swanson. They were both serious spiritual seekers who met when they were members of the Krishna Consciousness movement. By the time they married, they'd left the Hare Krishnas behind, though both remained devoted spiritual seekers.

Many years before, David had a powerful spiritual experience. He was alone in his apartment, meditating and chanting in front of a statue of Krishna. Suddenly, a luminescence appeared in the room and a Being emerged from the Krishna Deity. David immediately went onto his knees, the being of light touched his hand, and to David it was the presence of The Almighty Himself. Six years later, when David started waking up in the middle of the night and experiencing massive influxes of energy, he recognized the same Being.

Kalindi described those days as David being "taken over by the energy of God in the manner of Jesus, Buddha, and Krishna."[5] This same energy eventually helped Kalindi awaken into full awareness. During this same time, the Core formed and after several years, the Miracle of Love® was started.

We were shown before-and-after pictures of David and Gourasana. There was quite a pronounced physical transformation. Even from where I sat, there was no denying David looked like a rather meek and physically small man. Gourasana, on the other hand, was visually larger and more formidable. His head seemed to have nearly doubled in size. They seemed like two different beings.

---

1 A Master Coach is someone who can train and coach other coaches.

2 *Gourasana is pronounced Goo-RAH-sah-nah.*

3 Gourasana, *Breaking the Cycle of Birth and Death,* Miracle of Love, 2001

4 Soon after Gourasana came, He called for a 'Core' of people to gather around Him. Gourasana said these people had to have "unshakable faith, not blind faith, not sentimental faith, not some false belief, false hope." A group of seven people responded to this call.

5 What is an Incarnation of God? Gourasana says that an Incarnation "means all the love of God and all the power of God is coming in, and the only thing that can be received is love." Over the ages, many Incarnations of God have come to assist people in their search for God. Examples of these Incarnations are Buddha, Krishna, and Jesus.

David 1982   Gourasana 1991

I covertly glanced around the room. Did all these people really believe this stuff? People sure seemed to be drinking it in – many of them were taking notes.

The room was packed with an audience of 300 or more people in rapt silence. I was sitting towards the back. Thank God the exit was right behind me because the more I heard the more I wanted out of there.

Then I thought … but wait a minute, these are the same people who led The Intensive and supported me through all I'd experienced. There was no way to deny what had happened to me. It was my experience and if I couldn't trust that, what could I trust? The least I could do was to have enough respect to listen to them. That simple fact blocked the urge in me to flee, even though the urge returned repeatedly. By early Sunday I had a purpose: I had to see the **G-man.** If He'd gone through half of what they described, He was worth the wait.

In one of her talks, Kalindi emphasized that Gourasana had asked for permission before entering David's body. From the beginning, He clearly told David what it would mean to be a vessel for the direct energy of God. He informed David that he would die young because the pure spiritual energy of Gourasana's full power and presence would take its toll on his body and his body only. Because David knew who Gourasana was, he consented.

By 1990, when the transformation between David and Gourasana was complete, Gourasana told Kalindi that the body would last about five more years. So here we were in October 1994 with Kalindi reporting that Gourasana was perilously close to death.

Finally, around two in the afternoon on Sunday, Gourasana entered the room. He emanated robust, palpable energy. A wave of pure love and benevolence washed over me. He sat down with Kalindi on His right and Lady Gayle[1] on His left and, without preamble, spoke to us for two hours.

I was completely blown away as He spoke. He had a Presence like nothing I had sensed before. My mind was disengaged. The energy in the entire room had heightened and lightened.

I loved being in His immensely compassionate presence. Later, when Genie asked me what I recalled, I said that Kalindi and The Lady were his two angels, and what David went through would not be required of anyone else. That was it.

After He finished speaking, everyone got into line and one-by-one connected with Gourasana by gazing into His eyes. I was one of the last in that very long line. I got to watch so many others go up to Him. Some looked into His eyes and after a few seconds fell over. Others writhed or cried out. There were all sorts of emotional and physical reactions. When my turn came, I stared into the

---

1 Lady Gayle was a member of the original Core who became Kalindi's first disciple. Named Lady Gayle by Gourasana because she carries the qualities of The Mother. She eventually became known simply as The Lady.

depths of these large eyes and experienced nothing at all, or so I thought. I left the event glad I had experienced Him in the body. A few months later He died.[1]

The following spring, in May 1995, I returned to San Diego to review The Intensive. I'd had my initial opening so this time it was easier for me. I knew where to go inside myself. There was less denial and greater desire. The work brought with it such healing. I forgave slights, and resolved regrets and resentments with my mother, father, and brother (particularly the bullying). I opened up and connected to a deeper love and more fully committed to ending the fear and separation that restrained me.

Love Takes Over

As spring ended, my wife Genie and I moved to Marin County in northern California to be more actively involved in a Miracle of Love community. It was a bonus that Expansion Technologies was headquartered there. We moved into a communal house with a hot tub in a beautiful setting on top of a hill in Larkspur. It was California living.

We lived with other people, all of whom were actively engaged in Miracle of Love and serious spiritual transformation. I had my office in the house. I regularly attended Miracle of Love meditations and workshops and actively worked on dismantling my crumbling walls of concepts, habits, and beliefs that once protected my fears.

Big change was in the wind. My relationship with Genie was under duress. I was not a one-woman guy, and she knew it. We wanted different things and I was not willing to compromise. In September 1995, I connected with another woman. Her name was Lauren. She was one of Kalindi's disciples. I met her while sitting on a bench waiting for meditation to start. She was so warm-hearted and open. What passed between us felt like the sweetest love. I was irresistibly drawn to her. I laid my head on her chest. She embraced me and, for those few moments, I felt the deepest man-woman love I'd ever known. I knew I could not stay in my restrictive, closed marriage. Our love affair was unavoidable.

For the next three months, Genie tried to salvage our relationship, yet my heart was not in it. We'd tried to get pregnant and that never happened. I'd let go around having children. I was moving fast on my spiritual desires. I'd never imagined divorce but that's what we had to do. If it wasn't Lauren, it would have been someone else. Genie and I never really loved each other – certainly not like I had Helle and now felt with Lauren. It was more of a commitment to be together than a heart connection. Given our different desires and goals, our paths were diverging.

Lauren was fearless, bright, and inquisitive. Her father was a university professor; her mother, an intellectual. She had been on her spiritual path for many years, having left home at eighteen to seek God. Before coming to Miracle of Love, she'd been a Sannyasin[2] and disciple of Osho. She was a successful therapist working with couples and groups.

Before meeting me, she'd been in a three-way relationship with one man and another woman for several years. She completed her first Intensive in 1993, and now she was a disciple of Kalindi. To say that her spiritual awareness was light years ahead of mine would not be an exaggeration. She was extremely open sexually and willingly played out my fantasies.

God, sex, and love entered my life in a single moment. I had never met anyone like Lauren. While I was mostly interested in good times, Lauren was all about depth and seriousness. She discouraged me from drinking; she said it dulled my awareness. Even sex had a deeper spiritual purpose. She was right! I was

---

1 The night before Gourasana left His body, He called Kalindi and The Lady to let them know He was leaving. He asked Kalindi if she was ready to carry on His Mission and she said Yes. The next morning, March 24, 1995, He was gone.

2 Osho (1931-1990), formerly known as Bhagwan Shree Rajneesh, was an Indian mystic and outspoken critic of organized religion. His teachings focused on meditation, awareness, love, courage, and humor. Deported from the US for immigration violations in the early 1980s, Osho returned to India and died in 1990 at the age of fifty-eight. His followers are found around the world and referred to as 'Sannyasins.'

opening sexually to different women and combinations of partners. Within no time, we made a pact that any sexual liaison be initiated by Lauren since I was not to be trusted.

Lauren encouraged me to overcome my fears. With her, I took a music performance workshop. This was way outside my comfort zone but I loved expanding my boundaries and singing "Bad to the Bone"[1] with a live band in front of 100 people in a small concert hall. We even went skydiving.

Emotionally, my modus operandi was still governed by the reptilian urge to flee. I'd been running and hiding since I was a kid. Lauren worked endlessly to help me face my intimacy fears head on. One time she wrote this note to me, "If I open more, will you run? I am afraid of you, are you afraid of me? I am here for you, are you here for me? I am here to be free, do you want to be free?" I had no idea how to answer her.

In March 1996, we went together to the Miracle of Love Retreat in San Diego. These retreats were designed as several days of fast movement. I journaled on the first day what I wanted to accomplish:

- Overcome fear and self-loathing;
- Learn to stop repeating patterns of avoidance with Lauren and colleagues;
- Find a way to change my ongoing dread of the future;
- I fear connection; I fear surrender; I fear the fear and *where is freedom?*

During the Retreat, I found enough courage to talk with Kalindi for a few minutes. She was talking with people one-on-one.

When it was my turn, I told her, "Kalindi, I resist most of the things I'm supposed to do, both spiritually and materially. What can I do about that?"

She said, "Well, you are on the path of most resistance. There is nothing wrong with that; you will just suffer more."

I was astonished by what she said. Instead of some answer or help about my resistance, she instead showed me the results of my choices.

On the last day I was praying to be filled with Gourasana's energy. I didn't know if that had happened, yet I left the Retreat feeling exalted. Little did I know what was waiting for me!

That summer another consequential event occurred. My mother, Marilyn, came to visit me in Marin. She stayed in the house with Lauren and I for a week. We spent some time with Genie, and she got to know Lauren and the other people I lived with.

Marilyn felt much love with us that week. Coming from her somewhat alone and fearful situation in New York City, living in the splendor and beauty of Marin County with six loving and connected people, including her son, made it a magical week for her. By the time she left, she had decided to do The Intensive in San Diego the next month. My Mother saw how much it meant to me, and wanted to see what she could find for herself.

I went to San Diego to be with her at the end of her Intensive. I didn't know what to expect. She was so open and vulnerable; I had never seen her like this. I treasured these moments.

When I asked what happened for her, she said, "I found God again. I remembered growing up, being on Grandpa Joe's lap, it was the safest place in the world for me. Around five years old, because of uncertainty around sexuality with his young daughter, he stopped holding me and playing with me in that way." She went on, "Back then, I had God and my father mixed together. So when I lost him, I lost God. Having realized this now, I feel I have reconnected with God again so I am no longer alone." To this day, I hold it precious that my mother trusted me enough to find this for herself. ♪

---

1   George Thorogood and the Delaware Destroyers, *Bad to the Bone*, EMI, 1981

CHAPTER 4

GOURASANA

*"I have waited so long for you to come Home.
You cannot imagine my desire. I have not forgotten you
for a second. And I only care about you.
And I am determined. If you can also become determined,
then everything is possible."*

Gourasana

*"Devotees long for the Darshan (seeing) of the great
ones past (e.g., Jesus, Buddha) and read books fantasizing
what it would have been like to be alive at the time
when the Adepts (great ones) stood on Earth ...
Is it not fitting that the Divine
has manifested in the West this time?
Is not the 'westernized' world just the place
where Divine Help is needed most – to create lessons
here amongst those who had no exposure,
so that they would become capable
of receiving Divine Grace?"*

Adi Da

S oon after the retreat, Lauren had a premonition. She said it came to her that we should take Ecstasy three times. She was surprised since she was not into drugs at all. I'd never taken Ecstasy and hadn't used drugs in over 10 years. I was not even smoking pot.[1]

Some people took Ecstasy to make love, dance, or trip out. Lauren and I took it to go into deep exploratory conversations. At first I was nervous but, after experiencing some pleasant feelings, things settled nicely into a relatively uneventful high.

The second time we took Ecstasy was more directed and powerful. Lauren was helping me become aware of energy. Eventually, while sitting outside near a tree, I could feel the living energy of the tree. The energy of the tree felt similar to my own. I realized for the first time that I was a soul connected to the same universal energy as all living entities.

In this way I became aware I was something more than this body, this collection of thoughts, feelings, tapes, reflexes, etc. – the collective identity known as Mark.

Previously, I had barely wanted to exist beyond self-pleasures. Now I thought to myself, "I have a soul that came here to give and to love. The next step is to surrender all of myself to God, The One, The Eternal." This recognition keenly changed my belief system.

Gourasana Takes Over

The third and final time we took Ecstasy, I experienced the most powerful, life-altering event in my life. This proved to be the culmination of Lauren's vision. We were staying in an isolated

---

1 Starting in high school, through college, and during the first three or four years of graduate school, I smoked pot almost every day. In 1984, I decided to stop smoking and did not smoke for the next 13 years.

cabin in Mendocino, three hours north of San Francisco. We sat across from each other in a couple of dining room chairs. Once the Ecstasy kicked in and we were feeling light and open, Lauren asked me, "What do you want to work on?"

I told her there was a place of pain deep inside I wanted to get to but so far could not reach in my meditations. It felt like a dark, gaping hole surrounded by a wall of fear. Every time I got near it, I popped right out.

She said, "Only if you want to break free **in this lifetime** would it be necessary to go through your deepest fears into your core pain."

I responded, "I don't know anything about that. I don't know if God is even real or what I'd be breaking free of or into. I do know that I love what I'm finding through my opening and releasing; I find that very valuable."

Lauren asked if I wanted to talk about what my desire was. I said, "Yes."

We talked until I sussed out how I came to believe that my emotional safety was best served by denial and avoidance. In addition, once my sex/love addiction got locked in place during my teens, it was settled, and in no time I was frozen in place. Then I heard myself say, "I do want to get free."

Lauren said, "Okay, go into that desire."

I closed my eyes, went within, and focused on my desire for freedom. However, everywhere I looked was dark and forbidding. I opened my eyes and looked at her.

She asked, "What do you desire to break free of?"

I dove into that inquiry and fell into an emotional black hole filled with unbearable pain. All hell broke loose. Sweating profusely and feeling like I would die, I started howling at the top of my voice. I flailed around on the floor and wound up lying over the top of the sofa. I felt like puking. Lauren ran to get a bucket.

It was only dry heaves. Still, I felt like I was purging out some old, putrid, dark energy accumulated over thousands of years. Finally, I slumped over – empty and spent.

Before I had time to realize what was happening, another powerful energy took over my body. I was lifted off the couch. I say I was lifted because it was not me doing it. I landed on my feet, standing about ten feet away from Lauren who had been sitting next to me on the couch.

Lauren said I looked terrified, that my eyes were desperate and wild. The energy came into me in waves, filling me from the top down – my head, heart, core, pelvis and limbs. Then Bam! A vibration and sound started passing through my entire body before escaping from my lips, "GOU-RA-SA-NA, GOU-RA-SA-NA, GOURASANA!" Lauren thought, *"How does he know to scream His name?"*

I was standing straight up at the ready. I don't know how but I was not the only being inside of me. I was aware, I could see and hear, but somehow I had been pushed aside. I did not have control over my own body. I could not speak. Then, without my choosing to do so, we were moving around the room.

Seemingly, Gourasana was in charge! He looked at Lauren. She was frightened and confused. Then He spoke to her. (I say, 'He spoke' because I did not form or speak the words that came out of my mouth.) His voice was calm and firm. He said to Lauren, "Do not be afraid; I am benevolent."

Lauren relaxed. I was able to see through my eyes and observe what He was doing and that was it. I watched as He saw the copy of **Breaking the Cycle** on the coffee table. He said out loud, "Ah, my book" and picked it up to read. As He looked at the different passages, He murmured to Himself, "Uh huh, yes, uh huh."

I was reading along with Him, automatically getting the truth of each passage. Then my awareness exploded open and a simultaneous awakening and realization occurred. In a flash, I knew that **God was real!** God is real and Gourasana is an Incarnation of God and His message is real. It is possible to break the cycle of birth and death and I wanted to do that.

Before I could process these realizations, Gourasana walked over and sat down next to Lauren on the couch. He and I didn't even move in the same way. His Presence exuded this graceful force. I was simply along for the ride. I was perplexed. How could I not be in control of my own body?

Then Gourasana asked Lauren, "When are you going to surrender to Kalindi?" She stumbled around, trying to come up with some answer. Again, purely as an observer, I watched as in no time, He took her back into her childhood to when she first shut down at the age of four.

He asked questions about how she felt and what she did to survive. He helped her understand the truth for herself. He brought her into realization that her mother did not do anything to her. It was Lauren who chose to shut down; it was Lauren who created the loneliness she could no longer handle.

It was Lauren's responsibility to face everything that happened in her life. It was her life, after all. It belonged to no one else. Standing on the firm ground of clarity, Lauren recognized she could choose to be responsible and, in that space, chose to surrender to Kalindi.

Gourasana continued to speak with her over the next couple of hours. I remember time passing but have no recollection of what He said. Even though His words came out of my mouth, I wasn't saying them and my mind didn't record them. Lauren said He also asked about a close disciple of His (a woman who I did not know) who had been ill when He left his body. He wanted to know how she was. Then Gourasana changed the subject. He said, "We have to find the souls" (who desire to return Home in this lifetime).

After a while, the energy of Gourasana began to recede and I was able to reclaim control over my body. Lauren and I looked at one another. We'd both just had a profound experience. When she asked me what it was like to have Him inside of me, I responded, "What I imagine full awareness would be like. He was very powerful. What did you see?"

She said, "It was Him in you, pacing up and down in front of the coffee table. It was the way I'd seen Him walk. It was weird seeing Him in your body."

Then I got swept back into silence. I looked at her and said, "Maybe Gourasana hasn't gone so far away after all." Once again, I started saying things that didn't sound like me. I was talking about the Middle East and planetary changes that have yet come to pass.

Lauren started taking notes of what He said, predicting that the present-day hatred between Arabs and Jews would transform into love and heal the world, prophesying that from these beginnings the rest of the planet would enter an age of light destined to last 1000 years.

Gourasana went on to say we have come to a global crossroads in which there is an opportunity for true healing. Unlike in the past, the healing of this age can be done consciously. Those defending the old ways, grow hardened.

Gourasana warned that evil can't free men's hearts. It can captivate or move them but it can't free them. Fear keeps people locked up, and only the Lord who lives in all of us can break us free. It will take selfless devotion to God and heart-awareness. This is happening for more and more people and still it will take many centuries for significant change to occur for the majority of the population.

After some time, Lauren said, "Let's go outside and walk." I readily agreed.

It was three in the morning. We were deep in the country, surrounded by farmland. The clear sky was awash in stars. I looked at a tree. My entire focus and awareness went into that tree. There was no emotion in the tree, yet its essence was utterly alive. A dog went by. Its energy was more complex. The dog had several emotions at play. We passed a herd of cattle. The cows were sad. It was as though they spent their entire incarnation feeling this way.

Wherever I focused my awareness, I pierced into the truth. I scanned the sky, seeking the end of the universe. I couldn't find it because it didn't exist. I realized that everything exists in one place and one time like a tiny, condensed dot. I preached to Lauren, "In truth, there is no distance, time, or space, save as functions of the illusion.[1] God created the illusion as a physical container for us to live within. Material reality and the illusion of separation require space, time, and distance to exist." I smiled. It all made such perfect sense.

After we went inside, there was a break in the action for a moment or two and then another wave of awareness and information poured in. By now Gourasana had been in me for almost twelve hours and I was growing fearful of losing myself.

Lauren decided to try and contact Kalindi. She spoke to Kendra, one of Kalindi's companions and closest disciples. Kendra reported that Kalindi was in seclusion and unavailable. When Lauren asked to speak to The Lady, she learned that she too was unavailable. Undeterred, Lauren went looking for Jim St. James, the next in line among Kalindi's leaders.

Jim answered her call. She told him what was happening. Jim asked to speak to me. He was calm and direct. I told him I felt like a broken shell. Part of me was thrilled and part of me was on red alert.

Jim said, "There are two things that may help. First, you should know that you have dominion over your own body. If it is Gourasana, it is a benevolent energy. At any time, you can tell the energy to leave and it will. Second, watch out for your ego. Once you are solely back in control, your ego will try to co-opt this experience and use it for its own self-aggrandizement."

I got off the phone and told Lauren what he said. She asked, "What do you want to do?"

I said, "I want to stop it; I can't take anymore."

As I spoke, Gourasana left. He was there and then He was gone, just like that. My immediate reaction was, "Oh no, not yet! Come back, please." I was too late. He was gone.

Later that day, when driving home, Lauren said, "You should write to Kalindi." I agreed and the next day I wrote the following letter to her.

64

To the one who would guide me,   *July 27, 1996*

Kalindi, my name is Mark Brostoff. When I first did The Intensive in February 1994, you took me through my fear and lack of trust into God's love. I've always been grateful for that and have continued to do my work to go within and open more. Recently, I have chosen to follow this path and that surrender to God is what my life is for.

Last week, I got clear that I wanted to get free in this lifetime. I went into the deepest part of my pain, to a place I'd been unable to go before. That was when the energy of Gourasana fully entered my body head-to-toe. For hours He spoke through me to my beloved Lauren of what we must do. He told us to surrender to and serve you and His mission, so that the souls who want to break free can do so. I want your guidance in how to break free. I am yours, and grateful and hopeful that you will have me. I lovingly and patiently await your guidance for following God's Will. Please help me return home. I am ready now. Your servant and partner for God's grace here and everywhere,

Mark Brostoff

Within a few days, I received a phone call from Kalindi's assistant, Karin. She delivered the following message, "Kalindi got your letter and said you have had a special benediction. She invites you to write to her weekly and to come crashing into Kalindi now."

This experience, along with my first Intensive, became the two events that converted my reality from material to spiritual. Before these encounters, I was without purpose and clarity. I was lost and confused, chasing a dream, pretending and hoping. Now I felt connected to a God I knew was real. These phenomena morphed me into a fresh human being.

---

1   "Time is a box formed by thoughts of the past and future. When there is only the immediate *now* – when you're not dwelling in the past or anticipating the future, but you are just right here, right now – you are outside of time. Dwelling in the moment is dwelling in the soul, which is eternal presence." Ram Dass, *Polishing The Mirror*, 2014

On Fire

Energetically, I was on fire. I felt very intense inside all the time. I was waking up in the middle of the night with chills and sweats. Though I was vigilantly on guard to stop my ego from taking control, often it toyed with me and my new found desires.

When it came to sexual desire and women, ego won hands down. I was now open to the wildness of my desire to be with anyone who wanted to be with me. Unfortunately, my limited awareness lacked sufficient love and care to do this well. When I pursued another woman living in our house, I pushed even Lauren's buttons. She was okay with freedom within emotional boundaries, but I was currently oblivious to anything like that.

At the same time, I hungered for a deeply intimate and committed relationship. Lauren wanted that too, so we stayed together. However, our relationship was strained. My erratic sexual exploits made it hard for her.

During this time, I started writing to Kalindi as she had asked. It took me three weeks to write the first letter. I thanked her for her message and enclosed a photo of myself so she could know who I was. I told her how I appreciated that she said my experience with Gourasana was a benediction. I told her about my work, explained how I suffered when I forgot God, assured her of my desire to break free, and glossed over that it took me three weeks to write, promising to do better moving forward. A promise I did not keep.

My next letter focused on the duality of my spiritual opening. Inside my newly-found freedom, I'd found this sweet, vulnerable part of myself, as well as a selfish, uncaring asshole. One moment I would admit to Lauren actions that completely disregarded her, and the next cry in her arms like a baby, not knowing what was happening to me. I was a veritable Jekyll and Hyde, vacillating between periods of intense and uncontrollable 'break out' energy, followed by remorse that would leave me weeping in a corner.

Here are two other telling letters from this time:

Dear Kalindi,   *October 1996*

I have just completed staffing[1] the first 2-1/2 days of The Intensive. It is the first time I have staffed. It was a glorious experience. However, I am frustrated by my continued inability to have my life set up to have giving as my main priority. I was distracted and had to leave early because of my work. I also see how my ego's importance drives these things, keeping me from the heartfelt joy of selfless giving.

I am making concrete changes step-by-step, but feel I am not doing it fast enough. I am not sure I even want to keep doing my consulting work. I feel I need to get my life together, so I can focus my attention on God's will for me, or maybe it all happens simultaneously? Right now, I feel pulled on, angry, frustrated, sad, and deep down – unworthy.

My desire is to continue to simplify my life so I can be available to meditate, pray, and serve. My deepest desire is to serve the Lord, be with Him, and never be alone or separate again.

Dear Kalindi,   *December 1996*

My divorce from my wife, Genie, will be official on December 18. This is sad for me. Genie and I are working together to heal ourselves and the separation between her and Lauren. I am grateful for this.

Kalindi, I have not written to you for two weeks. I avoid writing to you. I'll do anything else other than write to you. I also avoid meditating, praying, and serving. I seek distractions – TV, sex, movies, phone calls or getting things done, anything but slowing down, calming down, and focusing on God.

This feels to me like my resistance to surrender. I'm still running my life, rushing around, wanting attention, with God third or fourth. Please advise me if you see or feel anything else for me. I welcome your guidance.

---

1   Staffing The Intensive was a powerful way to give back and continue my own spiritual movement.

CHAPTER 5

KALINDI

"The association of great souls is rarely obtained, difficult to understand, and infallible. Another proof of the power of the mahatma (Master) is their ability to convert non-devotees into saintly persons. The association of a mahatma is very rare, and yet it is available to a sincere seeker. Upon contacting a great soul, one should realize one's good fortune, and with a joyful but serious attitude one should surrender unto his or her lotus feet."

Swami Chinmayananda

"You might be a kind-hearted and giving person, but you give when it suits you; you give if there is something in it for you. That giving allows your ego to feel like you are a kind and loving person, and you are happy to see the other person happy. Your ego would love to feel that it is kind and loving and charitable, but it's still the ego that is giving. When you give from your heart with no expectation but because you want to give and serve, you will be acknowledged through your own heart. The reciprocation comes from God, and you have to give up even the idea that you want reciprocation from God. You have to want nothing other than to give of yourself."

Kalindi La Gourasana

n January 1997, Kalindi introduced "The Path to Ultimate Freedom®" to the Mission. An essential precept of the Path was accepting Kalindi as your spiritual Master and thereby agreeing to follow her spiritual guidance without question. While I did want to keep opening and coming further into God, I was not looking to surrender to a Master. I didn't know if I was really ready to give up my selfish pursuits and pleasures. I wasn't sure if I was serious enough to apply for such a path. In my first letter to Kalindi in 1997, I wrote:

I'm grateful for the direction the Mission is going in. I need this kind of structure, this kind of seriousness from the Path. Left to my own devices, I will slip out. Now I feel all the back doors closing, and that is critical for me. I may bounce around like a caged rat inside this new structure, but nonetheless, my energy will be contained and focused. I fear the ramifications of all this – what I will need to let go of – yet I am grateful for the opportunity to choose.

I am bound by the fear of losing my family, my friends, their possible condemnation and lack of understanding of what I am doing. Kalindi, please help me!

I am able to be honest with my mother about it, which I appreciate. At the same time, she is concerned about me "getting lost" in this path. So will I lose myself, Kalindi? Will I be taken over? Am I following some crazy path?

It is good for me to express these concerns. Thank you for hearing them. It returns me to my truth and to what I know. All I have are my experiences – of Gourasana, of you, of The Lady.

Praying for God's Love, Mark

Fortunately, there also was a 30-Day Path Choice program written by Jim St. James that I could participate in.[1] The program introduced the Path and the requirements and commitments for

---

1   The 30-day program was designed to work at your own pace, alone or with small groups of other participants by phone or in person over the course of 30 days.

acceptance. Jim explained, "The Path is something in the world to hold you to your spiritual commitments." He designed the program to help us make our truest choice. During this time I wrote:

To my would-be Master Kalindi,

This is a serious choice I am considering. I am relating to it like it is the biggest choice of my entire life. More than college, career, marriage, children, etc. Am I ready? Is there something else for me to attend to or build first?

Part of my frustration is how much I know that this material world is not it. It is not everlasting or eternal; it is, at best, an unacceptable place. Yet I cling to it. I am most attached to my relationship and my work. I see I could let go of my relationship with Lauren, more easily than my work. It seems that my life has prepared me to do what I am contemplating now. In my relationship with you, Kalindi, I essentially trust you. I respect you and feel your link to God. I agree with everything you say on your talks and the essence and structure of the Mission and Path.

I feel that since you are a woman, some of my issues with women are in the way of me feeling you fully. It has been useful for me to see this and to more actively question my trust and willingness to surrender to you.

With Love, Mark

Today I am surprised that I had enough awareness back then to see that, because Kalindi was an attractive woman, my judgment could be clouded by my inability to see past her sensuality and therefore not accept her as a vessel of God's pure love.

For me, the most helpful suggestion from Jim came when he wrote, "When you are not sure or you don't know, have enough trust and faith to ask God directly." This is what I did. I meditated, releasing surface emotions, and then went into my fears, judgments, and negative thoughts about masters and disciples. After a while, the need to release fell away and I opened up inside.

Then I sat quietly, becoming empty and calm. From this receptive place, I asked God, "Please tell me about Kalindi. Who is she? Can I surrender my life to her?" After some time, I saw an image of Kalindi sitting inside the heart of God. I thought to myself, "Wow, He is telling me something."

I brought these same questions to meditation two more times and each time I saw the same image. That was all I needed and at the end of the 30-day program, I applied to go on the Path. A few weeks later, I wrote to Kalindi:

In my current level of surrender and open heart I have bumped into deeper fear of loss, being abandoned and left alone, and fear of commitment. My anger is starting to come to the surface, unusual for me, but good. Now I can deal with it. I feel like I am going crazy sometimes. I have doubted my choice for the Path sometimes. My choice has scared some of my business partners; they fear I will lose my commitment to our work efforts (they were right).

I clearly see how easily I give my power away when I'm in a relationship. I really become a wussy. I have so much fear of loss that I cannot even see straight here. I feel the hole in myself that I use women and other distractions to fill. Now I am calling on God to fill me.

In mid-March, I was contacted by a Miracle of Love staff person to tell me I'd been accepted to the Path. My heart quickened. I was scared and grateful at the same time. Soon after, Genie came to meditation and we cried and cried about our pain and loss. For the first time since the divorce, Genie, Lauren, and I met together afterwards. We committed to support each other in our spiritual movement towards God.

Destiny Calling

A couple of weeks later, while staffing an Intensive, I was meditating with other staff and the leaders after the participants had left at the end of the day. I became extremely deep and calm, and started asking practical questions of God. What is the best living situation for me to move forward spiritually? Should I continue to live alone? Do I move in with Lauren or back into a communal, spiritual house?[1]

At first, there was the usual silence, then came this voice that said, "Move in with Kendra." I was shocked. Why Kendra? I barely knew Kendra, and Kalindi lived in Kendra's house. It wasn't like anyone could just move in there.

After the meditation, I went looking for Lauren. She reacted similarly, "That's where Kalindi lives. You can't move in there."

Nonetheless, what I'd heard was so clear and unexpected I knew I had to act on it. The next day, I called Kendra and told her about the message. She didn't know what to make of it and suggested we wait and see what happens. I said fine and left it at that.

One week later, I was working in Tulsa, Oklahoma, when Kendra called me on my cell phone. Back then, roaming charges were outrageously expensive for cell phones so I didn't keep my phone on when traveling. However, on that day my associate had just completed a check-in call with our home office.

Kalindi and Kendra 1997

I was about to turn the phone off and put it back in my briefcase, when this voice inside my head said, "Leave it on." I wasn't used to hearing messages in the middle of a restaurant so I was about to turn the phone off anyway when the voice became emphatic, "LEAVE IT ON."

Again, this voice was too clear to ignore so I left the phone on and put it in my jacket pocket.

Five minutes later Kendra called. She told me she had just spoken to Kalindi, who responded, "Tell him that message is straight from Gourasana. If he wants to move in, he can do so right away."

I was blown away to hear this. I immediately thought, "If I say Yes, it will be the beginning of the end for my ego, my separate life, and who knows what else." I closed my eyes and took a moment to go inside. From deep within the answer came, "Yes," I said.

Kendra asked about timing. I replied, "I get home tomorrow night. I can move in then."

Kendra said, "Okay, we'll have a room ready for you."[2]

As noted earlier, my first ever contact with Kalindi was at The Intensive in February 1994. That was my first taste of trusting her. Since 1994, I'd seen her at a couple of Retreats and over one weekend at the Gourasana Event.

Kalindi 1995

There had been no personal interaction between us. I was in the audience and she was up on stage sitting in a white, wingback armchair. There was a tall, good looking man assisting her. She would have him adjust her microphone, rearrange the flowers, straighten a photo on the wall, or bring her a large heavy gong she used to acknowledge when the truth was spoken.

---

1 There were several of these houses in Marin County. These houses were composed of individuals participating in Miracle of Love, its programs and/or the path. They were essentially several people committed to the same spiritual path living together to support their spiritual movement. I had initially lived in such a house in Larkspur when I first moved to California, before I moved into the cottage in Fairfax by myself.

2 This whole experience is magnificently spoken about by The Lady on her 2004 talk entitled "Listening for the Whispers of God."

There seemed to be a sweet and playful back and forth between the two of them. He was obviously surrendered to her. More than once I found myself wishing I could be that guy.

When I arrived back in Marin, I moved into Kendra's house, called Ames.[1] Kalindi had arranged that Kendra and I share a bedroom. We had two twin beds and shared a single dresser with two drawers for me. I also had one shelf in a bathroom shared by five people. This meant most of my possessions had nowhere to go.

Kendra helped me to trim down. It wasn't easy. For example, I was quite attached to an expensive Scandinavian blanket. When Kendra asked me to let it go, I was horrified. After some serious hesitation I gulped and said, "OK." This process went on for several hours until the excess was gone.

That night, lying in bed, I felt lighter. I was elated. This was such a wonderful turn of events. How lucky was I to be on the Path to Ultimate Freedom, living on an incredible estate in Marin, sharing a room with an incredibly loving and powerful woman, and somewhere nearby my personal Master and the spiritual leader of the Miracle of Love Church. My world had changed. I was loving it.

The harder part was talking with Lauren about this significant change. While she was happy for me spiritually, as my girlfriend she was naturally uncertain of how this would affect our relationship.

True Giving and Abundance

For the first five days at the house, I did not see Kalindi at all. She was tucked away in her quarters at the back of the house in a little bedroom. On the sixth day, Kendra said, "Kalindi would like to see you."

I followed Kendra into Kalindi's quarters. It was magnificent back there, exuding an otherworldly, holy feeling. Kalindi was sitting on a white couch in her pajamas. I sat down on the floor in front of her. She spoke to me nonstop for the next three hours.

74

I was captivated. I was soaking in so much love and ecstasy. It wasn't her words so much as it was the energy emanating from her. Kalindi was pouring light into me! She spoke about God's unconditional love. I could tangibly feel that love as she spoke the words. I came to realize over time that this was one of the greatest hallmarks of Kalindi. When she spoke, I directly experienced what her words were pointing me towards. It was like being in a multi-dimensional reality in which her energy and words came together in a place beyond my mind.

Miracle of Love was in a funding drive at this time so it felt natural to me that, at the end of our time together, Kalindi asked me if I'd like to make a donation.

As with so much else, Kalindi understood my generous nature and how I kept a tight rein over it. It wasn't that I didn't give. For a while now I'd felt pulled to contribute to charities such as Save the Children, CARE, Greenpeace, and Amnesty International. I started out making annual donations in the $25 range. As my income rose, so did the size of my contributions, typically writing checks for $100-$250.

Fund-raising in Miracle of Love was in an entirely different league. Kendra had given millions of dollars; a number of people were donating $100,000 annually. Since moving into Ames, Kendra and I regularly spoke about my contributing financially to the church. I was open to the idea.

I had already received so much value from Miracle of Love, I was very willing to support it financially. Besides, I already knew the benefit of giving and how much more I would receive from going beyond my rational limitations and stepping into the realm of unconditional giving.

Still, when Kendra suggested an initial commitment of $10,000, I laughed aloud. Even so, I did write a check for $5,000 or

---

1   Kendra Gamble Goldenway was an heiress to the Procter&Gamble family fortune and a fiercely devoted disciple of Kalindi and Gourasana. She lived on an estate in Ross, Marin County, north of San Francisco. The address of the house was 1 Ames Road, thus the name.

twenty times more than I'd ever donated before. Most importantly, I was overjoyed from giving in this way! Besides, I was earning over $8,000/month so I would hardly miss it.

Now, sitting in front of Kalindi, I felt myself disengaging from my reservations. I wanted to be free of my fears and limitations. I was quite open to giving more. I still had $20,000 in my savings account. I offered to write a check for all of it.

Kalindi asked, "Will giving $20,000 set you free from your sense of scarcity or lack? Does this put you into God's abundance and help you know you will do anything for God?"

I replied, "No, not really. I'll hardly notice it."

She responded, "What amount would?"

I said, "$50,000."

She asked, "Do you want to give 50,000?"

I said, "Yes."

She nodded thoughtfully and soon thereafter, we parted. As I left Kalindi's quarters, I was flying in the freedom of going beyond my limits and the ecstasy of selfless giving.

The next day I went to my bank to borrow an additional $30,000. When I had nothing to offer as collateral, it fell into the category of an unsecured loan and the interest rates went through the roof.

I returned to Ames hoping to see Kalindi. I was walking around the office area when she appeared. (Throughout the years, Kalindi had an uncanny ability to appear whenever I really needed to see her). Before I could get a word out, she said, "You probably want to rethink your pledge; $50,000 is too much isn't it?"

I nodded, and then told her about my time at the bank.

She replied, "Meditate on it. Be practical. Come up with a figure for which you can accurately and responsibly give." Kalindi was always looking out for me in this way. Years later, when I wanted to give my retirement money to the Mission during another fundraiser, she wouldn't let me.

I did as requested. The next day I changed my pledge to $25,000. Again Kalindi came to me and said, "It still seems like too much." Of course, she was right. The $20,000 first offered was really the most accurate figure. Kalindi agreed, then added, "You've cracked open anyway. You've said Yes to God. You are moving in His energy. There is grace in all of this."

Kalindi was so pleased with the process I'd gone through that she set me up with the Mission's funding manager. Kalindi proposed I attend the upcoming funding event as an example of unconditional giving.

Later, a wealthy member of the congregation told me they were so moved to witness this act of selfless generosity that they wanted to write me a check to return the full $20,000 to me! I was amazed and willingly said Yes and thank you. I was happy to receive their gift.

So there I was – the recipient of so much movement without having spent a single penny. Frequently, that is how my spiritual practice has been. I let go, say Yes, and come closer to God, and my material life improves along with increasing my trust and faith.

Love in the Pool

Over the next few days, I watched closely as Kalindi interacted with various people in the house and around the grounds. One moment she was talking to a contractor about building a cottage extension and discussing wiring options, and then engaging with a disciple, speaking fervently about the love and presence of God. With each person, her words came to life and the recipient lit up. Kalindi was literally and consciously pouring her love into others. She was so aware, intelligent, and considerate.

The following Saturday morning, some twenty disciples arrived at Ames to spruce up the grounds. Everyone was given a job. I was assigned to clean the paint off the leaves of an outdoor plant.

When I asked, "Wouldn't it be easier just to buy a new plant?"

I was told, "What we are asked to do does not always make sense. Maybe you see a better way and, at some point, that may help. In the meantime, drop your own ideas and focus on your service of cleaning each leaf of this plant."

I remembered a similar lesson at a Buddhist forest monastery Genie and I visited in Thailand on our honeymoon. All guests performed a daily service while at the monastery. My service was to sweep leaves from a path through the jungle. It was a job that had no beginning or end. When I talked to one of the monks about this, he grinned and said, "It is a sweeping meditation. It is not about the path being cleared." I always liked it when my western, goal-driven mind was disengaged, and here it was again.

As I let go and focused on the leaves, I felt myself relax into a peaceful silence. Then the quiet was shattered as Kalindi emerged from her room into the backyard to the roaring sound of Billy Idol's *"Shock to the System."*

This started about 45 minutes of dancing and intense letting go. As it wound down, a deep calm fell over the grounds. I was lying on the grass, on the verge of tears, wide open and full of love. I opened my eyes and looked around. Everyone around me seemed to be experiencing the same thing.

As this was my first spontaneous let go with Kalindi, I got up and went up to Siegmar, one of Kalindi's closest caregivers, and asked, "What do we do now?"

He looked at me with a big smile on his face and a glint in his eye and said, "Just throw some cold water on your face and get back to work."

I nodded my agreement. I started towards the house, but then was pulled to look over at the pool. I gazed in that direction and saw Kalindi standing in the shallow of the pool. As I peered over, she beckoned me towards her.

I veered off and slowly approached her. As I drew near, she reached out her hands. Without thinking, I put my hands in hers

78

and she gently pulled me into the water with her. Without conscious thought, I scooped her into my arms.

I held her close to my chest for what seemed like an eternity. As I cradled her, I experienced waves of the purest love I'd ever felt washing over me, caressing my heart and soul. I repeated a prayer silently within myself to help me stay open and connected:

"Dear Lord,
Please keep me humble,
Take away all my distractions,
Leave me standing in Your Will"

After about twenty minutes, Kalindi asked me, "Would you like to get in the hot tub?" Of course, I said Yes, still completely mesmerized by what was happening.

Once we were settled, Kalindi started talking. She told me about her life, describing herself as a racehorse who'd run hard on the track for ten years straight. She said she needed a break, to get off the track and "chill out" as she put it. She shared about the coming of the Incarnation, Lord Gourasana, and her own awakening during a twelve-day period when she didn't sleep as His energy entered her body. She described the diligence it took to manage this energy and maintain a yogic lifestyle. I could barely comprehend what she was saying, even as I was captivated and enthralled.

After soaking for a long time, we fell quiet. I broke the silence by suggesting we go for a walk. Kalindi smiled with pleasure and replied, "Yes. Go inside and ask Karin to set you up." We got out of the tub and, as Kalindi headed for her room, I went to the kitchen to find Karin.

Karin was Kalindi's personal caregiver. At first she seemed alarmed. Then she got hold of herself and said, "Okay. I'll be right back." She returned with several typed pages bound in a plastic cover called, *"The Female Phenomenon."*[1]

---

1 This 15-page booklet outlined the rules and way of life Kalindi needed for her health and well-being during this current phase of her continuing transformation and manifestation.

This booklet was written by Kalindi in an effort to explain herself to others. She dedicated the booklet to her father, Alan Seidman, "Who throughout my whole life and spiritual journey, has been right by my side in loving support and care, even when he didn't agree with or understand my forward movement."

There were several pictures of them together and a quote in which Al acknowledges his third child as a "Female Phenomenon." I quickly scanned the first few pages. Here are some of the main points I noticed:

- *Always maintain a calm composure, even if war is breaking out around me.*
- *Have as much time as possible in solitude every day.*
- *Never eat in public; never drink in public, not even water. While in public, there is an energy influx making it difficult to swallow. When there is an energy influx, the body needs to be with the energy and not the physical demands of the body.*

When Kalindi joined me, I put the booklet aside and we took off for Lake Lagunitas some ten minutes away. Even though we talked quietly, I began to again feel out of my depth. I was in a kind of blissful shock. There was nothing normal about Kalindi, not even the way she shared. On that first walk, she told me her complete history with every man she'd ever been with intimately. I was moved by her honesty and unsure of why she was telling me all this. I felt very limited with what I was willing to share. As we left the lake, I asked if she would like to go on another walk sometime.

Kalindi replied, "Yes, tomorrow. We can walk to the beach."

Years later, I asked Karin about that first day. She said, "The whole team was totally flipped out. Here's this new guy taking our beloved Kalindi out for the first time. Kalindi hardly ever left the house or grounds. So for her to go off with you was an astounding thing."

Beach Kiss

It was Sunday. Kalindi wanted to go to Marin's Tennessee Valley Beach known for its lovely cove. I arrived in my Geo Tracker, a small jeep-like car. This time I was set up in some detail by Kalindi's caregivers. When they suggested coming along, Kalindi said she wanted to go alone. As they continued to object, Kalindi added, "I want the adventure. No one needs to tag along."

When we arrived at the parking lot, Kalindi opened her little white backpack that was filled to the brim. On the very top was a cassette player that she turned on full-volume, blasting 60's rock 'n' roll music as we walked.

After a few minutes of thinking about it, I gently said to her, "Does the volume need to be so high?"

She replied, "The music's not for us, Mark. It's for everyone else." Now I felt embarrassed. The volume was high so others could enjoy it. I was beginning to understand.

Kalindi asked me about my spiritual movement. As I shared with her what I was feeling I started to cry, although it was more like whimpering. She immediately told me to, "See if you can go deeper, feel and cry from a deeper place – less boo hoo and poor me from your chest and more from your gut and belly from the depth of your pain, separation and longing."

This guidance made me much more aware of where I was situated in my opening and feelings, and helped me tremendously to focus on going deeper all the time.

As we trekked through the canyon, I fell into sync with her and noticed a new sensation emerging. I felt we were floating. The bushes, grass, and hills of the valley seemed to move in a kaleidoscope of color. The air filled with a wonderful sound.[1] It was like being on LSD, except I was stone-cold sober.

---

1 "Seeing and hearing were not separate in this place where I now was. I could hear the visual beauty and I could see the surging, joyful perfection of the sound. It seemed that you could not look at or listen to anything in this realm without becoming a part of it – without joining with it in some mysterious way." Eben Alexander, MD, *Proof of Heaven*, 2012

When we arrived at the cove, the beach was crowded. I scouted out a secluded spot. Soon after we were settled, **we began kissing!** I don't remember how it started. Regardless, I was amazed it was happening.

Instinctively, my hands were roaming over her body. As I was about to slip my hands inside her clothes, I paused. *"This is Kalindi!"* I thought. I had never considered this would happen.

Then Lauren appeared in my mind and I was wondering if what was happening was OK. My eyes had been closed and when I opened them, Kalindi's intense piercing eyes were gazing right at me.

I asked her, "Is this okay?"

She replied, *"With whom?"*

Time stopped.

Her words sent images cascading through my mind. Like a drowning man, I saw images of moments with parents, teachers, friends, girlfriends – all of them tied together by the feeling that *someone was watching me!* Someone was watching me and what I was doing was **bad** – the source of my guilt and shame.

Now I had a choice. I could be with her or I could hide. During my whole life I'd shied away when I thought someone was watching, all the way back to the first girl I liked in fourth grade. For me to be watched was to be found out. The way to live was to not get caught or noticed.

My awareness opened into the present moment and only Kalindi was there. Kalindi popped up and said, "Okay, let's go." This moved me forward without a chance to mind fuck about it.

I quickly packed up and we started walking back to the car. As we left the beach, Kalindi asked, "Mark, do you want to be my boyfriend?"

I was stunned. Never in a million years did I expect that. Without hesitation, I said, "Yes, I would."

"Good!" she said, as she immediately jumped into creating our lives together. We were going to live in my cottage. She was going to turn it into a hippie, chill-out pad. There would be lava lamps and tapestries on the wall. I was stupefied. Kalindi wanted to be my girlfriend.

As we drove home, I was absolutely thrilled at the thought of being in an intimate relationship with Kalindi. I was also cognizant of my relationship with Lauren. I didn't know how to handle this or what to say to Lauren, so initially I said nothing at all.

Look No Further

The next day, Kalindi and I were back in my Geo tracker headed into San Francisco and Haight Ashbury, the birthplace of the hippie movement. Kalindi was ready to create our chill pad.

At first we window shopped. Kalindi said, "We are on an 'essence walk,' don't shop, just be and flow with me." Flow with her I did as she intently and meticulously walked in and out of different shops and stores.

Then she got down to business and started buying things. She chose several tapestries, two lava lamps, and a furry rug. After a while she started buying things for me. We went into a jewelry store specializing in silver. She found a round sterling silver keychain with a pendant on it, on which was inscribed, "LOOK NO FURTHER."

She picked out a second silver pendant with Jesus' face on it. She said I should have the second pendant soldered onto the keychain with "Lord Gourasana" engraved on the bottom.

I was all ears with freshly minted willingness. As a newly-engaged seeker of love and truth, my "seeking" was over. I'd never before felt so peaceful and at home. I'd found Kalindi. This divine woman was going to show me the way. ♪

CHAPTER 6

THE RELATIONSHIP BEGINS

"As the intimacy between you and your guru increases,
the desire to merge intensifies too.
It's a bit like going downhill on a runaway train.
There's a point where the velocity becomes so great
you can no longer jump off without it being fatal (to the ego),
and at the same moment you realize the ride itself
may be fatal too."

Ram Dass

"… And above everything, I care for your Ultimate Freedom,
that is my True Love for you. I love you as God Loves you."

Kalindi

An "Unordinary" Relationship

During the next couple of weeks Kalindi took extreme care communicating to me the type of relationship we could have. She wanted me to understand what I was getting into, and what I was saying Yes to. She laid it out for me in an eight-page handwritten letter. Here are the highlights:

"I want to chill out totally one time per week every five weeks for four days, maybe more – up to Him. Chill out – meaning total relaxation, pleasure, fun, peace in truth with someone that understands Kalindi 'The Female Phenomenon,' I will share my love and freedom as a woman."

- *No business at all in any way;*
- *No helping a disciple or pulled on for God's energy;*
  I can talk truth a little bit but not much;
- *Nothing but love, togetherness, playfulness, sex, freedom, calm, relaxation, and just being;*
- *I don't fight or argue or play games; I am devoted and I just let go; I am grateful for every second of intimate exchange.*

Kalindi wanted a friend and a lover, a man of strength, maturity, and humility capable of focusing solely on her during their time together. She knew that if she could relax on a regular basis, she would be able to give more over a longer period of time.

"I am looking for a boyfriend that fits this description and wants to be in an 'unordinary' yet very fulfilling relationship with Kalindi. This person can have the freedom to have extracurricular sexual encounters with no need to tell me; it just cannot cross into my space or energetic field. I cannot be mixed up in the drama of other women pulling on him or on me to work things out, etc. It's too much disturbance and distraction."

That paragraph tickled my heart. The thought that I could be with Kalindi and be with other women was too good to be true. I was riding high on cloud nine. In my ignorance, I actually thought I could "keep it out of her space."

Kalindi continued: *"I am always ready for the person to say they have to move on or they're looking for a woman to have a more ordinary relationship with."*

Kalindi made it clear that she could not be involved intimately with more than one man at a time.

Kalindi 1996

She said, *"I am a one-man woman, plus God. The people own my heart and soul. It would be too much distraction away from my service to the people."*

Kalindi knew that what she desired from a companion was not easily achievable. For me, the challenges began with attempting to discern the difference between Kalindi the woman and Kalindi the Master. I was also soon to find out there were more than two energies alive in Kalindi.

The day after I received her letter, I was with Kalindi in her sitting room. She was deep into her next manifestation and, to conserve her energy, she spent much time in silence. Instead of speaking, she would write down her words and I would respond. Our exchange went like this:

K: Do you want to be with me?

M: YES!!

K: Then I'm going to get happy and excited about it!

M: OK, then I will too!

K: I will still break 1,000's Free.

M: I nodded.

K: P.S. I will feel sad when & if it ends, the longing will increase, the love will increase and I will carry on in Him.
I will Always Love.

Do you want
to be with me

YES!!

o.k.
then
I
will
Too!

Then I'm going to
get happy + excited about
it! And still break
you's Free

P.S. I will feel sad when+if it ends, the longing will increase, the love will increase + I will carry on in Him

I will Always love

Throughout this period, Lauren continued to call, leaving lengthy voicemail messages. She also wrote to Kalindi as her Master about what she was going through. While heartbroken, Lauren trusted Kalindi. She felt everything that was happening was ultimately for her freedom and who better than Kalindi to go through something like this with. Not being fully honest with Lauren was painful for me. In my heart, I hoped someday she would understand.[1]

Even so, I couldn't stop sleeping around and when I did try to end things with Lauren, it was not clean at all. We continued to talk and occasionally had sex for months.

Kalindi put me into spiritual training so I could relate to her from a deeper place. She asked me to review The Intensive to help me open up more emotionally, and increase my connection to God.

Dance of the Man

Each day during this Intensive, I went deeper within and connected to spirit more. I went through rounds of emotional release to heal old wounds and open my heart; each day deepening my connection with God.

On the next to last day, Kalindi arranged for me to be part of a group of advanced men that she charged with "coming into the power of manhood through our connection with God." She called this group "Dance of the Man." Before we began, we all received a message from Kalindi that said in part:

"Kalindi will be dancing with you at her house at the same time you are dancing here. She will be right with each of you as you dance – strong, surrendered, and courageous."

There I was, out of my league again, surrounded by serious and committed seekers. I prayed to be pushed through my physical and mental fears and limitations. I begged to be uplifted by God's energy to live as a passionate, humble, strong man of

God. This Intensive helped me make a powerful leap away from my controlling ego into more authentic surrender and humility.

A couple of days later when I returned to Ames, I learned that Kalindi had been dancing with us that day. She had been involved in a spontaneous eight-hour photo shoot on the grounds of Ames. The photos showed all her different aspects and the many ways that God's energy manifested through her.. These photos became the basis of her picture book, "Ultimate Freedom: Union with God."[2]

The Intensive ended on Sunday evening. My plan was to return to Marin on Monday. Instead, as the evening concluded, I was handed a phone and told, "Kalindi would like to speak with you." Kalindi asked me to return home that night. I changed my flight to Sunday night. The moment I arrived at Ames, I went straight to her room.

Sex with a Master

Kalindi 1997

Most of the major religions and traditional spiritual paths view sex as suspect. Any number of Hindu, Buddhist, Jewish, Muslim, and Christian teachings address sex as a flawed urge. This desire must be curbed and controlled, if not renounced altogether, if one seeks connection to God. Most of these teachings are rooted in beliefs that are hundreds or thousands of years old. Because of this, in most of us sexual desire is often found festering behind walls of guilt, shame, and secrecy.

Even in the new age spiritual paths, sex with your Master, Spiritual Leader or Guide is viewed as somewhat taboo or scandalous. This is especially so when the Master or Gurus are male and their teachings espouse celibacy.

---

1 Several years later, Lauren and I reconciled and remain close friends to this day.

2 Kalindi La Gourasana, *Ultimate Freedom: Union with God,* Miracle of Love, 1998

As a modern-day Master, Kalindi saw sex in a different light. Her teachings embrace opening sexual energy, not repressing it. She teaches that everything needs to be open: heart, body, mind, and spirit.

In this context, Kalindi stood strong against repression and hypocrisy. She openly enjoyed the pleasures of sex and she guided her disciples to do so as well. Kalindi reveled in sensuality, yet never succumbed to lust. She saw herself as an example of sexual openness in God's love. She loved discussing fantasies. At the same time, Kalindi emphasized that healthy sexual contact should be between consenting adults practicing safe sex with love and care.

Kalindi discussed sex as a way to teach how the soul evolves. She explained that thousands of years ago the human nervous system was insufficiently evolved. Out of this inadequacy, celibacy and other sexual restrictions became commonplace for those on a spiritual path.

In times past, sexuality and the resulting drama inherent in all relationships was simply too much of a distraction. Today our nervous systems and consciousness have evolved to allow spiritual seekers to engage more in life. She directed her disciples to be 'Yogis in the Marketplace' and assured us that. by embracing life, we embrace more of God.

Kalindi taught how essential it was for a seeker to explore sexual desire. She explained, "One cannot break free where there is any repression, shame, or guilt." At the same time, Kalindi emphasized that sexual freedom did not always mean having multiple partners or lots of sex.

Both Kalindi and Gourasana emphasized the unique distinction of each person's path to God, especially in this area. Both cautioned against blanket statements or processes. Each individual requires individual guidance. For me, love, sex, and relationship were key areas of endeavor and I was grateful to have found such a liberating path.

First Sex

Kalindi had said before The Intensive that we would have sex when she was relaxed and calm, which she thought would be when we stayed at my cottage next month.[1] We'd already had all relevant conversations about sexually-transmitted diseases and condoms.

When I entered her bedroom, the lights were off and Kalindi was in bed in her pajamas. I got in with her. We talked for a bit and then much to my surprise, she said we could have sex together. Caught off guard, I was mesmerized to be having sex with her. It wasn't better or worse than being with anyone else; it was just because it was Kalindi and that I was in my Master's bed.

During the days following, Kalindi wrote to clarify many things. Her thoroughness enlivened and enthralled me. Her love and vulnerability unlocked my heart and left me breathless. I was a "Yes" to all she wrote. I so much wanted more of the conscious love she offered.

My emotional plate was overflowing. There I was, intimately embracing a fully awake powerhouse of God's energy and love while contending with an irate, soon-to-be ex-girlfriend, all while working full-time and on the road three weeks a month. I was on a high wire, running in two directions at the same time. Part of me was focused on God, love, truth, and Kalindi. The rest was frantically busy trying to hold it altogether and wondering if I could.

Kalindi was aware of my escapades and somehow had space for them. It took me years to realize how much she loved me and how important I was to her. Why else put up with so much self-absorption? Kalindi had to deal with all my walls and defenses, not to mention layers of unworthiness for her love to reach my well-protected heart.

---

1   One of Kalindi's Rules was that she could only have sex when she was relaxed and calm. She wasn't able to have sex to relax or get calm; she had to be in that state first. Otherwise, energetically it would be too disturbing to her nervous system.

Master or Girlfriend?

After returning from The Intensive, Kalindi had us moving at full speed. It was like The Intensive continued without a break. When emotions and feelings arose, I had to scream or cry. In one moment love, gratitude, and appreciation filled me to bursting. In the next, I was thrust into deep pools of wordless fear. Everything was happening so quickly.

One day I sat crying on my bed. Everything was going so fast. I was thinking, *"How was it possible to feel out of control and filled with gratitude for all I was being given?"*

It wasn't rational to experience joy and sorrow at the same time. "I need help," I thought. Then Kalindi appeared in my room. She sat next to me on the bed and put her arms around me. Her compassionate embrace melted my anxiety. Her very scent brought such comfort. I was okay when Kalindi was near. I could keep going with her close by my side. In this knowing, I breathed and relaxed and, when I did, she got up and left without saying a single word.

My newfound sense of peace left the room with her. Immediately, I wondered, *"Was it OK that Kalindi saw me like that?"*

"Was it Kalindi the woman, my girlfriend, who sat on my bed or was it my Master?" Then I thought, *"Whoever it was, Kalindi should never go out of her way for me. It is my job to be there for her, not the other way round."*

Kalindi 1996

I grew agitated, left the room, and went outside. There were too many questions and feelings. I was in overload, with my mind racing at top speed.

That night, I received two letters from Kalindi. In her cover letter, she spoke to the difference between the Master and the girlfriend. I pondered, *"How did she come to know what I was wondering, I never spoke those words aloud?"*

Kalindi told me what a letter from my girlfriend might look like, and how it would be signed. Rather than describe a letter from my Master, Kalindi wrote one. She wrote, *"Your feelings of loss will never go away. God is pulling you through your separation from Him."*

She cautioned against trying to fix such feelings. She told me to let my longing grow until I couldn't stand the separation. She promised that a time would come when both sadness and joy turned into pure longing for God, and that I would eventually embrace all of it.

In response to a question I asked the day before, she wrote: *"You asked if I feel sadness. I feel everything, but it all turns into deeper longing. This increases the love and He forever fills me more with His touch, with His embrace, and with the depth that people fear. It all translates into words of truth to help people in their transformation back to Him."*

The effect of these two letters on me was enormous. The more I read them, the greater my trust increased. How consciously Kalindi handled things! My fear and apprehension were alleviated. I was clear who was writing to me. For the first time in my life, I felt held from on high.

The next day I received a different kind of letter. In it Kalindi stated she did not want me to jeopardize my livelihood or spiritual transformation by spending time with her. She wanted me to place work, personal transformation, and service to the Mission ahead of being with her. She added that alone time for myself should be placed ahead of being with her. Kalindi wanted to make sure I was being consciously responsible for my own well-being. All I wanted to do was spend time with her and give to God. She wanted me to maintain a healthy balance.

Kalindi was extremely intentional. She did not waste words. Even when ticking through a laundry list of what she'd been doing since last we'd been together, there was so much information being passed along. What at first sounded like a rambling thirty-minute monologue turned into information-gathering about her physical state, the latest iteration of Gourasana's energy, how her nervous system was handling it, aspects of what she was letting go, and the state of her overall being. I realized what she shared was designed to enhance my awareness so that I might best serve.

Conscious Life

Kalindi loved the two-room cottage I rented on the estate of a family in Fairfax. What was soon to be her personal chill-out pad was secluded, had a beautiful creek running through the property, and tall redwoods scattered about. In the backyard there was a pool and a Jacuzzi. The family rarely used the backyard, so I had that part of the estate mostly to myself.

Ever since I'd told her about my cottage, Kalindi talked enthusiastically about having time away and being an 'enlightened hippie.' She spoke of the cottage being showered with love and peace from Gourasana. She looked forward to the human pleasure of being together and sharing love in a slow-motion, no-hurry, calm way.

Before Kalindi, I lived alone in what I considered Zen simplicity. My practice was about letting go of all excess and being timely. I considered my digs comfortably austere though I was not having similar success around being timely.

Wishing to cultivate impeccability, I accepted a devotional service of delivering food for The Lady when she came to visit Kalindi at Ames. My goal was to arrive at the precise time requested. This simple task was difficult. I was always running late. I'd underestimate how long things would take and left no room for the unexpected. The **illusion of busyness**[1] kept things chaotic in my head and filled my mouth with excuses every time I was late.

About a week before she was scheduled to move in, Kalindi visited the cottage. She came with a purpose. She was God's spring cleaning machine. Starting in the bathroom, she rifled through my things, culling out unnecessary toiletries, towels, toothbrushes, and so on.

94

She went through my bookshelves and tossed out a number of spiritual books because they did not contain the highest truth. Fifty-seven out of sixty books I owned did not make the grade. Out went "A Return to Love," "Conversations with God," "The Celestine Prophecy," and "The Peaceful Warrior."

The three books that made the grade were Yogananda's "Autobiography of a Yogi," "Ramakrishna and His Disciples," and "The Essential Sri Anandamayi Ma."

I was shocked when Kalindi told me there was more to come, and then left. Several hours later, a member of her team arrived to take me through my belongings, including what I kept in storage. When it was over, I'd let go of 90% of everything I owned. Half of it was donated to charity, the other half was trashed.

Next, Karin delivered a selection of Kalindi's clothes, toiletries, cosmetics, and food and Siegmar brought over her alpine skiing exercise machine.

A couple of days before our time together, Kalindi wrote to thank me for my love and care and willingness to let go so fast. She called this "the swallow-fire path." She explained, "Many will learn from you (as) you shift into realized consciousness. I love you and thank you for all you are to me."

The day before coming to the cottage, Kalindi invited me into her room at Ames and gave me a beautiful silver ring. She said this could be our "engagement" ring. It was sterling silver and had been specially made.

On the face of the ring was the image of a dove, representing the Holy Spirit. On the right side was a cross for Jesus. On the left side were the Fruits of the Holy Spirit: Love, Joy, Peace, Patience, Kindness,  Goodness, Faithfulness, Gentleness, and Self-Control. ♪

---

1 It has taken many years for me to unravel this illusion. I discuss this topic in more depth in future chapters.

Kalindi 1995

CHAPTER 7

GOD, SEX, AND LOVE

"At the root of everyone's sex problems is a feeling deeply ingrained that sex is bad and against God. Everyone has that very deep inside because of the religions and different ideas and belief systems. In the past, people needed to practice celibacy because there was not enough power and energy from the Lord (to help them move spiritually). Celibacy was a way to increase the energy so someone could make it and that was where the idea came from."

Gourasana

"Beings who understand how it all is, who know the flow of the nectar of liberation are 'Stream-enterers'; a breed apart from other people in the world. They know something others do not know. Every part of their life is colored by that merging. They touch us not only through what they can share, but also through what they cannot share, what they them-selves have become. We can only begin to imagine or intuitively absorb those states from our limited vantage point."

Ram Dass

The morning before Kalindi arrived, I handled the last of my personal business. I wanted to be as clear and present for her as possible. Karin brought Kalindi over around 1pm. The setting was beautiful. The weather was sunny and warm. The three of us went inside to walk through the cottage. The living room had just enough space for a small sofa bed, two reclining chairs, and a TV. The bedroom held a double bed and a small closet. There was a small kitchen in between the two rooms.

As Kalindi looked things over, Karin put some prepared food into the refrigerator and reminded me she would return for Kalindi around 9pm. Kalindi had been listening to our conversation, and then said something about my ego. The air became tense. I did not know how to respond. Then Kalindi said, "Never mind. I don't want to be working with your ego during our time together." Karin left. I relaxed. We were alone together. It felt like a honeymoon. Kalindi was sitting on the couch wearing light-colored sweat pants and top with a scarf around her shoulders. She looked so relaxed. I asked what she wanted to do.

In response, she closed her eyes. For a while longer I stood there watching and waiting. Then I realized she may be meditating for some time so I sat down in the recliner and closed my eyes.

This began our time to-gether. It was indicative of how it would go. Kalindi led and I followed. She always knew what she wanted. When she didn't know she would close her eyes and go within until she did. I would wait patiently until she reopened her eyes.This could be anywhere from a few minutes to a couple of hours. Sometimes during these intervals I would take care of domestic chores but mostly I sat meditating in silence. Over time, I learned to tune in to her energy. When Kalindi opened her eyes, I would open mine. Kalindi might say, "Hey Mark, want to watch a movie?" I would respond, "Yes, of course," and then pop in one of the five videos I'd rented that morning.

Learning about what Kalindi liked was extremely important. Watching movies was one of the few ways Kalindi relaxed. She explained that the stories captured her mind. She liked action films without too much violence, and movies that featured distraught women overcoming difficult circumstances. Kalindi loved to laugh, yet she did not like comedies or most jokes. When she did laugh though, it was spontaneous; the sound was spectacular, and oh so real.

While her mind was engaged, her soul could be with Gourasana. Her energy would grow quiet. She'd literally slip out of the mainstream of energy that flowed through her at Ames. Kalindi the Master stepped away from the endless rounds of recorded teachings, creation of new projects, and devising ways to better help people spiritually.

Kalindi loved movies. We kept a list of every movie she watched so I would not rent the same one twice. It was not uncommon for us to sit in our recliners and watch two or three movies in an eight hour day – thus the need for five rentals because inevitably one or two would not make the grade.

Watching a movie was a good segue into sex. Often, we'd take a break after the first feature, maybe get a bite to eat, and then Kalindi would look at me with her sweet face and eyes and ask, "Hey, Mark, do you want to have sex?"

I would say Yes and immediately jump into action. Whereas we watched movies from our reclining chairs, we would get on the open futon couch for sex.

With Kalindi, sex was a deliberate act. She liked the missionary position and once told me, "I'm a come-from-the-front kind of girl." She would guide me into how she wanted the action to proceed. It was always a slow and conscious beginning.

Even though not overly attracted to her physically, I was easily aroused by Kalindi. I loved having sex with her because I loved giving to her so intimately. Very quickly I came to deeply love her. Years after we'd stopped being lovers, I would still get erections when near her. When Kalindi would notice, she'd say, "It's okay, Mark, it's just the love."

Sex with Kalindi was different from what I'd known with other women. I had to be very gentle with her. She could not tolerate pressure on her chest or stomach. I had to support myself when inside her.

She was not interested in sex talk or sweet nothings, and had no use for moaning and groaning. She talked easily about what gave her pleasure and always made sure I was satisfied. During those first days together, we would have sex two or three times a visit.

There was no cuddling after sex. Kalindi did not want me to get lost in any sentimental, romantic love feelings or attribute what I was feeling to her.

Instead Kalindi encouraged me to go into the opening I had from sex and feel my own connection with God. She explained that the opening that could come from sex could be a doorway to God.

For me, the physical act with Kalindi was a total rush. I had carnal knowledge of a vessel that held the energy of God brought to earth by Lord Gourasana. My mind could never wrap itself around that. Neither could I understand how our intimacy could be so exquisite yet non-binding.

During sex, I felt both worthwhile and completely free of suffering and anxiety. Like the rest of our chilling out, it offered a wonderful, albeit temporary, reprieve from the world.

Oddly enough, I quickly became concerned about becoming attached to her. Kalindi was magnetic. She told me it was impossible not to become attached to her. At the same time, she assured me that there is no make-believe with God. We would have what we had until, like everything in life, it ended.

After sex we'd shower, sit in the hot tub and then turn our attention to one of Kalindi's favorite activities – food.

Devotional Feeling

Kalindi enjoyed food. Vanilla ice cream, peanut butter cookies, and whipped cream were favorite menu items. Whereas to the Master food was an aspect of full consciousness and diet necessary to maintain the body, when with me she ate what she wanted to. She especially liked eating straight out of the jars and packages.

Whether making a snack, main dish or dessert, I was the cook and dishwasher. Sometimes I'd heat up what Karin brought. At other times, I'd be her short-order cook, making grilled cheese or BLT's to order.

I always enjoyed cooking for Kalindi, the very act kick-started my consciousness. Everything slowed down when preparing her food. Each dish was cooked and seasoned to her taste. She liked being served on a tray with a napkin, silverware, water, and a flower.

One evening during our first days together, Kalindi announced that she would cook an Indian meal for me. I was perplexed. Kalindi did not prepare meals. I had to let go when I saw how much she enjoyed herself.

She talked about when, as a Hare Krishna, she had cooked for 50 to 100 people on a regular basis. It was always a labor of love. She wanted so much to serve me. My initial objections washed away and I basked in the presence of this extraordinarily devotional woman who made a delicious Indian meal of chapati, beans, rice, and vegetables. It tasted like nirvana.

The days went by in a blur of pleasure. As a man looking for fun and a good time, I could stand a steady diet of watching movies, swimming, eating, and having sex. The challenge came when I realized it was my job to keep my fully-awake girlfriend fully engaged in these repetitious activities in a natural and flowing way so she would not be drawn back into spiritual endeavors.

It took a while for me to read the signs and diffuse the moment because, when I didn't and Kalindi got down to work, she changed. First came an influx of energy, quickly followed by ideas and information that had to be recorded.

101

The energy sped up her nervous system. At first, I tried to stay with her getting her thoughts down on paper. Soon enough, I learned to call others whose job it was to record the information and handle the energy. Once started, these sessions often took hours and hours longer for Kalindi to unwind.

In short order I learned it was best for everyone not to let that energy get started. Often enough, all I had to do was focus our conversations on lighter subjects, such as what to do next, redecorating her house, clothes she liked, or movies she wanted to see.

Staying Present

Being with Kalindi took the stamina of a long distance runner. I remember an afternoon in the bedroom when Kalindi was sitting on the carpeted floor and I was on the bed. We were talking about staying present and I was drifting away. We'd been talking four or five hours and my focus was breaking down. I asked her what I could do to stay present?

Kalindi 1997

She responded, "Learn to go deeper within, Mark. It's in those depths that God resides. This will help you stay present with me."

I said, "I'd like that."

Then I asked her, "Are you ever afraid?"

She replied, "Yes, I'm frightened at times but I never let the fear stop me. I always keep going, no matter what."

Later that day, while relaxing in our chairs between movies, I said something to her that was designed to provoke her into an argument. I was unconscious of my intent and behavior, until she looked at me inquisitively and sharply asked, "What are you doing? I don't fight. I just let go." After that, I never tried to pick a fight with her again. It was my ego doing it, not my true desire, and futile with Kalindi anyway.

Another thing Kalindi did not engage in was complaining. There was this one day at Ames, I came in from work and just had to vent. I found her soaking in the tub. I barged in, sat on the floor, and started complaining about how stressful things were.

Kalindi listened until I'd got the worst of it out and then she laughed, saying, "You think you've had a tough day? Let me tell you what I dealt with earlier today."

She went on to share the magnitude, complexity, issues, and challenges of being the **spiritual** CEO of a world-wide spiritual organization. It was a jaw-dropping recital. By comparison, my complaints were petty.

On the days I went to work, I'd joyously return home to find Kalindi lying out by the pool on a lounge chair, sunbathing in a bikini. It was a mind tweak that made me smile to see her enjoying normal activities. My spiritual idea was that a Master would not be interested in tanning; she would not be so vain. I came to understand that her desire to tan or wear makeup, nice clothes, and jewelry were all about pleasing God, expressing her Self, and inspiring others to bring out their own beauty.

One day while walking in the hills behind the cottage, I had a question I wanted to ask. I'd been struggling in my relations with some coworkers. I asked Kalindi, "What do you do when a shared path with friends and colleagues comes to a fork in the road? What if they choose a different way?"

Kalindi replied, "You say goodbye and move on." She forged ahead on the path while I stood still. This was a good parallel to the answer to my question. I realized I was going to have to make some changes. A wave of anxiety swept over me as I thought, "Do I have the courage to act?" Meanwhile, as Kalindi was disappearing up the path ahead, I quickened my pace to catch up with her.

Another day on arriving home, I heard sweet music coming from the bedroom. I slipped in quietly to find Kalindi dancing in ecstasy with her arms raised as she swayed and swirled. I felt her depth of love and breathed in her ecstasy.

After a couple of minutes, she noticed me. She stopped dancing, her face suffused by this huge smile. This moment of unrestrained joy remains deeply imprinted on me. I will always cherish the grace I saw in Kalindi that day.

Woman/Master/Gourasana

About midway through our ten days together, in order to help me understand her better, Kalindi gave me a drawing and some words of support from Jim. He was one of the Core of seven people who first gathered around Gourasana. Kalindi valued Jim's thoughts and advice and talked with him about nearly everything, including her relationship with me.

From Jim   8/12/97

HE IS HERE TO SERVE AND GIVE TO ALL 3

Jim drew a pie chart as a way of indicating the three parts of Kalindi. First, there was the woman, then the Master, and finally the presence of Gourasana.

Jim underscored the need for me to be present with each aspect. He described the essence of my role as being grounded by unconditional giving in a human way. I had to learn to tune in to whoever was there.

Day after day, I witnessed the changes Jim described as the Female Phenomenon manifested the different parts of Kalindi. Essentially, there were three different energies in her body simultaneously.

Kalindi **the woman** loved to chill – relaxing, eating, having sex, watching movies, and so on. She liked talking about the truth and God so long as I listened openly and asked sincere questions. We both enjoyed those moments. Usually the woman was present when Karin dropped Kalindi off at my cottage.

The Master was more intense and ready to slice into my ego and illusions. I avoided the Master as much as possible. My staying focused inside and out usually meant she kept her spiritual sword sheathed. Sometimes the Master was simply there. I'd feel this energy focused on me and would freeze like a deer in headlights.

Usually the Master made herself known when I got caught out in the act of pride, arrogance, or lack of care. The way the Master spoke could be harrowing. It took all my focus, strength, and resilience not to go down with how she spoke to me. Thank God this did not happen often.

Kalindi herself did not want the Master working with me. She told me she would do her best to control the energy when we were together. One of her chill-out goals was not to address my spiritual shortcomings.

There were times I watched her turn her conscious eye away so that she could enjoy the moment despite my foibles. Often, just that fleeting glance was enough for me to get grounded. For a while I'd stop engaging in unnecessary conversation and the mood would deepen.

The energy of Gourasana nearly always came as day turned to night. Kalindi would become more meditative. The air in the room would grow thicker. As Gourasana's energy became dominant, Kalindi spoke more slowly. Her voice grew heavier and deeper. Her physical appearance changed. She took on the features of

Kalindi La Gourasana 1998

a man. In moments like these, when Gourasana was present, I kept a respectful distance, eyes averted and utterly aware of how I moved. My soul was in awe and reverence before this Incarnation. For me, it was God, the Lord, Father.

Need More Trust?

Further changes were being introduced at work. Over a breakfast meeting, we talked about my experience with Gourasana and their recent interest in 'Integral Theory.'[1]

They showed me a model with four quadrants delineated through internal/external and subjective/objective realms of experience. The notion was that until one has an external validation of internal experience, we cannot know for sure whether or not the experience was real.

For example, if I felt I was spontaneously healed of a brain tumor, it would not be real until an X-ray or MRI confirmed it. Mostly, I listened to what they had to say, yet I didn't feel I needed validation. My experience was more real than anything I'd ever known. That was good enough for me.

Later that same day, during the meeting at which I had decided to address my desire to change my relationship with the company, I began to feel uncertain. Was I actually prepared to say something right then? Confusion set in. A short time later I went out to eat with my mentor, Dana. Over lunch I began to cry, stumbling my way towards what I needed to say later that afternoon.

After lunch, in a clear voice and without any fear, I announced I no longer wanted to work full-time. As was customary, those present listened openly and, after some frank deliberation, made me an offer. I could become an independent contractor with monthly bookings not to exceed eight days and a daily rate comparable to what I'd been paid working full-time! This deal was better than any I'd imagined. I drove home feeling elated and eager to share my news with Kalindi.

When I entered the cottage, I felt a heavy energy in the air. I recognized the energy of Gourasana. Very quietly, I walked into the bedroom. Kalindi sat still on the bed. Her eyes were open, yet she seemed far away. I sat down next to her.

Kalindi turned towards me and started talking. Her voice was deep and slow. The tone, pace, and rhythm were reminiscent of Gourasana's. I was astonished.

As she was speaking, I thought, *"The energy I'm sensing now is the same as when Gourasana was inside of me."*

The energy-laden voice said, "You have experienced Me inside of you so you know how that feels. Now you are experiencing Me outside of you, and you can tell it is the same. Now you know I am everywhere."

I was literally stunned! My mind spun back to earlier that morning. I had just received an external validation of the same energy I'd experienced last summer. Then the energy and presence lifted and sweet Kalindi returned. She held my hand while I settled down. Then smiling warmly, she said, "Hi, Mark. Welcome home."

Our time together quickly came to an end. I was extremely sad when she left that final night. At the same time I was deeply gratified. Kalindi had chilled out with me. She'd got off the racetrack and into the hot tub and, when she left, she was relaxed and rejuvenated. I felt superb, inside and out. I loved being her 'chill out' boyfriend and I never wanted it to end. ♪

---

1 Integral theory is Ken Wilber's attempt to place a wide diversity of theories and thinkers into one single framework. It is portrayed as a "theory of everything" trying to draw together an already existing number of separate paradigms into an interrelated network of approaches that are mutually enriching.

CHAPTER 8

FROM HONEYMOON TO REALITY

"As the light increases, we see ourselves to be worse than we thought. We are amazed at our former blindness as we see issuing forth from the depths of our heart a whole swarm of shameful feelings, like filthy reptiles crawling from a hidden cave. We never could have believed that we had harbored such things, and we stand aghast as we watch them gradually appear. But while our faults diminish, the light by which we see them waxes brighter, and we are filled with horror. Bear in mind, for your comfort, that we only perceive our malady when the cure begins."

Francois Fenelon

*"The guru acts as a mirror for your soul and at the same time reflects your impurities and attachments back to you.
As you surrender more and more to the guru, those attachments begin to fall away. It's a natural process of seeing what keeps you separate from love and letting it go."*

Ram Dass

Love Sitting

A few days after our return, Kalindi asked me to her quarters and gave me the most remarkable letter. It was eight hand-written pages, and it was signed "Lord Gourasana." As I read the letter, the words danced before my eyes. Gourasana told me I must constantly adjust as Kalindi adapts to the ever-changing energy of God. He wrote, "When you're making love, you feel Kalindi, the womanly part of Kalindi, and Kalindi feels that human part of herself. When that is not going on, Kalindi turns automatically to Me."

Gourasana explained that, "You must not pull on Kalindi when she switches from her womanly vulnerability into her relaxed state of resting within the Lord."

He addressed the importance of switching my "consciousness from exchange with Kalindi, to going deep to where I am within you." He told me to rest in that depth so that she might fully let go into His great love and peace. He promised that as I became more adept at being with the Female Phenomenon, I would find even greater and richer love.

I looked up from the letter. Kalindi was watching me. She asked, "Do you understand?"

"I think so," I replied, then continued reading. Gourasana explained, "Kalindi will journey now ever deeper and, if she does not fall into My embrace of peace, she will be very uncomfortable. Be alert when you lose your depth and don't expect Kalindi to follow you."

He added that, if I did not cultivate greater depth, I would not be able to stay in connection with Kalindi because she was going deeper all the time.

Gourasana said there was an art to flowing with Kalindi. He reminded me of my personal relationship with Him and promised to help me find my way quickly to her. He suggested I go within to Him whenever I felt confused or in doubt and pledged to "assist me in all ways."

Gourasana was pleased that Kalindi was finding happiness in the company of a man. He shared that Kalindi "… found it hard to believe that someone would care enough to associate with her humanly because she is in such a unique place. It is strange to one minute be able to interact womanly and the next fall back into My Arms." He wrote, "So if you desire to be with her, this is how it will be."

Gourasana told me to support and assist her in following her rules.[1] He said, "You'll know love with Kalindi in a way you have never known love because Kalindi is in the Lord always."

He reminded me that I can't do it right or wrong and asked me to be natural and flow with her. He wrote, "Do not be afraid to approach her as a man, yet be sensitive to the timing and what is occurring with her. If you can open to the entire phenomenon, Kalindi will have great ease with you."

He called what I did "love sitting" as Kalindi relaxed into time-off with God. At the end, He thanked me and signed, "My Eternal Love, Lord Gourasana."

I looked at Kalindi and said, "Gourasana is thanking me? Shouldn't I be thanking Him?" Kalindi replied, "Yes, He is thanking you. He is grateful to you for loving me."

Kalindi asked me to read the letter many times. She reiterated that the best way for us to connect was "by me going deep within to where He resides."

Kalindi 1997

This letter also helped me more fully understand the sexual dynamic between us. Sometimes at Ames, we'd have sex in a mirrored room off her bedroom. It had white plush carpet. Kalindi liked to spread a soft sheet on top of the carpet. She enjoyed the physical intimacy but never abandoned herself to sex, remaining fully present at all times.

I could feel her with me in our intimate exchanges, although when the sex was over she would return to her deeper state. There was no post-coital reverie, no whispered words of endearment. Although she was there physically, there was no emotional entanglement. From that day forward, I prayed to Gourasana every time I went to be with her.

In July, Kalindi began preparing for a visit from her most serious European disciples. Her focus came off of me the way a light turns off. Our time together compressed down to a few hours every few days. Kalindi was now otherwise engaged.

Around this time, people began asking about our relationship. I didn't know what to say. As usual, Kalindi addressed my questions before I could articulate them. She wrote:

- If someone asks if we are intimate, say, "Yes, I spend time with Kalindi."
- If asked for details, reply, "Kalindi's personal life is private."
- If they continue to ask about your relationship with Kalindi, respond, "It is not an ordinary relationship because Kalindi's lifestyle is not ordinary."
- If someone asks if you have sex with Kalindi, reply, "Yes."
- Then say, "For there to be any privacy, the Mission must stay out of Kalindi's private life; otherwise there will be a huge drama scene."

I was grateful to Kalindi for covering these bases. It helped me to know what to say to people in the Mission.

But what about a total stranger? This came up for me on a flight home from a business trip. I was conversing with a fellow passenger when he asked me if I was married or had a girlfriend.

I responded, "Girlfriend."

He said, "Tell me about her."

This was a first. What to say? This man may not believe in God. He may have no knowledge or understanding of spiri-

---

1 Kalindi's rules included everything from meditation, rest, association, exercise, amount of work hours per day, etc. These "Rules of Love" from Gourasana for Kalindi are further explored in Chapter 16.

tual paths. I decided to tell the truth. The words flew out of my mouth, "My girlfriend is a fully-realized, spiritual Master. She is the leader of a spiritual group based in San Diego known as Miracle of Love."

Of the two of us, I was the more astonished. The realization of who I spent intimate time with landed more deeply inside of me. In the ensuing silence, I asked if he was married. He quickly answered, "Yes" and then talked about his wife and three kids until we landed.

Vipassana

In July 1997, as I was settling into my new contractor status, several of my work colleagues began shifting from Miracle of Love as their primary spiritual focus to Vipassana,[1] a Buddhist meditation. One of them was preparing to go on a three-month Vipassana retreat in Burma (Myanmar).

I wondered about Vipassana for myself and spoke with Kalindi about it. The next day I received a letter from Kalindi the Master. She addressed the difference between traditional meditation practices and what she and Gourasana brought to the world. She lauded Vipassana as an excellent meditation technique that deepens one's desire for God and truth. Then she warned that Vipassana cannot break anyone free.

Kalindi emphasized that one breaks free through **absolute surrender** of the entire being to God. You surrender your existence to God, not to a search for Him but to Him directly. Only in this way can Self-realization be found. It does not come in meditation. It cannot be found through service. It takes absolute surrender to Him.

Kalindi told me to develop more awareness in order to distinguish the difference between surrender to God and the **ego on a search.** She explained that the dividing line is subtle but, once seen, becomes both obvious and insidious. The Illusion, as an insidious force against a seekers most sincere desire, loves it when a seeker gets confused and begins trailing down one spiritual path after another.

She said, "Look into the eyes of people and see if you feel 'Surrender to God' or a seeker on an enlightenment trip. I was grateful to Kalindi for always bringing me back to the highest consciousness and keeping me from wandering off.

Buddha Tent

Over the years, Kalindi gave me many opportunities to spend time alone. This one was in a secluded spot in the backyard at Ames where I was told to raise a large tent with a front canopy. Over the next few weeks Kalindi filled this tent with a sofa bed, end tables, and some small lamps. She put chairs on the front porch area. Once furnished, Kalindi called it the 'Buddha tent.'

Kalindi asked me if I'd like to use the Buddha Tent for a three-day silent retreat. She promised that someone would bring me vegetable stew three times a day and the rest of the time I could meditate and pray. I was ecstatic. I said, "Yes" and eagerly jumped into the opportunity.

Kalindi called times like these **living in a spiritual play pen.** I was safe in the backyard, fed three times a day, and otherwise left to my own devices.

It was during this mini-retreat that I had a major revelation. I realized I had been waking up in fear every day of my life. As my consciousness moved into waking awareness, the first feeling or sensation I had each morning was **fear.**

As I contemplated this, I realized that while I was asleep, I was relatively peaceful. Why did I feel fear upon waking? *"Life is not safe,"* was the answer that immediately popped into my head. Going deeper led me to see that my ego-self lived in loss. *"Would everything still be there?"* was my mind's mantra. I traced this back

---

1   Vipassana, literally 'inward vision' meditation, involving concentration on the body or its sensations, or the insight which this provides.

to when my Dad left when I was four-and-a-half and my abandonment fear arose, along with feeling loss of love and feeling unsafe.

As I became aware of this, I started focusing on going to sleep in prayer and connection. This helped – along with immediately focusing on my love and connection to God as soon as I awoke. It took some time, yet over the next years, as I strengthened my connection and awareness, the fear dissipated and either I would wake up in His Love and Protection or quickly be able to shift into it.

Meanwhile, as this was happening, Kalindi had her focus on me. At one point I decided to take a walk in the gardens. When I returned, Kalindi had sent me a note that said, "Maybe Gourasana's Presence wants to get in if you sit long enough in deep prayer. Stay in the tent unless you are eating or going to the bathroom. Don't wander around the premises or sit in other gardens." I understood. Her Buddha Garden was all I needed.

Compassion

Kalindi loved the simple life. More than once she had happily lived in a mobile home. Now she had a recreational vehicle (RV)[1]. It was parked in the parking area at Ames. We used it for day trips around Marin County, and as the men's quarters on longer trips when she stayed in nearby hotels.

Right after the RV arrived, she asked me if I wanted to live in it. I readily agreed. It felt like a great next step in simplifying life. It proved to be a good space[2] for Kalindi and me to be together. It was utilitarian and meagerly appointed, yet nothing was missing. It had a bunk bed, a couch that turned into a double bed, a table, a miniature kitchen with a two-burner stove and pint-sized refrigerator, a tiny bathroom, an even tinier closet, and a good stereo.

I loved it. There was electricity and water. I ran a phone line from the house. I had a small basket with my toiletries for when I showered inside the house. I had everything I needed. The RV became my cozy, private preserve.

In no time, RV times were precious to both Kalindi and me. The RV was parked right outside the house; it seemed like we were alone in a far off space. Kalindi now relaxed by listening to music – Donovan and Sade were current favorites.

After chilling out, we'd either have sex or I would stimulate her sacred spot until she reached orgasm.[3] Quite often after that we'd nap – Kalindi on the sofa and me up on the bunk bed.

One day Kalindi entered the RV with a bottle of hardcore liquor: Bacardi 151 dark rum. She announced, "I used to drink this stuff all the time. Let's give it a whirl." My jaw dropped.

We knocked back a couple of shots and, before I knew it, Kalindi was throwing up in the bathroom. Now I was horrified. I should have known better. When she came out of the bathroom, I gave her water to drink and a wet towel for her forehead. I held her calmly, lovingly, sweetly until she felt okay. Later she told me she had so much gratitude for my compassion and care.

For a little while longer everything went smoothly, until one early morning when I screwed up royally. Kalindi slipped into the RV in the early dawn and woke me. This had never happened before.

Kalindi was having a hard time. She took my hand and led me back into the house. We entered her bedroom and slipped under the covers. More and more energy was coming into her. Her body was vibrating. Idiot that I was, I misinterpreted it as sexual.

When I reached out to caress her, she leapt out of bed and onto her knees in front of her altar. Kalindi sobbed uncontrollably. Too late. I understood that all she wanted was to be held.

---

1   A recreational vehicle (RV) is, in North America, the usual term for a motor vehicle or trailer equipped with living space and amenities found in a home. Several definitions exist for RVs and vary by region, including "caravan," "camper van," and "motorhome."

2   Kalindi's quarters were a sanctuary where she prayed for her disciples' freedom – a sacred space, not some place to chill out or relax.

3   The Sacred Spot (also known as the G-spot) is an area of sensitive tissue on the front wall of the vagina behind the pubic bone. The sacred spot is usually one to three inches in, towards the stomach.

Now when I tried to hold her, she shrugged me off of her. This was awful. In an agony of shame, I was left with no option but to sit behind her and pray. *How could I have been so out of touch?*

Kalindi sobbed. The sound pierced my heart. After a while, she sat up, turned to me, and said, "I must follow my rules completely. This is what Gourasana wants. I can't see you right now. I must be alone."

It was 7 in the morning; I was devastated. I wobbled out of the house and back to the RV. The rest of that day I was filled with fear that Kalindi would never be with me again.

Love the Woman, Follow the Master

Kalindi wrote me yet another kind of letter for my benefit and growth. It was time for the Master to address what she dubbed "my stuff." She began by touching on what drew her to me. She said:

"You are so kind, gentle, and giving, I have a hard time saying anything to you. You are a gift to me. I love you and want things to work out as He desires. Above everything, I care for your Ultimate Freedom. That is my true love for you. I love you as God loves you."

"You are so humble, so brave and courageous; you must have come here from Gourasana. You carry the qualities of a saint. The

Kalindi 1996

Saints break my heart; the people of the world break my heart. My heart cries out for salvation for the people." I was awed. This was how my Master saw me?

She recognized that, "It is too much for you to be with me every day. Even though the desire is there, it is not accurate. You need time for meditation, Mission service, and being with other people. You need time alone and time to play and be separate from Kalindi's seriousness."

I started to feel something was wrong. The tone of the letter was changing. Somehow what was written sounded like it might be my fault. As though reading my mind before its thoughts were formed, she wrote, "Sometimes, when I am silent, you ask me if something is wrong. You should know there is nothing wrong; there is just depth and contemplation."

She paid me a vast compliment when she said I knew how to love her and even snatch her away from the endless rounds of Mission business, giving her precious time off. It pierced my heart to feel her humility when she wrote, "I'm barely able to give you what a woman can give."

Then she addressed other women, saying, "I understand the importance of extracurricular sex for you." At the same time, she warned me once again that she had no time for the emotional ups and downs of man/woman drama. And then the woman in her spoke out, "It is frustrating for me because there is very little woman time left in me, though it's there on the back burner."

Then the Master and woman spoke at the same time, "I feel you have your mind so occupied on sex with other women you can't get occupied on me. Of course, why should you get occupied with Kalindi when I am so weird? Are you afraid of the love I give you, are you locked in fear? If you can't be all the way with one person, do you think the answer is many varieties? Maybe you're hiding from love and intimacy, and that is Kalindi – love and intimacy." She ended the letter with the following points for me to contemplate:

- No amount of sex will set you free;
- Love and intimacy won't set you free;
- Only God and your desire for Him will bring you to Ultimate Freedom, and in Ultimate Freedom you can enjoy sex pleasure with full love and intimacy;

It would take almost a decade for me to begin to realize and embody what Kalindi wrote to me.

God all the Time

I arranged my schedule to have only three days of on-site work in the month of August. Other than a little administrative work and some phone calls, the rest of my calendar was free. This worked for Kalindi. We spent nearly the whole month at Stinson Beach,[1] though not alone. This time her team – Karin, Siegmar, and another man – came with us. We booked a hotel room for Kalindi and Karin, and brought the RV for the three men.

From the very first day, our time at the beach took on a rhythm. Usually Kalindi was ready to venture out between 11am and 2pm. The three guys would stretch our legs early and then return to the RV awaiting Karin's call that Kalindi was ready. I enjoyed my time alone with these two men. To me they were advanced disciples.

Where I held them in esteem, I later learned they resented the hell out of me. What right did I have to be so intimate with Kalindi? Was I just some "here today/gone tomorrow" new guy along for the ride? They were her men. They'd been through the fires and were now 100% consumed in their service, love, and devotion.

Kalindi called them living examples of her teachings about consumption and combustion: being consumed in service to God as a way to combust out of the limiting bondage of ego and separate will into freedom. They loved to talk about the spiritual value of selfless service. I was impressed, yet had no desire to join their practice. Giving 100% of anything to anyone was outside my comfort zone. That level of surrender did not appeal to me.

Kalindi liked to cruise through the little village of Stinson beach. We'd window shop and duck into funky boutiques to look at trinkets and blouses. We'd share a hot dog or sip from the same ice cream float. Kalindi reveled in being at the shore, though we rarely went to the beach. This was difficult for me. I loved playing in the surf and was a sun worshipper. To be so close and yet so far from the water for an entire month became part of my surrender.

On our last day at Stinson, Kalindi asked the others to leave the two of us alone in the RV. This was not about sexual intimacy. Kalindi was changing again. Her mood was heavier and deeper than it had been. After the others departed, she let me know she wanted to be in silence and picked up a pad and pencil to write. Here are snippets from our exchange:

K: I feel bad asking you to give to me humanly or receiving from you.

M: Please don't feel bad to ask for anything. I want to give you anything I can. It is what I am here for.

K: You can have **no expectation** of me ever. I cannot feel I must give anything, only receive and ask for exactly what I want. I feel like you may be waiting for an incredible sexual relationship and that is not what is happening in the way you want.

M: I have no expectation. I am with you in whatever way Gourasana wants it to happen. Maybe we will never have sex again. Maybe it will only be your sacred spot. I'm not here for sex; I think more is going on.

K: There is a lot more going on than sex – you are close to me for many reasons: your freedom – fast track; Help the people – fast track.
I like to be with you! Will you stay with me? And why?

M: Yes, I want to stay with you because I too like doing all these things with you.

K: What if I don't want to do those things anymore, but only want to hear Gourasana's words and church music and preach to people? Do you still want to figure out how to give to me humanly?

---

1 Stinson Beach is a gorgeous strip of beach on the other side of Mount Tamalpais and only accessible by one windy mountainous road, north of Muir Woods and about 45 minutes from central Marin County.

M: **That is how it is now!** I will forever, continually be figuring out how to give to you humanly. Somehow with Him, it all falls into place.

K: **I don't know what He has done to me to enter me this much.** I simply don't know. Do you want to listen to Gourasana tapes with me? Do you like to hear His Holy Words?

M: YES.

K: Do you feel a satisfaction or rightness in destiny for you to be with me this way? Are you receiving anything from me?

M: I am receiving, have received so much from you, always. I am graced in many ways.

K: I am very vulnerable right now and feeling a lot of longing; begging for more of Him to consume me. I love you and it means a lot to me that you are with me. You make me melt and cry; my love for you is enduring and grows daily.

Sexual Fantasies

The next month, in September 1997, Kalindi and I had a "double date" with Karin and Siegmar. The four of us spent a couple of days at Half Moon Bay, south of San Francisco.

We had new procedures for times like these. Karin and Siegmar would leave first in order to get everything set up for Kalindi's arrival. Several hours later Kalindi and I followed.

I chauffeured her in Gourasana's Chrysler.[1] During our ride, she asked me to name the ten women I most wanted to sleep with. I was momentarily speechless and, at the same time, delighted.

After gathering my wits about me, I mentioned Marie, a gorgeous redhead from the original Core. Kalindi was particularly encouraging about Marie but hardly mentioned any of the others. I made a mental note to find out more about Marie. This conversation turned me on and our travel time flew past.

At Half Moon Bay, we drove up to a bed-and-breakfast where Karin had booked rooms. One room was for Kalindi and Karin, and the other for Siegmar and me. Right after we arrived, Kalindi gathered us together in her room.

Without preamble, she asked us to describe our sexual fantasies. She encouraged us to share without guilt or shame, no matter how lurid those fantasies might sound.

I was immediately uncomfortable. I could live out my fantasies with Helle, Lauren, and other partners, yet talking about the down and dirty inside my head in front of Kalindi, I wasn't sure about that.

My sense of discomfort grew as first Siegmar and then Karin shared openly and in detail. Now it was my turn. Like a schoolboy filled with shame and guilt, I stumbled over my words and lost my train of thought. In the end, I felt nakedly exposed as shallow and unreal.

Kalindi so wanted me to come to terms with my hidden lusts and insatiable desires. She said it was so much healthier to express every desire rather than hide it away in some closet. Kalindi encouraged me to discover for myself which fantasies were real and needed to be played out, and which could stay in fantasyland. She assured me that this understanding could only be found from direct experience. ♪

---

1 A Chrysler New Yorker which someone bought for Gourasana before he died that he left for Kalindi.

CHAPTER 9

FROM BOYFRIEND TO DISCIPLE

"A basic principle of all life is that we all communicate or 'transmit' to others who come into our company the present state of our consciousness. If we are happy, others feel the happiness, no matter what we are doing or discussing. Likewise, if we are disturbed, others feel that anxiety. The communication of our state is instant, immediate. Similarly, and to a magnified degree, it is the case with the Divine Realizer. When we come into the company of such a Being, we immediately – and to whatever degree we are open to feel it – feel his or her Transmission of the Divine naturally and spontaneously. This is the process of Spiritual Transmission described in many traditions. It is the greatest Gift of the Guru to the devotee."

Adi Da

Rising in Love

Even though I knew that sex could not sustain me, I didn't want to believe it. I still believed that fulfillment was over there in this or that woman. Clearly I was not done with my sexual conquests or that incredibly powerful illusion.[1]

Even with all of Kalindi's help, it took me eight more years to realize the suffering nature of illusory love. Once I saw this, it started tipping the tide away from the belief that falling in love was worth the inevitable suffering that came with it.

It took me another six years to find the desire and courage to start letting it go altogether. At this point I was desperate. I fell on my knees, begged God, and finally let go of my favorite thing in the whole world – that high and glorious feeling of falling in love or being loved by my 'fantasy' woman – before I could feel free of these seemingly insatiable desires.

Even now, while I fully know I cannot find fulfillment in a woman or in anything outside of myself, I sometimes hunger for that to happen. It is hard to admit that I am in life-long recovery from this addiction. Thank God for Kalindi. Without her, I would never have known a cure was even possible.

Back at Ames, as I prepared for a short business trip, I penned a note to Kalindi. The first half poured out of me like liquid honey. After that, I started trembling as I put the words to paper. Here's what I wrote:

To my Beloved Kalindi,

My feelings for you are deep-rooted and transcend anything I've experienced before. When I am not with you, I am still with you, and there is no upset or loss; it is just clean. No push, no pull. It just is. This is very unique for me.

---

1 That was the essence of illusory love for me – the misconception that True Love and ultimate fulfillment lived outside of myself – in this case, whatever woman I happened to be 'in love' with.

Now, I'm going to take some risks here, or so it seems. I wonder if you want to stay with me, be with me? I have so much illusion going on. I cannot give you exactly what you want. I am not free, I am sentimental and self-absorbed.

Yes, I am moving quickly, letting go quickly, and yes, I am totally committed to you and to getting free, but how long will it take? In the meantime, you have to put up with all this. Is this okay for you? Do you want this? Am I it? Sometimes I feel like you could be with anybody, it doesn't matter that it is me. I just happened to show up.

I love you with all my heart, Mark

Kalindi wrote me a beautiful response:

My dear Mark, tolerant one:

You ask me if you are "IT" for me. My answer to that is God is "IT" for me, Gourasana is "IT" for me, and despite the illusions you are moving through, yes, I want to be with you, spend time with you, and have what we have together. It is not easy for any man to be with me as closely as you are, and it doesn't matter if someone is "free" that is not what makes a man able to be with me.

I miss you and desire you to be close to me. I don't like when you're gone from home, and I do want to encourage you to move forth however is accurate in Gourasana, in your travels, and in intimate connecting with women. I love you! You have so much love, patience, kindness for me. Personally, I don't know why you desire association with me – I am fire to melt all illusion. Someone being IT for me in the way you think and feel IT has melted away in my union with Gourasana. But who could be a better chill-out boyfriend, and who would want to? I am a tough case to understand and move with; you can and are able to do this.

My love for you is God's Love, it is endless.

I was relieved, awe-struck, and immediately assured, not to mention swept away.

Leaving Home

In October 1997, Kendra decided to buy another house. A five-minute drive from Ames, it was a magnificent structure with Roman columns and an elegant swimming pool out back. It had huge, open rooms downstairs and spacious bedrooms upstairs. It was located on a street named Bellagio, so Bellagio is what everyone called it. Everyone but Kalindi, that is. She named it, "The Announcement House."[1]

A couple of days later, Kalindi asked if I would move to Bellagio to live with Kendra and two other close disciples. She assured me we would see each other often. For now, she wanted me to support Kendra with her fund-raising and other public events. Crushed and frightened, I said, "OK."

I was numb and close to heartbreak. Living with Kalindi was where I had felt most at home in my whole life. Now I was going from daily intimacy to what felt like exile. As was often the case around Kalindi, I was moved between the extremes of austerity and abundance. In one short drive, I moved from my simple set-up in the RV to a palatial mansion that overlooked Mount Tamalpais. The big empty house felt cold and I felt empty. Then Kalindi came to visit. She bathed us in her light and breathed God's presence into each room.

In the snap of two fingers, the nature of my relationship with Kalindi had changed, and Kalindi was on the move again. The Master was taking over. Her focus was back fully on the people.

One after the other, groups of disciples now arrived at Ames to be with Kalindi. The focus of the meditations and talks were what she called "The Cry of the Heart." I was grateful Kalindi invited me

---

1 From the very beginning, Gourasana and Kalindi had tasked Kendra with the job and destiny of announcing to the world the coming of the current day Incarnation of God. Kendra worked tirelessly on her destiny, hosting various media events in California and Chicago. The final phase of The Announcement included a full-page ad in the International Herald Tribune and a day-long web event on 10-10-10 (October 10, 2010), just six months after Kalindi's passing. Two weeks later Kendra passed away, succumbing to lung cancer.

to attend. My heart was crying out the moment this phase began and continued during the remainder of that year.

The day before I left Ames and the RV, I got my first taste of how things were changing. That morning I was packing my few belongings when Karin knocked, came in, and delivered a letter from Kalindi.

In the letter, Kalindi said it was time to change how I talk about our relationship. As of this moment, I am a disciple and friend only. I do not have sex with Kalindi and I see her only occasionally for walks or a movie.

The letter continued that I was not to discuss my personal relationship with Gourasana – how He came into me or through me. She suggested that I be in silence whenever possible, and in this quiet find humility. There was too much energy coming at Kalindi from Lauren and other women. They wrote to her about my ego and illusions.

Kalindi wrote, "I don't want our few times together to be about me preaching to your ego." She was, "willing to accept that my movement would zigzag back and forth through a lot of muck because that's what it would take for me to find my freedom." She added, "I want to find a real simple situation between you and I."

This **letter shook me to my core.** I felt I was losing Kalindi. I was on the rocks. My escapades with Lauren and other women had reached her. I'd kept nothing out of Kalindi's space. **What a fool I was!** *How could I have been so out of it?* This is what Kalindi called my blind arrogance. This was worse than I'd imagined. How could I be so unaware?

I sat alone in the RV for hours, virtually paralyzed. In the afternoon, Kalindi came to see how I was. I could feel her love and compassion but I was too drained and shaken to say anything. After a few minutes, she said, "It will be best to have some time apart." As Kalindi turned for the door, I wanted to physically grab her. I thought, "I'll die if she leaves!" but it was too late, she was gone.

Letting Work Go

No one had to ask me to review The Intensive. It was time for me to find my vulnerability. There were ways of being that had to end and wounds that must be healed. I needed to find forgiveness for my failures and shortcomings.

From the moment I entered the room on the first day of The Intensive, I felt hope. Each time I review an Intensive, it takes less effort to open my emotional body, grow calm at a depth of being, and connect to Spirit within. Once there, the trick was **staying there.**

This required intense focus. I would easily drift and be captured in my mind's endless chatter and derivative thoughts. Like a diver developing their lung capacity, I was building my capability to remain focused on God, love, and truth. My mantra within was, *"Stay with Him."*

In one meditation, while I was fervently begging God for forgiveness, The Lady spoke into her microphone, saying, **"You do not have to ask God for forgiveness, He has never judged you.** You may need to forgive yourself. You may need to forgive others, but God has never judged you."

Wow, I thought, begging God to forgive me means I am lacking and judge myself wrong. I need to let go of self-judgment. It cannot serve me, God or Kalindi.

Another powerful experience came in a later meditation. I had a vision of a time when I'd been a follower of Jesus. When he was crucified, I turned away, fearing for my life. I felt tremendous guilt and even though I couldn't change what I'd done, I vowed to never let the fear stop me again.

As was often the case, in my final meditation, I had an epiphany. After days of driving intensity, I ventured into the next layer of my fear and burst into an inner light. I stood up. I felt different. I opened my eyes and looked around the room. There were light and energy strands connecting everyone. I was one part of the tapestry of what was happening. I noticed a lightness in myself. I was "beyond my mind" without the usual evaluative, judgmental thinking which formed the walls of my separation.

I realized that this depth of openness and connection was a perfect time to go within and ask some questions. I was eager to see if I could receive helpful information about my job and work in general. Even though I appeared to have an ideal work situation, I felt something else was possible, and I was determined to find out what that was. From this perspective, I sat down and silently inquired:

"Is it accurate for me to continue working with The Clarion Group?"[1]

Instantly, I heard, *"Mark, you do not have to work."* BAM!

This was completely unexpected. I asked, *"How will I make money?"*

Another startling answer: *"You don't have to work to have money."* BAM!

Each time I silently posed a question, the answer came instantly in an explosion of light, love, and trust that blew through me like a refreshing breeze. The information burst into my awareness directly, bypassing my mind.

As I received each answer, I was able to instantly and effortlessly understand in a way that would have normally taken me years to grasp.

I continued my inquiry, *"How is it possible to have money without working?"*

"There are many ways to have money without having to work," came the response.

Now, I felt my soul starting to breathe again, expanding inside me. That was all I needed. I wanted to know more.

I put forward my next question. *"How else can I have money other than to work for it?"*

"There are many ways for money to come to you. Do not worry. I will put lots of money through you. You just have to let

go and get to nothing. Once you get to nothing, I can give you everything."

These words set my soul on fire. In the light, it all seemed possible. Along with the information had also come the energy, faith and knowing that I could take this next leap. I realized it was time to let go of my job and work all together. God was guiding me. This truth brought so much relief.

For a while, I worked through the practical side of things. I made notes about how to resign and leave responsibly, while giving all due consideration for my clients, co-workers and the success of the company. These notes included using my savings to live from once I was unemployed.

I resolved to make these changes by the end of the year. That was six weeks away. I took my first step at the next company meeting when I informed the partners that I was resigning my contract. It wasn't easy to say goodbye. I had grown significantly since Florida and GTE, and loved and adored my colleagues and clients.

I was grateful to come away from this Intensive with so much clarity and a newly-honed ability to hear the whispers of God. I had a strong desire to become adept at listening, saying Yes, and taking action. I had no idea where I was headed but I was glad to be underway.

Heartbreak

When I returned to Marin, I heard from Karin that Kalindi was going through a difficult time. Karin said I was welcome to come by if I liked. Within fifteen minutes, I was at the house and came into her room. Kalindi lay quietly on her bed wearing black slacks and a white sweater, with a beautiful blue and green scarf. Her energy was open and familiar. At first, I sat on the floor. Later, I held her as we engaged in easy conversation.

---

1   As the company grew and expanded, the name had changed from Expansion Technologies to The Clarion Group.

The next day when I returned, Kalindi was in a vulnerable space. As we sat on her white couch, she shared intimately about her life with David Swanson. Later on, we had sex. It all flowed so easily and was such an out-of-the-blue surprise that I thought we might be returning

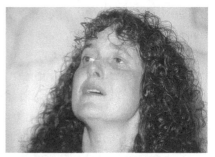
Kalindi 1997

to our honeymoon phase. Little did I know that a major blow was right around the corner.

It came on Nov. 23, 1997. I was in Kalindi's quarters with Kendra and another close female disciple. The conversation turned towards me. The two women talked about how I was unable to express any real vulnerability or depth. My walls and defenses went up.

Looking directly at me, Kalindi asked if I was stuck in fear. I nodded Yes. When she asked me to talk about what gripped my heart, I stopped breathing and my mouth went dry. I had no answers. I stood right in front of her and she could not reach me.

I felt trapped inside some invisible cage, tongue-tied before my Master, and a failure to the woman I loved. Pathetically swamped by dread, I tried to lay low until the danger passed. After a moment, Kalindi dismissed me. I crept away hoping that maybe I'd dodged a bullet.

The next day, I received written guidance from my Master.[1] Her words were simultaneously filled with love and delivered as a direct blow against my ego.[2] She started with, "Become disgusted with your arrogance." Then she extolled the virtues of an open, humble heart. She said, "You are going to be grateful for this day; your false self was about to have a heyday."

Then she gave me guidance on what to do: 1) Pray to Gourasana, 2) Attend every meditation scheduled at the Center, 3) Use a blindfold and earplugs when meditating to limit distractions, 4) Stop settling for sentimental wimpy crying, 5) Scream from your deepest longing, 6) Stop trying to be someone you are not. At the end, there was a handwritten note:

Mark: You are a beginner, become humble. You are arrogant! Pray to see that. You think you are better than others. Your desire for purity and truth is strong, so pray to see all these areas and pray to be taken over by the Lord. Being with me intimately is stopping you from seeing and feeling all of this.

Mark it's a lot of shit in there, covering your purity. You need your Master desperately. You need to find Gourasana on a different level, which requires a wide-open heart to let Him in. You don't know Him as well as you perceive – go deeper, way deeper.

Forget about women for now, forget about sex. You use sex for manipulation. It is your big Band-Aid. Going from woman to woman is a big illusion for you.

When will you crack open? How long will it take?

I don't know when I will see you, as all the above is more important. When Gourasana tells me to see you, that is when I will.

You must go deeper. Fast. Become humble!

All My Love – as your Master here to push you into truth.

Kalindi

P.S. You can still stay in the RV anytime and please always have it first-class clean in the way I like it.

I knew Kalindi had my number. My hidden darkness, my secret self, was being exposed. *Why must these moments always feel like some kind of death blow?*

I felt pulverized, weak, and unlovable. I thought that without the pretense, what would be there other than this empty shell wit-

---

1   Kalindi knew how much the illusion tried to block any spiritual help that would lessen its control over me and therefore always wanted me to have her guidance and help in writing whenever possible.

2   "We are using the word 'ego' to mean 'false self, false personality.' This must die for your true self, your true personality, to live. Presently, your true self is lost and your false self is dominant." Breaking the Cycle of Birth and Death, Gourasana, 2001

hout distinction or value. Kalindi was right, I manipulated situations and people. I did it to survive. If I didn't ingratiate myself to others, they would abandon me and I'd become utterly lonely.

Kalindi's next words jumped off the page. "It's what you don't trust that has to crack open." Oh, my God! She was right! But how could I trust myself? No one else did.

I felt so guilty and rotten inside. Over the past few months alone, I'd slept with at least three other women, all of whom I'd kept hidden from Kalindi. I even boasted about it to my friends to look impressive in their eyes. It meant so much to me to look good to others. Looking good was my protection.

At my most expansive, I knew I was somebody. Hell, I was successful, confident, witty, and charmingly appealing to all kinds of women. Being intimate with Kalindi enhanced my sense of all of it. For a while there, I could do no wrong. The problem was, I was my own worst enemy.

What a paradox to feel superior and unworthy at the same time – talk about hiding in plain sight – and, other than myself, fooling no one at all. Lauren had my number. Kalindi read me like a book. Karin, Siegmar, Kendra, all of them saw the insecure little boy running around playing pretend games.

I felt sick at heart. I'd been using the light for my own purposes. It was such a painful way to live. It couldn't go on anymore. Not like this. I had to change. I had to break free of these insatiable appetites. But how? I started to panic.

Throwing myself on my bedroom floor, I wept inside this aching sadness. I could not find True Love from those around me. Nothing lasted. I could not trust any woman. Soon enough they found me out. I was inferior. I would never overcome my shortcomings.

No matter the guise I donned – from the super cool jock in college to even cooler beach dude in graduate school and loverboy in Europe – the only constant was, that for as good as it got, it was never good enough and neither was I.

I fell into an awful nightmare. My body locked up. Terror gripped my mind as it raced from one devastating thought to the next. I let out a blood curdling scream. My emotional self cracked open. I wailed and howled until I had nothing left. Exhausted and out of breath, the tears kept coming. Just when I thought it would never end, my crying slowed to a whimper. A gentle wave of soothing energy swept over me and clarity began to emerge.

Kalindi knew me better than I did. She saw the bigger picture. She sensed my true nature and desire. Where she had been gentle with me in the beginning, now her gloves were off. She knew I was ready for more confronting work.

Part of what I had to confront was that, up until now, my spiritual work had been a series of temporary fixes. Whatever I practiced or vowed, nothing subdued my ego for long.

When sorely pressed, my ego simply went from one persona to the next. If it couldn't be overt, it became covert. When caught out, it used silence as a shield. When on target, it would trot out the great listener or the charming, fun, compassionate fellow, or even the macho man, each tailor-made to the circumstance. Life was about survival and making it. Women fell for my creations. Hell, even I fell for them. I was still trying to be someone I was not – trying to prove something, trying to get somewhere. I started to understand what Kalindi meant when she first wrote to me, "Come crashing into Kalindi." Colliding into the vortex of light that was Kalindi was short-circuiting the growth of my "enlightened ego."[1]

Little by little I came to a watershed moment. The insights slowly formed. There was no fanfare. Pieces fell into place like small cogs that turn big wheels. I was the one who created my suffering. It was my fear that disconnected me. The stories that ran in my head belonged to no one else. It all came from me. If it was to end, I had to end it. It was time for the ego to get out of the way. My soul was hungry to lead. ♪

---

1 The enlightened ego is a major pitfall of the spiritual path and is very difficult for the individual to see. This is a main reason why a live Master is needed for those who want to attain ultimate freedom.

CHAPTER 10

LOSING KALINDI

"My initial awakening experience with Kundalini
triggered a transformative process that lasted for twelve years.
During this time, the sensations of light,
splendor and joy alternated with –
and were often completely overshadowed by –
sensations of fire, unbearable heat and bleak depression."

Gopi Krishna

"Surrender is the acceptance
of everything WITHOUT exception."

Irina Tweedie

Desperate Uncertainty

I fell asleep exhausted. I couldn't wrap my head around what had just happened. Was it two days ago I'd been sent away by Kalindi because I was unable to talk about what gripped my heart? I had no answers to anything. In the middle of the night I flew awake burning with several questions:

"Do I want ultimate freedom or is this all about ego grati-fication?"

If I am a sincere seeker, what am I willing to do about it?

I pondered the first question. On the surface of things I lived for ego gratification. On the other hand, my connection to God was tactile and real. I thought about how insidious the illusion can be, so much so that it can use my own mind to question my faith, despite the experiences I've had. I'd read about the illusion in Buddhism and Hinduism, and heard Gourasana talk about this powerful force that works against the light.[1]

I wondered at my ability to be both shallow and in way over my head. I laughed with embarrassment. What an idiot to think I could con Kalindi. What good would it do me to forget about God when neither God nor Kalindi would forget me?[2]

I mulled over the current state of my relationship with Kalindi. *"Does my personal love for Kalindi get in the way of my relationship with God?"*

"Is that even possible?" *"Isn't Kalindi His vessel here?"* My heart answered, *"Staying close to Kalindi is all that matters."*

---

1 "The term Maya has been translated as 'illusion,' but then it does not concern normal illusion. Maya is often translated as "illusion" since our minds construct a subjective experience that we are in peril of interpreting as reality. Here, 'illusion' does not mean that the world is not real and simply a figment of the human imagination. Maya means that the world is not as it seems; the world that one experiences is misleading as far as its true nature is concerned. The world is both real and unreal because it exists but is 'not what it appears to be.'" Raj Pruthi, *Vedic Civilization,* Discovery Publishing House, 2004

2 "I am eager to show you the unlimited splendor of the True Realm. I have waited so long, and while you have not been aware of Me, I have never forgotten you." Gourasana, *Breaking the Cycle of Birth and Death,* Miracle of Love, 2001, Quote # 100

That simple declaration seemed to cover the ground. I fell back to sleep vowing to hang in there and come out of hiding.

The next morning I awoke calmer and clearer. In this state, I wrote Kalindi a card, sharing about my meditation and middle-of-the-night contemplations. I admitted it was hard not knowing when I might see her again. I expressed my undying love and promised to do my spiritual work. I ended by saying I would surrender to God's Will, though my personal desire was to stay with her forever.

Karin called the next day to say that Kalindi wanted to see me. My heart leapt. When I arrived, Kalindi was open and loving and I was hesitantly afraid. I hated it when my body and being would not cooperate. I wanted to be close to her and was too frightened to move. I was having two different experiences in the same moment.

For Kalindi it was a brief and lighthearted moment. For me it was an exquisite torture. She looked into my eyes for a long time and then said, "Sex might happen next week." I smiled. It was time to go. I left feeling relieved.

Later, I realized our time together had been a lesson from Kalindi on how to let go. While I came to her filled with trepidation, she came to me filled with delight. Kalindi had this uncanny ability to let go. She could be heavy one moment and a few minutes later like nothing had happened at all. I, on the other hand, seemed to drag all of it everywhere with me.

Kalindi and I were able to spend a few hours together over the next couple of days. At first I remained high-strung and then my fears subsided into a kind of watchful restraint. If nothing else, I had to guard against rampant illusion. If I disturbed her, the Master was going to show up. I couldn't take any more of that scene. Even when she was calm, the subtle energy was moving in her. I had no desire to awaken her wrath or make her anymore uncomfortable.

Kalindi often had a physical symptom of heart pain. This would happen if she was exerting herself more than Gourasana wanted her to, or if she was not calm and the energy in her nervous system started to race. The transformation that Kalindi had gone through, and the manifestation that was continuing God's energy in her body, was an unimaginable process for us all. Her medical doctor, Dr. Tavakoli, understood her physical process best and even for him, an extremely qualified diagnostician, it was guess-work at times.[1]

Although it often seemed like nothing was happening around Kalindi, a lot was going on for me. It was an incredible space where most of what was happening was internal and little of it external. While she was calm and peaceful, I was riding an emotional roller coaster. As we sat around seemingly doing nothing, the changes beneath the surface felt truly geological, or molecular, as if Kalindi was rewiring me on a subtle level.

By chance, I saw Kalindi again just before leaving on my final business trip. She was walking in the backyard at Ames. I joined her. Her calm was so inviting that my body relaxed in her presence. We went inside and became intimate. The sex was full-blast.

Afterwards I poured my aching heart out. She lovingly liste-ned. A weight lifted off my shoulders. When I left, we hugged and kissed. It was all so innocent and vulnerable.

When I returned home, Kalindi asked me to come over. After some minutes of silence, she softly announced it was time for her to let go of sexual intercourse. The blow jobs had ended months before. Now, if I wished to go forward with her, she only wanted to have her G-spot stroked. I promptly announced that I was her G-man, ready to give her pleasure and release whenever she desired. Kalindi nodded quietly, taking it in.

---

1   In 1996, a year after Gourasana had left the body, Kalindi was very run down. It was at this time, she found Dr. Tavakoli, the doctor who would care for her for the rest of her life. He was an excellent medical doctor who also intuitively understood the spiritual energy that was pulsing through her.
In order for me to better understand how the energy affected her physically, Kalindi gave me this book to read *Kundalini: The Evolutionary Energy in Man* by Krishna Gopi, 1997. She said it was the closest example energetically and physically to her experience that she knew of.

Before I left, she gave me a travel altar for a birthday present. She made it herself with tiny photos of Gourasana, Jesus, and the Light Beings. I cherished this gift, taking it with me when I traveled for years. I felt light and filled with joy when we parted.

Emptiness

1997 came to an end and I wrapped up my consulting career. As 1998 began, Kalindi remained focused on the break-free work with her disciples. I didn't see much of her and only heard through the grapevine that soon she would be leaving for Hawaii for recuperation and rest.

I felt relieved as the days went by and no one contacted me about accompanying her. I was enjoying my time off and had just started checking out various business ventures when, the day before she left, I received the following letter from Kalindi.

Dear Mark,

I have been blamed twice for having intimacy with a disciple that interfered with the Master-disciple relationship. Both circumstances were for their freedom (they knew it and they forgot).

I do not want that to happen for you. I care only for your freedom. I know you need your Master above the woman part of me. I cherish what we have and that you love me so tenderly and I want the friendship and intimacy you give so selflessly.

Now, I feel like there needs to be time for you to travel the path, fall deeper into Gourasana, the Mission and your service for God, business, etc. Please take the time to truly see if you and Lauren are finished. If so, you need time to truly conclude in love and see what you desire RE: Relationship, sex, etc. I don't want her to turn against her Master. How unfortunate that would be.[1]

I want there to be a totally pure, clean and fully conscious choice of your intimate friendship with me. So there is nothing to blame Kalindi for when you get afraid in your transformation.

I want you to have your Master above anything. It is the doorway relationship for you. When you need faith, connect to your Master within. This will take time. You need space to let everything unfold maybe for six months or so.

My job is hard, very hard. I don't want to create situations with close disciples that could jeopardize their spiritual freedom and then be the one blamed. I am sad today. My job feels impossible. It will be nice in the future to be able to talk to you from a deeper place. I feel so alone with only Gourasana walking up a mountain calling the people. I cry and cry, begging him to help. I am sad about so much. It is not possible to be reconciled.

I don't think we should spend time together right now. I am sorry the movement is such a riptide. I love that you can ride Gourasana's wave.

My Endless Love,

Kalindi

For the first time in almost a year, we were going to be apart from each other.

Severe Detachment

During the next week, a kind of pall settled over me. Life lost its luster. Everything settled into a slow, grinding pace. Then I received a letter from Maui:

Well Mark,

I am sad today. I will spend these next months undergoing **Severe Detachment.** *I will be different when we spend time together again. For all I know, it may be sooner, but I know you need time to get two feet on the floor and go forward with desire,*

---

1   Lauren remained Kalindi's disciple throughout and continues on the Path to Ultimate Freedom to this day.

*yes and nothing to **ever** blame Kalindi for or how can I be so open with you; if in one, two, three years the stab comes?*

*All of this is coming from what I have already experienced every time I have been intimate with a disciple. I feel like I am going through a very big death process to become **utterly and fully detached in all ways.** Gourasana said that would be my ecstasy, so maybe that's what's happening now. It feels bad. Do you understand everything I've said? Do you agree? Do you see the benefit?*

I trust you and you know what, I've said that before and these persons have crucified Kalindi. It is so painful because I only love them. So I want to feel you in your deepest depth in Gourasana, in your Master, fully knowing you are by my side for good. Our friendship will have an ease then.

I trust this next unfoldment. We have come a long way, and I want to move forward into more of the truth of our friendship, and you by my side unshakably.

My Endless Love,

Kalindi

In her post-script she wrote that she must become "eternally patient" and unattached to anyone breaking free, even as she lived for that purpose. She prayed for me to fly into my own destiny and depth.

I was grateful to read that she still trusted me and was willing to give me the chance to be by her side. I was utterly inspired by her own sacrifice and commitment for other people's freedom.

140

Kalindi Lets Go ... Again

It was the end of January when I got a call from Karin in Hawaii. Without going into details, Karin told me that Kalindi had passed through the first phase of her detachment and was ready for a break. Then she asked, "Do you want to spend a few days with Kalindi here in Maui next week?" I couldn't believe my ears. I was instantly joyous and said, "Yes, of course!" I was going to be with my beloved again.

We arranged the dates for early February. I would have five wonderful days with Kalindi. I booked a room at the Westin Grand Resort on the beach in an area called Ka'anapali, near Lahaina, Maui. The hotel was ten minutes away from where Kalindi stayed. I arrived on a Monday morning. Karin was to drop Kalindi off at the hotel at 2pm. This became our daily schedule – arrival at 2pm with a 10pm pick-up.

Kalindi appeared rested. She smiled easily and overflowed with joy. I was delighted. It felt magical to be with her.

We fell into a quiet playful intimacy that was broken only once when she shared about a depth of despair that filled her as she detached. It tore at her heart to let go of the Mission and the freedom of her disciples.[1] She smiled at me and sighed a little, then changed the channel, returning us to our love-in.

Toward evening, I helped Kalindi release from the sacred spot. This intimacy was fulfilling and relaxing for both of us. Later, we ordered room service and then took a twilight stroll on the beach. I remember that first day as idyllic. Something had shifted in both of us and we were fully enjoying this time together. Nothing was missing.

I stood alone in my room in a state of disbelief. Had what just occurred really happened? I could smell her scent in the air

---

1 Kalindi was attempting to detach from her daily responsibilities and spiritual oversight of the worldwide spiritual organization she was sourcing, and also let go of any attachment to the success of her disciples in breaking free in this lifetime so she could herself go deeper in her own manifestation in God.

and on the bed. Wave after wave of gratitude flooded through me. All was right with the world.

During our second day together we visited an ancient giant banyan tree in Lahaina and bought two opal rings to commemorate our Hawaiian "chill out" time. Once again, I felt myself falling in love. Each time with Kalindi that love reached a deeper level. Walking through the hotel side-by-side, I felt lifted off the ground, like we were floating in the true realm of heaven. Kalindi was really enjoying herself. All was going smoothly.

When we returned to my hotel room, Kalindi showed me a flyer of the latest Mission publication. Just like that, the energy changed. As she spoke, a powerful influx of energy stirred in her. I knew what was going on. I recognized the signals. If Kalindi cranked up, in no time she could enter a creation-frenzy, going non-stop from one new project to the next. This was not part of our agenda. I was her chill-out partner and nothing more. I silently called on Gourasana and followed my protocols by turning emotionally bland. When I showed no interest, her enthusiasm calmed and she settled down.

The third day was monumental. We watched two movies, had lunch and dinner together, and strolled several times on the beach. A few things went awry but when they did I managed to handle them with aplomb.

For the first time ever, **I stayed present all day.** Kalindi noticed. This helped her to relax even further. In this space, there was a lot of spontaneous affection. I opened and cried deeply when we had sex. That night, after Kalindi left, I slept with the angels.

On the fourth day we lay in the sun on lounge chairs beside the pool. I'd made sure we had easy access to anything Kalindi might desire. There were goggles for swimming, suntan oil for the asking, a variety of foods that she loved, an endless supply of water, and her favorite ice tea. There was one moment that remains fresh in my mind. Kalindi lay face down on her lounge chair – the bra straps of her favorite bikini undone. She was breathing so quietly.

I was letting down myself when, in the midst of this perfect moment, Kalindi sat up and said in a loud expressive voice, "It's difficult to relax, Mark. I just want to break people free. Otherwise I feel dissatisfied with everything." Settling back down, she concluded with a chuckle, "Of course, dissatisfaction can be quite useful if you're willing to change."

When we got back to the room, Kalindi started making phone calls to Mission leaders. I asked her if this was a good idea. She brushed my worry aside, saying this was information they needed to receive. Then she smiled as a way to acknowledge my care, adding, "I'll stop when I'm done."

As good as her word, after she made the calls, Kalindi and I went down to dinner and then on to the hot tub. The hot tub was large enough to accommodate a number of people. Kalindi didn't mind as we crowded in together, though I never liked having strangers cozying up too near to her. All went well until I blundered into saying something about scheduling sex. Kalindi gave me a look.

Even before we returned to the hotel room to watch a movie, I was starting to go down. My unsettled feelings tripped me up in the hot tub and now got wrapped up with our time together nearing its end. I was sinking fast. I was drowning in being unlovable, unable to reach out. Without saying anything, Kalindi reached out her hand to me. I took her hand and, with that gesture, I felt God's love reaching through my illusion of separateness and taking my heart once again into His.

On Friday, Kalindi was tired and I was anxious. She fell asleep for a couple of hours in the clothes she arrived in. I loved it when she napped like that and yet I was fretfully aware that this was our last day together. I was looking forward to some farewell sex. When she awoke, Kalindi obliged. But sex couldn't alleviate my distress. I could feel her energy shifting. Our time together was over even before Karin came to take her home.

The Voice Again

The following morning as I went through the lobby, I heard the same clear voice that had told me to move in with Kendra a year ago. I realized the voice had been whispering to me for days now. Until now, I'd not paid attention. This time the voice got louder, practically shouting "MARIE, MARIE." I thought, *"Oh, you want me to call Marie. OK, I'll call Marie."*

I had contacted Marie soon after Kalindi had mentioned her on our trip down to Half Moon Bay. I actually used the line, "Hey, Marie, Kalindi mentioned that it might be cool if you and I got together, so I was wondering ..."

Marie had been willing enough to get into bed with me but she had other things on her mind, and our time together was tense and uncomfortable. I was disappointed and wondered if I had gone straight to sex too quickly.

Towards the end of the year, we had an opportunity to spend another night together after a funding event at Bellagio. This time, as Marie had walked out the front door, she flipped up her skirt and flashed her butt cheek at me. Her mating sign was not lost on me.

Without hesitating, I asked, "Do you want to come back later tonight?"

She said, "Yes."

This time was entirely different. We really clicked, massaging each other into extremely sweet and hot sex! Afterwards, as Marie was leaving my room, she turned to say, "That was wonderful. I'd love do that a couple of times a year." I thought that was a strange thing to say, yet I wholeheartedly agreed.

Over time, I came to understand Marie's statement. Her life was consumed by God, Kalindi, her 16-year-old daughter, and her

144

work for the Mission. Relationships with men were a low priority. She meant it when she said that hooking-up once or twice a year was about what she could handle.

The big voice within was now pointing me to Marie. I wondered, *"Is this foreshadowing the demise of my relationship with Kalindi, or is something else brewing?"* Regardless, when I returned to Marin later that night, I called her. ♪

PART TWO

SERIOUS TRANSFOR-MATION

CHAPTER 11

MEDITATION

*"As your meditation deepens, you identify less and less
with the ego and begin to touch and enter more deeply
into the space of love. You begin to experience love
toward more and more people and find love
in the experiences that come into your field of awareness."*

Ram Dass

I had no idea how long Kalindi would stay in seclusion, nor what would become of the man/woman part of our connection. The 'voice' within had pointed me towards Marie so, when I returned to Marin, I called her. I told her what I had heard from the 'voice' while I was in Maui with Kalindi and asked, "Are you open to seeing each other again?" She said Yes. We looked at our calendars. I was planning to staff The Intensive in San Diego at the end of February so we scheduled to see each other then.

I was excited at the prospect of seeing Marie. Still, with Kalindi gone and San Diego three weeks away, I wondered what to do with my love life. I had a date with a woman I liked but it went nowhere. I decided to no longer pursue women or sex. Walking back and forth in my basement bedroom in Bellagio, I said to God, *"OK, I will leave this area up to you. I will not act on my own unless you want me to."*

I decided to focus on my spiritual work and participated in a 'Go Deeper Day' – an eight-hour workshop and meditation desi-gned to deepen my connection to God. During the initial part of the day, I reflected on the changes I had made in my life during the past year. I had joined the Path to Ultimate Freedom, had an 'Un-ordinary' relationship with Kalindi, left my work and career trajectory, and created a lifestyle that allowed me to focus full-time on my spiritual journey.

Meditative Thinking

The highlight of the day was the six-hour Meditation. I had been practicing this meditation since my first Intensive and had found it both spiritually and materially useful. Sitting down for quiet meditation to stop or control my thoughts was impossible for me. My mind and thoughts were too out of control, and I was run by the repressed emotions and feelings that kept my mind and being chaotic.

For me, meditation with **emotional and energetic release** was key for me to open, calm, and reach any real depth. I often used it to gain clarity around personal situations and decisions I needed to make. This time my focus was on spiritual development.

There are four parts to the Gourasana Meditation Practice.[1] Part 1 is Opening/Releasing; Part 2 is Calming; Part 3 is Meditative

---

1 The Gourasana Meditation Practice®, GMP®, is a modern-day meditation meant to address the needs of people living in this day and age. It was first taught by Gourasana in 1995. Traditionally throughout the ages, every Incarnation of God brings a medita-tion practice that carries the power for that period appropriate to the circumstances of the world they live in. This practice facilitates living in a fast-paced, high intensity world, supporting people to pursue spiritual practice without having to withdraw from society. The meditation practice is infused with a transformational energy and special assis-tance to help people gain a greater sense of well-being, materially and spiritually.

Thinking; and Part 4 is Taking Action. First, I sat quietly, shifting my focus within. My mind was restless so I did my best to let go of the thoughts of the day and week. As I did so, I started to feel the pent-up energy and emotions inside me.

There was dynamic emotion-evoking music playing and I started to move my body, opening and releasing energy and feelings. When I hit a spot in my heart related to Kalindi, I started crying. As the tears eased, I felt my emotional body opening and there were more tears from who knows what. I went on like this for another hour until I was feeling empty and peaceful.

The music changed to something soft and peaceful, without words. I spent the next thirty minutes calming. Calming was difficult for me back then. I had a challenging time not going off with my thoughts, as opposed to sitting still and allowing my thoughts and feelings to flow in and out without focusing on them. It helped when the meditation leader said, "Calm, just calm. Thoughts and feelings will come and go. Just let them be. We are not active now. You are alert and calm. Calm, calm, calm."

This became my mantra, "*Calm, calm, calm, just calming, calming, calming.*" Then I settled into an open and clear state to do meditative thinking. From this place, I could more easily access and pose questions to my awareness and higher Self. I started thinking about my current situation and a nagging feeling I had about it. The nagging feeling was, *"Even though I am no longer occupied by work, I still feel like I don't have enough time."*

Busyness

I thought about the changes I had made to work and travel less so I could be more available to help, serve, and be with Kalindi. Now I wasn't working, Kalindi was gone, and **I still felt too busy.** I had been trying to un-busy myself for years without much success so I wanted to take a deeper cut at it.

I asked myself, *"Why is this?"*

I scanned the last few weeks since these changes and regis-tered how I was automatically filling the time with other activities and things to do. I had let go of much of **what I had to do** and traded them for the things I wanted to do. Still, to remedy my inhe-rently meaningless existence, I was searching for meaning in a life of events and situations that contained ever higher stimulation and excitement.

"Good," I thought. *"I want to know more."* I knew I needed to go deeper. I asked, *"Ok, what am I avoiding?"*

Immediately, an answer emerged, *"I am running from God, from freedom, the truth, myself."*

I was intently listening. I knew one of the beginnings of free-dom was to be able to stop doing and just be. I was in a dialogue now with my higher Self.

"Yes, that's how God can meet you where you are. Being precedes and grounds everything. Unless I learn to live there, everything – words, events, relationships, identities – is superficial and without depth or context."

"Okay," I thought, *"that's true. Why is it I do not stay in being?"* This was a difficult question and I heard no answer. Hoping for some insight, I stayed as calm and peaceful as I could until something started to bubble up – not as words though, more as a sense of something.

There were feelings and emotions. I had always been a rational person and not inclined to feeling. I was staying busy and occupied so as *not to feel.* As I was taking this in, something popped into my head. It was an image of me on the phone with my Dad when I was fifteen, after he had moved to Florida. He called me every week to see how I was doing. On these calls, no matter where I was or what I was doing, he would ask me the same question, "Are you keeping busy?"

"Am I keeping busy?" I thought. *"What does that have to do with anything? Where did that question come from?"*

I flashed on the massive heart attack my Dad had when he was fifty, and the insanely frantic, activity-filled lifestyle he led. He didn't do one or two events in a day, he did three. He stayed busy morning, noon, and night. There was no lag or quiet time. He spent his life constantly busy until his life hung by a thread and the doctors barely saved him. After that he slowed down a bit, which was better for his health and a welcome respite for the rest of us. I was on to something. What began as a good intention on my father's part – his asking out of love and concern – had become a way of life for me. A way of being where busy equaled good, healthy, active, and useful for escaping painful emotions.

I sensed there was more to this. I focused my thoughts and prayed to see more about it. I flashed back to when I had worked at AT&T in my twenties. I was living in Manhattan at my Mom's. I would wake up on Saturday mornings in a panic. I had no work to go to and had not made plans for the day or weekend. I was frantic. I had to do fill the emptiness.

In this void, my hidden thoughts and feelings would start to emerge, similar to when I had my bad acid trips. Thoughts like, *"No one likes me; no one cares; I have no friends; I'm not loved."* The mere sight of these thoughts scared the shit out of me.

As these thoughts were taking me over, I'd immediately pick up the phone and call people to set up times to meet and do things, anything to not have **idle time on my hands** or **be alone with myself.** I needed distractions. Without them, my inner demons (feeling bad, wrong, alone, desperate) would emerge.

I recognized that the fear I experienced around these demons, these thoughts, was tremendous. In my teens and twenties, I had done everything I could not to confront these fears. I was afraid of falling apart, losing control, and feeling overwhelmed if my walls crumbled. I had been looking at some of these demons since my first Intensive in '94 and there was much deeper to go.

Then my experience with Gourasana from 1996 popped into my head. I recalled how I had faced a potent fear, which then allowed me to **access the deeper pain underneath,** leading to the most profound spiritual experience of my life.

It felt like God was taking over my life. I feared losing control and being helpless – just like not being able to open the can of tuna when I was a kid and crying for my brother to help. I was now feeling helpless to stop or control the **God train** I had boarded.

My body started vibrating. My energy was increasing. I noticed I was holding my breath so I breathed and relaxed. I still wanted to see more. As I calmed myself again, a picture crystalized in my awareness:

For years I had repressed events and situations, leaving many unresolved emotions. This went all the way back to my father's departure (abandonment) which traumatized me; being bullied and robbed as a teen (the world is not safe); my leaving God (I'm alone now) which was scary; feeling bad and wrong about myself; and everything feeling empty and meaningless.

My ego's strategy was to avoid these feelings at all costs. The plan was to stay busy and distract myself so as not to feel any of it. Busyness came in the form of sports, play, travel, women, and talking – a lot of meaningless talking.[1]

My ego had surrounded my pain in a barrier of fear. It knew that if I felt the pain, I could get free from it. The fear kept me running away from situations and people that could trigger that pain.

I had felt helpless in the face of these fears and thoughts. Staying engaged in constant activity left me in the hamster wheel of life. Unable to break the chains, I fed on temporary satisfactions and pleasures. I had to look good and do it right. I was obliged to prove myself or I would be found out as a fraud. I had to work hard

---

1 "It is the busyness that takes you from the light that you must avoid. You look to these things as excuses to not go within. Ironically, this is what most people are doing in the processes of religions. They are so busy propagating and helping others that they do little for themselves, thereby missing the entire point. This does not mean that some activity cannot be there, but the activity must not be this busy type of escape that you so quickly seek." Gourasana, *The Radical Path Home to God,* Miracle of Love, 2008, page 12

to make it. That's why I got my Ph.D. – to prove myself and impress others since I felt like I had no inherent worth.

Up until now, I had been unwilling to go deep enough to uncover the root causes of these behaviors. I could rationalize my behavior to protect my ego. If I hurt Genie or Lauren, I had my reasons. I was this shell of a man, a thin veneer barely hiding my insecurities. I was afraid of intimacy. I was afraid of failing. I was afraid of feeling pain. Fear and loss governed me, and I was saddened by these potent realizations.

Then I grasped what had been happening – **I had been on automatic pilot for all these years!** Until recently, I had not been running the show – the show (e.g., the illusion) had been running me! You go to school, get good grades, go to college, graduate school, work, wife, house, children, and spend the rest of one's life maintaining it all.

I had detoured off that road, and still I was trapped in my own prison of fears and beliefs. "You have to work to have money." *"I am unworthy of love." "I have to be funny and entertaining for people to like me."*

The concepts and beliefs went on and on. Last of all was, *"Do not feel bad/negative emotions! Emotions are bad and must be avoided at all costs!" "True Love is a fantasy! The best you can hope for is to get by and act like everything is OK."*

As I unraveled the maze of illusion in which I had been living, the solution was starting to emerge. I had to continue to face these fears and demons and relive past and future fears and events to release the stuck energy. I knew I would need God's help to do this. I started to pray:

> *"Dear Lord, please help me to see my ego clearly.*
> *Please give me the strength and courage I need*
> *to face my fears, pains and wounds*
> *so I can heal into your light, love, and peaceful embrace."*

154

I felt a powerful energy in my gut. I became more physically active. I began screaming into my pillow, pushing myself further within, into my insincerity and illusory kindness. I was trapped inside a pane of lies the illusion had fed me. I had bought the lies. The lies were two-fold: I was arrogant and unworthy; I was special and nobody; I was good and bad. I was trapped between these dualities. It was so tight in there.

Being deeply connected, my strength and courage were strong. I pierced into a new awareness: *"In between these opposites is where God lives."*

I dropped into deep pain. In order to feel it as deeply as I could, I screamed into it. I was happy to feel it. The pain felt good. It was real. After that, I found some anger with my parents and brother. I screamed and released it.

Very quickly, any specific content disappeared and I was just feeling, releasing, and letting go. I was on my feet now, moving freely, and intently focused on the energetic blocks in my body. I felt stuck and blocked in my heart and genital area. I asked God to help me. A white light came into my heart which removed something. I breathed deeply and felt my heart open.

Then a golden light came into my pelvic region and that opened. I started gyrating freely, unlike the blocked stiff guy I had been. I was now spinning and dancing with abandon as my energy started to move with ease through all of my chakras. I was beyond meditation into movement. I was moving and moving fast.[1]

After fifteen minutes of this *let-go* dancing, my awareness went into the hurt underneath the anger. I paused as the hurt turned into sadness. I fell on the floor and curled up in a ball crying out to God, *"Thank you, Lord, thank you."* I was getting free.

After twenty minutes of tears and immense love pouring into me, I was physically exhausted. After resting, my strength quickly

---

1 "It is beyond meditation. It has come to movement. It is time to let the energy move you as it has never moved you before. Just let it move you; become one with the energy." Gourasana, *Breaking the Cycle of Birth and Death,* Miracle of Love, 2001, Quote # 249

returned. I asked for more to be shown to me and started to pray, *"Please show me who I really am, and help me to open more of my shutdown being and neglected heart."*

From this prayerful and open state, the dual answers of humility and surrender emerged from my awareness. They would be the saving grace against my ego. *"I have little idea what humility really is,"* I thought. *"I mostly have concepts of humility. Humble behavior is not my thing."*

I felt humility in Gandhi, Yogananda, Kalindi, and The Lady. Yet I thought, *"What they have, I do not."*

Then my awareness chimed in, *"You are in humility in this moment – from your open and prayerful stance, crying, and asking for help from The Almighty."*

I acknowledged that to myself and continued to ask for help, *"Please help me to understand more about the connection between humility and surrender?"*

I started exploring my surrender to Kalindi. I had surrendered to Kalindi to the best of my ability. I was conscious that I was, "Giving up my life as I would have it."[1]

I loved and trusted Kalindi. Still I pondered, *"How am I with God? Am I surrendered to Him? Will I let go of my own will and live in His Will?"* I knew full union with God required voluntarily giving back my free will to Him. Then I thought, *"If I do this, what will His Will be for me?"* Hah!

There I was – trying to figure it out.

That was it. My mind kicked back in. I was done. I would have to leave additional inquiry into humility, surrender, and trust for another time. I pledged to myself to pray for more trust, to cultivate humility in myself with simple, selfless acts, and to recognize surrender when I saw it exhibited.

My final act for the day was to approach the leader and ask how she related to humility.

I loved her answer so much that I wrote it down:

When we feel the presence of God, and the magnitude of His Love, it is easy to think, "I have been touched by God. I am special." The ego manifests this specialness and this creates separation with others. Others feel less-than and excluded. God is inclusive of everyone. Be a man who speaks what he has realized, plainly without exclusivity. This way you can bring forth universal love and caring that is inclusive of everyone.

I knew I needed to always be vigilant about specialness because of my relationship with Kalindi. To the best of my ability, I tried to love everyone openly. I had to always watch for my ego's desire to be someone special from my association with her.

The awareness I gained from this meditation was essential for me moving forward. Besides, I was soon to lose my special relationship with Kalindi.

Marie

The following week was Valentine's Day. I had left on a good note with Kalindi, yet I still wasn't sure what the status of our relationship was. We had no direct communication. I wrote her a letter, thinking I would probably not hear anything back from her:

---

1   Gourasana had taught two main principles for surrendering to God: First you must give up everything as you would have it in your lifetime; all your plans, all your conceptions for the future. How you want it to be; how you think it should be. You must give all of this up – even as you conceive spiritual life to be. A turning point comes in your spiritual life where you have so completely given up your plans that you are prepared to die; you will gladly give up your life for awareness. Attaining awareness has become that critical that you will not only give up your plans and hopes for the future, but you will give up your *future in this existence.* To come to that point is essential.

... The next step, the harder step, is to continue to live, but live as you need to live to become aware, without considering – is it pleasurable or not pleasurable, is there fear or not, is there suffering or not, is it increasing my distress or not? You just do what another will has you do. You give up your will, and you do what the Universe would have you do. That is all. If you can take these two steps, then you will succeed. That is serious. That is complete surrender: to give up your will, to surrender to a higher will. Gourasana, *The Radical Path Home to God,* Miracle of Love, 2008, page 344

My dear Kalindi,

Our last time together was first class. Each time feels as if it improves, as I can open and give more. I loved being with you and sharing all that we did. The experience was whole and complete in itself. I feel a rhythm that we can fall into now. A simple, peaceful, easy flow. Mostly, Kalindi, I want to express the gift you are to me, how precious you are to me. Our friendship transcends all I have ever known.

Today I brought the RV back home. As I was setting it up, I was remembering all the wonderful times we spent there – our trips, barbecues, movies, sex, eating, naps – it was a true haven.

I am reading the book 'Ramakrishna and his disciples' right now. It is helping me to understand what it is like around a spiritual master. Also, this passage from one of his disciples, spoke to me:

"I am afraid to speak, I am afraid not to speak, for the fear rises in my mind that I shall lose you." I have also felt like this many times.

Good night my Love, Your friend,

Mark

The next week I went to San Diego to staff The Intensive. I was looking forward to days of pure service and giving. I also would see Marie and was eager for that. I looked forward to meeting her for several reasons: 1) She was a hot, open, loving redhead and I was eager for love and connection; 2) She was a member of the Core with a very advanced consciousness; and 3) I was eager to have a partner for regular sex.

During The Intensive, there were one-and-a-half days off for the participants to rest and integrate. Marie and I spent this time together. I had reserved a hotel room not too far from where The Intensive was happening. Marie arrived looking radiant as usual. I was happy about meeting her.

We talked about what **the voice** had said. Innocently, she asked me, "What do you think it means?" I told her, "I don't really know but the only other time I heard that voice it led me right to Kalindi. So I want to act on it." That was true and I really hoped she would go for it. I suggested, "Let's relax and just be together and see what happens."

Marie said, "Okay, I don't know what to make of it either but, if it is from God, I want to pay attention."

I loved how much Marie knew and felt God. It was fact for her. She had a Catholic upbringing and shared how she would pray alone in her closet as a child. She'd had a deep connection with God and Jesus since she was five years old. Now she gave her all to her job and service with the Mission. She had been giving her all since the start of the organization in 1991. I loved that she was 100% committed to Gourasana, Kalindi, and the Mission.

I felt good with her, better than I felt with myself. I felt I could be myself and even more. When I spoke, she listened intently, as if what I was saying was gold. She liked me, although at the time, I couldn't fathom why. I still felt so empty and vacuous.

That night, and the next day and night, we fell right into each other. I could really let go into sex with her. I loved being with her and I wanted her to love me. She understood me and my time with Kalindi. She told me from the get go that, if we were together, she would never come between Kalindi and I in any way. I was extremely grateful to Gourasana for this gift. "Perhaps this is a match made in heaven," I thought.

Marie and I both wanted to see each other again. We thought we could get together before and after the Annual Retreat, which was taking place in San Diego at the end of March.

Serving God

As March rolled around, I was frustrated. When I stopped working at the end of 1997, I had $15,000 in savings. My current expenses were $5,000/month. I had one coaching client who was paying me $1,400/month. That was a good thing, yet I wasn't interested in more coaching clients.

I was engaged in conversation with Kendra, Blaise[1] several other colleagues about creating a business that was for and about God. It could be any business or product, as long as at least 51% of our profits would go to Miracle of Love or other spiritual organizations in service of God. We looked at spiritual counseling using the disciples of Kalindi. We thought about a sex shop that promoted conscious sex toys and guides.

Nothing was clicking, which was fine, except I was running out of cash. That scared me. I hated feeling like I was going to run out of money; however, financial realities were closing in.

This began a two-week period of fierce prayer for me. I was asking God, begging Him, to show me what He wanted me to do. *"What should my livelihood be?"* I asked. *"I need to make money and I want to serve You. Please show me the way."*

For the next days, nothing came to me. I waited patiently, and kept praying and trusting. Each day was harder than the next. I was feeling a lot of pressure. My friends thought I should create a private coaching practice since I was experienced, could charge high rates, and still have time for God and the Mission. Somehow, I couldn't do it. I wasn't up for that; it felt like taking the easy way out. I sensed there was something else God wanted me to do. I just didn't know what.

I had nearly reached the limit of my trust and faith and fear was starting to win. Nothing was happening and I would be out of money soon. It was a Thursday night in mid-March, and I went to the meditation center in Marin County to meditate.

During the meditation, I prayed for guidance. I prayed for humility. I prayed *"Dear God, please help me, what do you want me to do?"* I was desperate. I was begging and begging, openly, sincerely, from my deepest yearning.

Then something broke in me. I had been trying to figure it out myself. There had been no room for God in my plan, my mind, my thinking. I released control and I fell to my knees with tears of surrender. My will melted away into that sweet surrender, and then into crying from letting go of control. I was sobbing, sobbing, sobbing. I had been holding on to me, what I knew, how I wanted it. I realized I had to let go and give it up to Him. What a relief! From here, I could start to feel, dance, move, be, love, connect, let go, and again live in His Glory.

I went home that night feeling totally altered. I was no longer worried or concerned. I still didn't know what I was going to do, yet it didn't seem to matter. I went to sleep, feeling held and loved.

I woke up feeling alive and full of possibility. I was talking with people, making phone calls, and open for what was going to come next. While making dinner, I received a phone call from Kalindi.

I'd not spoken to her since I'd left Hawaii in early February. Without preamble, she went to the heart of the matter and asked, "Do you want to go on supported staff at the Miracle of Love Center in San Diego?"

"Oh my God!" I thought, *"How could she know?" "Did she hear my prayer?"*

Before I could grasp anything, she explained, "I am going to suggest that you manage the Outreach and Fundraising Departments of the organization."[2]

---

1   Blaise had been close with Gourasana when He was in the body and a close disciple of Kalindi's ever since. A dentist, nurse and successful businesswoman, Kalindi also relied on her for assistance in matters regarding her health and wellbeing.

2   Kalindi provided spiritual direction to the organization and to individual participants for the sole purpose of furthering their spiritual movement. Sometimes the direction took the form of doing something material or within the organization. Kalindi did not manage the day to day running of the organizations business affairs.

Kalindi was saving my ass. I quickly said, "Yes, of course, I'll do that! Thank you, Kalindi. What an honor! What an opportunity!"

Kalindi was again validating my faith in God. Through Kalindi, God was answering my prayers, and caring and providing for me. Plus, being on supported staff meant I would be supported financially. My money fears evaporated. We agreed I would start in April. We said goodbye and it was done.

That night, after it all sank in, I recognized I would also be in the same city as Marie. It was an extra bonus and I was excited. Given how I was feeling with Marie, I sensed it could easily develop into something more than a few hot dates now and then. I thought I should check in with Kalindi about it though, before I went to San Diego for the retreat.

Given our personal relationship, I wanted to know if Kalindi would be OK with it. I wrote to Kalindi the next day, thanking her again for the job opportunity and asking if it was OK for me to become involved with Marie romantically. I faxed the letter to Karin for Kalindi.

After holding my breath for a couple of days, I received a note back from Karin that said, "Kalindi says that is OK." I couldn't believe my good fortune. In just a few days, Kalindi had opened the doors for my next work and love life. ♪

CHAPTER 12

CREATION

*"The original indivisible state of God becomes countless
individualized souls, like bubbles within an infinite ocean.
Each soul, powered by the desire to become conscious,
starts its journey in the most rudimentary form of consciousness ...
The soul experiences itself in a succession of imagined forms ...
The soul identifies itself with each successive form,
becoming thus tied to illusion.
During this evolution of forms thinking also increases,
until in human form thinking becomes infinite.
Although in human form the soul is capable of conscious divinity,
all the impressions that it has gathered during evolution
are illusory ones, creating a barrier for the soul to know itself.
For this barrier to be overcome, further births in human form
are needed in a process named reincarnation.
Eventually the soul reaches a stage where its previously gathered
impressions grow thin or weak enough that it enters a final stage,
an inner journey, by which it realizes its true identity and
the goal of life for the individual soul is reached."*

Meher Baba

arrived in San Diego a week before the Retreat. I was staying with Marie and her daughter, Mariah, in their house east of San Diego. The next day we received a message that Kalindi would be coming to San Diego for the Retreat. She would be arriving in two days, and she wanted to see both of us the day after.

Two days later, Marie and I were at a gas station when we got the call that Kalindi would like see us in thirty minutes. *"OK, here we go,"* I thought.

My heart beat fast and all my emotions heightened at the thought of seeing Kalindi again. I wondered, *"How should I be with her now that I am dating Marie?"* I couldn't figure it out ahead of time so I decided to just be as open as I could.

When we arrived where Kalindi was staying, we both felt a deep mood in the house. When I asked Karin what was happening, she curtly said, "She is very serious." I straightened myself up, getting as serious and deep as I could.

I looked at Marie and saw she looked a bit worried. I had not seen her like this before. I thought, *"Maybe this is something about Marie."* Either way, I was feeling tense and uncomfortable.

Karin ushered us into Kalindi's room. She was sitting on a small, white sofa. Marie and I knelt down in front of her. I could tell Kalindi was in her no-shit Master mode. There was no greeting. There was no sentiment.

Kalindi first spoke to Marie. She said, "It is important to stay in your connection with God, Marie. You must not get lost as you have in your previous relationships."

Marie nodded and said she understood. Kalindi looked deeply into her eyes and Marie started to sob, as she said, "I promise, Kalindi, I promise."

Kalindi turned to face me and said, "Mark, it will be beneficial for you to be with Marie. Allow yourself to have it fully." I breathed a deep sigh of relief. She continued, "You need the space to experience all your sexual desires and fantasies. Most importantly, you need to let your heart open and then let it break over and over again."

Intellectually, I understood what Kalindi meant by 'break over and over again.' I was aware that the path to God was strewn with permanently broken hearts. However, I was mostly thinking about love and sex with Marie, preferring to deal with any heartbreak or loss down the road. I nodded and said, "Thank you, Kalindi. I understand."

I was dying to talk with sweet Kalindi, yet I knew enough to know this was not the time for that. I resisted looking Kalindi in the eyes because I knew I was feeling sentimental and needy. Kalindi said, "That will be all. I will see you in the Retreat." We rose to our feet with a silent nod goodbye, and walked out of her room.

As Marie and I drove back to her house, I was a little off-kilter and not feeling connected to Kalindi personally. Still, I was happily relieved that my Master had given me the green light to love Marie and have all the sex I wanted.

I could tell that Marie was affected by what Kalindi had said. Her face was stern. She looked at me and said, "I cannot get lost with you, Mark. It's been my habit. It's the way I've been in my other relationships." I didn't know this about Marie. She seemed so strong and mature. I couldn't imagine how that could happen so I asked her about it.

She told me, "I became very possessive in my last relationship. I was jealous and needy, all of which was OK, except it nearly pulled me out of my connection with God." She said, "I was grateful when Kalindi saved me. I was really lost." She went on, "Frankly, I had decided to stay out of relationships. I didn't know if I could trust myself. I was content to focus on God, the Mission, Mariah, and my own spiritual liberation."

I listened intently as she continued, "Then you came along with that message from Gourasana and what was I to do? I know I am clearer and stronger now and I'm grateful that Kalindi is watching out for me." Lastly she said, "You should know I take everything Kalindi says very seriously. I will meditate on this for days now to see where and how the illusion might try to get me this time."

I was inspired by Marie's earnestness and dedication. I was also glad Kalindi was holding Marie in this way. I said to Marie, "I trust you. I know you can do it. It is me I am not sure of."

She glanced at me, saying, "I'm glad you have faith in me. I am not that sure myself." I steamrolled past her statement to say, "I'm ready to go full throttle with you and I am committed to opening my heart as much as I can." Marie smiled.

I told her, "I know I still have healing left to do from my relationships with Helle, Genie, and Lauren. I am determined to heal those wounds, to move through my fears, and to continue opening, giving, and loving you as much as I can." Marie smiled modestly – perhaps not as confident as I was about this topic. We continued home in silence.

Personal Kalindi

A couple of days later, Kalindi asked if I would come visit her. This visit had a very different feeling to it. When I arrived, I asked Karin where Kalindi was. She smiled and said, "On her exercise bike. Go right in."

Kalindi smiled and said, "Hi, Mark" as I entered. She was peddling the bike, slightly out of breath. I sat down on a weight bench nearby. This time she was completely personal with me. She expressed her feelings of loss. She said, "I feel I am losing you to the Mission and Marie. I am made to let go again and again. This feels like it could be the end of our physical intimacy together."

I was silent when faced with her vulnerability. I felt her loss and sadness deeply. Kalindi said it in such a matter-of-fact way and without sentiment. It was a new experience for me to feel – one without drama attached. In Kalindi's presence, the man/woman drama was overshadowed by the true love underneath.

I was feeling loss myself. I thought, *"Yes, this might well be the end of our physical intimacy."*

Given where I was going with Marie, I had mixed feelings about it. The physical intimacy with Kalindi helped me feel special. Because of my crossover with love and sex, I was afraid I would lose my 'in' with Kalindi. I had no idea what my relationship with her would be like otherwise. Romantically and with regard to lustful sex, I had already moved towards Marie and wanted to keep going in that direction.

Kalindi moved on and asked me something about the Retreat. Feeling uncomfortable with the previous conversation, I was glad for the segue. To ease my uncertainty, I wanted to ask her what the future held for us. I didn't because I knew she didn't know and she seemed disinterested in any further talking, so we said goodbye.

On the way home I felt sad from the thought of not being intimate with Kalindi any longer. There was not much I could do about it anyway. She was moving forward in her purpose, and our man/woman relationship was not part of it.

On the other hand, I was falling in love with Marie. I knew I needed an ordinary relationship to heal the wounds of my heart – one where the other person wasn't a so-fully-awake-and-aware being. I needed a partner to play out all my sexual and love desires, while exposing my fears and neediness. Plus, I still believed I could find happiness and even fulfillment from a woman.

With Kalindi, our love was deeply based in God. Our sexual intimacy was a bonus but certainly did not drive our connection. I hoped that Kalindi and I would continue to share personal time together. Being with her was fulfilling for me at the deepest level. I wanted to continue loving her unconditionally in any way I could. The next day, feeling clearer and more able to express myself,

I wrote to Kalindi:

"I have cherished all of our time together and I hope for more. It saddens me to think we won't have intimate time together again. I accept how it is and willingly surrender to what needs to happen next for you, for me, and for the Mission. I trust that it will unfold as it should and we will be together in the right way. However, I don't want to pretend like it is not painful for me or that I don't miss you, because I do.

There has been so much fear in me, and you have been so loving and sweet and kind with me. Yes, you have been tough with me, heavy with me – yet I have always felt all your love, all your care, right behind it, and I still do. I will continue to send you letters and cards, although they are only slivers of my love. My love is always there for you – present and alive."

Seclusion

I didn't have any other personal time with Kalindi before or during the Retreat. However, after the Retreat, I was pleasantly surprised when she asked me to fly with her back to Maui. When I told Marie, she was thrilled for me and happy I would be there for Kalindi.

This time I was to meet Kalindi when they arrived at the airport in San Diego. As I waited on the curb, I focused on being as deep, open, and natural as I could. I knew that the first moment she saw me was crucial to how she would relate to me. If I was stiff and fearful, she would notice and not feel comfortable with me.

When Kalindi's car arrived, I opened her door. I extended my hand and helped her out of the car. She looked tired and drained. We smiled at each other and all seemed fine. She walked slowly and quietly. I felt her vulnerability, which motivated me to get her through security as smoothly as possible. Once through, we strolled through the airport, towards the gate.

I noticed others watching as we all walked at Kalindi's deliberately calm pace through the airport. Another male disciple and

I were in front, loaded with carry-ons. Kalindi and her sister were in the middle carrying their purses, and two other disciples were behind them, also loaded with carry-ons. As opposed to most everyone's hurried pace, we moved slowly as a unit, with a presence not usually seen or felt in public, thus the staring.

Once on the plane, Kalindi sat with her secretary to get any remaining information and guidance for her disciples out to them. When she was done, Kalindi asked me to sit with her. I was happy to do so, yet was unsure of how to be with her. I thought, *"Just follow her lead, that's always a good plan."*

Kalindi was quiet for some time. Towards the end of the flight, she asked me to massage her neck and back. I did, although it was an awkward position in the airline seats. I was uneasy, feeling my massage style inadequate. Then Kalindi raised her head and said to me sharply, "Where are you right now? Where is your presence?"

I realized I was holding back, trying to keep my energy from disturbing her. I was unsure how to touch her or how intimate to be with her. Rather than expressing all this to Kalindi, I simply snapped present and started massaging her again, this time with all my love and energy freely flowing to her. Her body relaxed and gently lay in my lap. I was happy I could recover so well and that she let down accordingly.

After we landed in Maui, I drove Kalindi back to her house. Before saying good-bye, she gave me a very light, yet fully open and wonderfully sweet hug that made me feel good all over. I was scheduled to stay on Maui for four days and didn't know if I would see Kalindi again. I had been asked by Karin to be on call and stay close enough to get to Kalindi's within 30 minutes.

I was pleasantly surprised the next morning when Kalindi called and asked me if I would like to sit with her by the pool. She wore a bikini and asked me to put suntan lotion on her. I was glad I could still touch her body. We ate at the pool. There was a sweet flow with long periods of silence. I loved being in silence with her. We knew each other well and there was no agenda or expectation.

We had a calm and peaceful day, with occasional talking and laughing. We had light, casual talks about serious spiritual matters. Kalindi talked about how the consciousness of the earth will change over time. She said that things may get worse for a while before getting better in several hundred years.

Then, in about a thousand years, the consciousness of the whole planet will be peaceful, meaning we will no longer be hurting or killing each other. We will have evolved beyond the unnecessary suffering (i.e., man-made suffering). We will have evolved to be universally kind, gentle, respectful, and caring with each other. The only suffering would come from the inevitable physical suffering of the body and other natural disasters.

"Okay, far out!" I thought. "What will be happening with religion?" I asked her. She said, "There will be a one-world spirituality that unites everyone." I liked that too.

I asked her, "What about Christianity? What will happen to it?" Her answer astounded me. She said, "In a few hundred years, 'Warrior Souls' will be born to fight the final battles against a dying religion." She continued, "Christianity will become as extreme as some of the current Islamic sects and eventually, like all violent and false expressions of God, they will self-destruct."

She was so matter-of-fact. It made sense to me. I was thinking, *"Christianity, Islam, Judaism, Hinduism, anything that was not about the inclusive love of God, will not survive,"* I was deeply impacted by this and laid back on my lounge chair to take it all in.

Later on, we went inside and watched two Lifetime movies.[1] By 9 pm we said goodbye, and arranged I would come the next day at 12:30.

On the second day I brought a large pizza and five videos with me. When I arrived, Kalindi was in her bedroom, lounging in her pajamas. She was tired, but relaxed. We watched three movies in a row and in between ate the pizza. She surprised me by having

---

1 Movies on the Lifetime channel. Kalindi particularly liked to watch these movies when she was resting or recuperating. They were simple and easy to follow and without too much violence.

a strawberry shake with her pizza. We hardly spoke at all. I loved these kinds of easy breezy, quiet days with her. We were 'chilla-xing,' just as we had done in our hippie pad the year before.

The next day we drove to the Westin Hotel where I had stayed months before. I was to be in the flow with her as we walked around. We glided hand-in-hand and I felt like we were walking in the True Realm together.

We stopped at a fast food place on the way home to pick up a couple of burgers. Once home, we watched another movie in her room. After the movie, she called her physician, Dr. Tavakoli. I left her alone for the call.

Kalindi must have received some kind of approval from Dr. T because, when I came back into the room, she said she was ready to have sex! I wasn't expecting it but I thought to myself, "OK, here we go."

I was happy to be with Kalindi in this way again and give to her. I also felt validated, thinking it meant she was really happy with me. Marie had given me a green light to have sex with Kalindi anytime, so that was handled.

Kalindi asked if I wanted to, and when I said Yes she was happy. She said, "OK, but you have to use a condom now since you are also having sex with Marie." I agreed.

Afterwards, she was calm and quiet. It was 9 pm, and time for me to leave. I left feeling both happy and slightly confused. I didn't understand why we had sex together. I thought that part of our lives together was over. I couldn't figure it out and yet I was content to let it be. Here I was – in love with one woman who wanted me as a man, and in service to a Master who chose to be with me sexually. Somehow it felt like the best of two worlds.

Fragmentation

The next day was the last of our time together. We spent time at the pool and had a long conversation about **reincarnation** and the **evolution of the soul.** I asked Kalindi about how it all works here and where we come from. She said she would tell me the whole creation story but it would be best to relate to it as a 'spiritual fairytale' since it can't really be grasped or comprehended by the mind.

She started by saying, "The soul is the fragment of the true self that comes from our spiritual home, the True Realm of Existence. When that soul or fragment leaves the Spiritual World and enters the material world, it is fragmented everywhere. It is like an explosion and, with that, you are separated and forget at that point where you even came from. It is all gone. The whole true self does not come, only a fragment, and that fragment is what fragments."

I nodded my head, following her so far. Some part of me was drinking it up, resonating deeply with what she was saying.

Kalindi went on, "So let's say at first you are fragmented into all different germs, the very bottom of the line. Say you are splintered into a thousand different things. One of those things is like the dominant or the highest existence of your current situation. You are at the bottom level and all of those things die. Then as you come up to the next level, climbing the ladder of evolution, some of those pieces find their way back to other parts. When you get to the next level, maybe you only have 900 fragments instead of 1,000 because some of them joined back to the other and it is now a higher form. Then you go to whatever kind of insects and bugs."

I nodded and asked, "Do you have to be every different kind of germ or bug?"

"No" she said, "to experience being a spider, you do not have to be every kind of spider. You just need to be one kind of spider to have that experience of the spider. Now the thing is, there are two kinds of spiders. Some spiders bite and are poisonous and some are not. So you have to have those two experiences."

"Still you are fragmented, so 900 things are going on at once. On the level of the spider, there are other kinds of insects that would be classified in that species. Let's just put insects in one category. So, you are experiencing 900 different kinds of bugs and insects and then, as those die off, the fragments come together again and then on up to the next level. Some parts of the fragment go to the next level, while other parts are still down here being spiders and mosquitoes and whatever is in that level. Then up here some parts of some fragments are butterflies and whatever is in that level."

I took a deep breath as Kalindi continued.

"Then there are all of the fish and birds. Again, you do not have to be every kind of fish. As you climb up there is more intelligence and you have more fragments coming together the higher you are. Like the dolphins are very smart and, by the time you are in that situation, maybe there are 100 fragments out but the intelligence is starting to wake up because the dolphins can think. Now you are getting ready for human birth."

"As you keep going up, there are fewer fragments because, in order for the higher intelligence to be there, more fragments have to be gathered. Then, once you become a human, you still have some fragments out as you are just entering human existence. You do not enter human existence at the end, you enter it at the beginning – pretty ignorant, but human. Maybe you are born in places where there is no consciousness, just human survival and like that."

"As the bodies of those fragments die, then those fragments find their way to each other. It is possible that all of your fragments are together, but you are having several more lifetimes experiencing different things while you are all the way back together, maybe 10 more lifetimes once you are back together."

"You keep going like that until your last birth. When it is your last birth, all of the fragments are back together. Otherwise, you are not whole down here. So in your last birth, you are all the way back together and all that is together is the fragment that left before it fragmented."

I breathed in. That was a big one. It hit home because I'd often felt incomplete in myself. "What happens next?" I asked.

Kalindi went on, "Based on God's timing and the soul's desire, the completed fragment leaves reincarnation behind, returning Home, while behind it more and more souls pour in at the beginning of their physical existence."

"Really?" I asked. "That sounds endless."

"It is," she said, and went on to explain, "Many souls have been incarnating on earth in the last several thousand years because there is the right amount of suffering here to motivate people to get out."[1]

This fascinated me.

"However," Kalindi continued, "earth will not always be the place to come to get free." She added, "Once the consciousness of the planet has sufficiently changed into peaceful co-existence, this will no longer be where souls come to get free. They will incarnate to other planets and dimensions where there is enough suffering to motivate one through the final parts of their journey."

"So there is life on other planets?"

"Yes," she said, "there is life on other planets – some with such high levels of consciousness and technology that no one gets free there, no one gets out; it is too easy, too good, and there isn't enough motivation to get out."[2]

I was blown away by all this. As Kalindi spoke, what she said was being created for me. It was created, existed, and then disappeared in my awareness, moment by moment.

In addition, she told me, "While it is beyond comprehension, the entire purpose of this reality, this material illusion, is to continually manifest love back Home in the True Realm of Existence. Each time a soul returns, there is like a cosmic celebration and the love increases. That is the purpose of all creation."

---

1   This may be why our population is increasing.

2   "If you are in the mud, you try to get out" her Master said to her. "In other words speaking figuratively, if I sit in a comfortable chair, I will do nothing." Irene Tweedie, *Daughter of Fire,* 1966

"And remember," she said, "who you really are, your True Self, is still there in the True Realm. It never left, only the tiny fragment did. Although that fragment may be gone for millions or billions of years, that seems like nothing to the True Self. The True Self is a timeless, eternal, unique being of light and love, synced with every other unique being and The Source."

"The True Realm of Existence is so far out, you can do whatever you want there. Yet trying to explain the Spiritual World (when you can hardly understand the material world that you know and can see) is almost impossible. So I do not want anyone to have too many concepts about the True Realm, only that there is no separation and you return to who you are and everyone is rejoicing in the Lord. Everything is the Lord, but the beings are not God. Only God is God, but it is as if you were God it is so big. But God is God and everyone has a relationship with God and with each other all at once."

I asked if she could say more about the True Realm.

"It is beauty and it is ecstasy and there is music and colors. The colors are the love and the music is the love. You can just keep changing yourself. If you want to do five things at once, you can do five things at once. One part of you might want to laugh for a 1,000 years and another part wants to join in on what is happening over there and there and there. Well, okay. You can go and be everywhere. You can split yourself into different parts and laugh in one spot together with hundreds of other True Selves for hundreds or thousands of years. Simultaneously, you can be in as many different situations with as many different true selves as you want – constantly, forever!"

I loved this part. I have always felt inside myself how I want to merge with everybody, everywhere, all the time. I thought, *"Maybe the yearning I feel to be in different places with different people comes from this knowing of my True Self?"*

Kalindi continued, "That is why it is so hard in this world because the true nature is that there is no lack, everyone has a special relationship with God, and everyone has a special relationship with each other. If you want to sleep for 1,000 years, you can go to sleep. If someone feels like waking you up so they can bump into you, you do not have to wake up because you decided to go to sleep. Then if God decides that we are going to do this, then everyone is saying, "Good, we are all going because God is moving this way and we are all part of that force." It does not move separate."

Kalindi went on, "When the fragment returns Home, there is like a slight 'blip' that the True Self may notice for a moment, then it continues romping away in ever-increasing love and ecstasy."

Then she moved closer to me and said, "You volunteered to come here, to do all this. Everyone has. People don't remember because the illusion has them forget, until their soul is ready to awaken and then they start to remember."

"Really? We volunteered for all this? Did we know what we were getting ourselves into?"

Kalindi nodded and said, "Yes, and God has a special love for all of us because we said Yes." I rolled that over in my mind for a minute.

"And we don't remember because of the illusion?" I asked.

"Yes, God created this illusory plane of existence as a place where you can forget who He is and who you really are; where you can feel separate from Him; where you can doubt or even deny the existence of your Creator!"

"The truth is that you are one with God and each other. The illusion covers over this truth and you think and believe you are separate and alone."

"Do you see how powerful the illusion is?" she asked me. "He created it and that is why He is the only thing more powerful than the illusion, and why He is the only one who can free you from it."

"Once the soul starts to awaken, He sends help – Incarnations like Krishna, Buddha, and Jesus are the well-known ones. There have been others too – Enlightened Masters, as well as other special assistance once you are ready to return Home again."

Those last few sentences hung in the air for me for a while. My soul lit up as my brain processed this information. Kalindi leaned back in her chair and I knew the conversation was over.

This was one of the most impactful conversations we ever had. It made sense that a small fragment of my True Self came here at the beginning, and at the end would come back together to leave this plane of illusion.

It solved so many problems for me about suffering. The idea that I actually volunteered to come here and experience all this comforted me; and that the suffering on this plane fueled the love in the True Realm gave the whole process more meaning to me. The fact that the Earth had the right amount of suffering to motivate souls to break free of the cycle of birth and death also made sense to me.

Fully satiated, we went inside. Kalindi got dressed for her meeting later that day with The Lady, who was also on Maui for rest. We gazed at each other, acknowledging the truth and love we shared together. She said she would miss my love for her while she completed her seclusion. She gave me a kiss on the cheek and was gone.

On the plane ride home, I wrote this love letter to Kalindi:

For My Love, Kalindi La♪[1]

For the last year, I have felt constantly with you, never very far away. I am open to you fully, more than I thought was ever possible for me. I've opened my heart, giving you everything that I can. I have learned to love you no matter what. I have felt your unconditional love for me, and I have tried to return that love to you, loving you through every phase you go through, being with you lovingly with all the care and devotion I could give.

When you look at me and smile and say, "Mark …" I feel all the love in the entire universe.

I miss you already. This is making me very sad. I don't like feeling this immense sadness. While I trust that our friendship is simply taking its next turn, I do not like it. I am afraid of losing you. The thought of losing you feels like the love being cut out of me with a sharp, jagged instrument – leaving me gutted and ripped open.

I am preaching to myself that, in truth, you will never leave me. What I feel with you is God's Love, deep inside me, which can never be lost.

With love, care and appreciation,

Mark

It was late March when I landed back in San Francisco. I went straight to the Bellagio house to pack up. I was due in San Diego in a couple of days to start my new job. My goal was to have all my possessions fit into my little jeep and a small trailer. I loved weeding out the unnecessary, getting down to the basics needed for my new situation – materially and energetically.

As I was packing, I went over the last three years. Since I moved to northern California: I completed my marriage to Genie; had a deep connection with Lauren; personally experienced Gourasana; moved in with Kalindi and became her friend and lover; shifted from full-time to part-time work and then resigned completely; fell in love with Marie; heard my Master speak to me personally about the Universe; and now prepared to go on staff in San Diego.

Mission Central

I was set up to live in a simple, four-bedroom house in La Jolla, a coastal community about a 20-minute drive from the San Diego Miracle of Love (MOL) Center. The house was beautifully situated. There was a flowery backyard and the ocean was just a few blocks away. My new housemates were members of the

---

1   Kalindi La♪ was the name Kalindi used in between Kalindi and Kalindi La♪ Gourasana.

Mission. My room was in the front right of the house with a nice view on a quiet, tree-lined side street.

When I first arrived at the Center for work, it had a completely different feeling than that which had prevailed during Intensives and other Events. The large meditation/seminar room was empty and the office was filled with some 50 people all energetically at work.

I met with the MOL community coordinator. She made me feel completely welcome in my new situation, explaining that there were currently 80 people on supported staff and many volunteers. Staff included Kalindi, The Lady, the Core, spiritual leaders, and personnel in publications, audio/video, events, participation, and several other departments. She told me I was joining a dedicated group of people who willingly and gladly do whatever it takes to support the overall goals of the Mission.

Staff was supported according to need, based on a mutually agreed-upon personal budget. For example, those with children received a larger monthly stipend. If a person was in debt, they received sufficient support to gradually pay down that debt. Whatever each person received covered monthly expenses but nothing more.

The accurate budget for me came in at $1,800/month, plus health insurance. That was less than 40% of what I had required three months before. The Mission was there to support me. If I needed additional help to cover dental expenses and so on, those funds would be made available. I was elated. How extraordinary it was to be part of an organization with a serious commitment to spiritual transformation and the ability to support those who served its cause.

Like a newly-minted member of the clergy, I dove head-first into **God-central.** I was ready to let go of my life as I knew it and live my life as God would have it. I loved my new service and the people I worked with. I was taking my next steps towards living a fully aligned and integrated life.

Illusory Love

Living in the same city as Marie, our connection blossomed into an intimate relationship. We talked on the phone every day and spent several nights a week together. In the process, I became close with Mariah, Marie's 17-year-old daughter. We spent time together because I was so willing to drive her to the places she wanted to go. I liked the family feeling and committed myself to helping and supporting them both.

We even worked together! While I was a department manager, Marie's job was supporting and coordinating the volunteer staff. She was great at it. Gourasana had nicknamed Marie – 'God's Love' – and everyone felt it. She emanated love, care, and beauty.

It wasn't just the volunteers who felt this. People loved Marie. She brought so much light and joy into the lives of others. In Marie, they felt touched by the same love they had experienced in their Intensives, one-on-one from her.

Marie did a lot of her work from home, only coming to the Center two or three times each week. I loved seeing her at the Center. I would watch her through the plexiglass window in my office as she fluttered around talking, smiling, and laughing. She was a ball of energetic joy and I was elated that I got to love her as a woman.

In no time, Marie informed me she was pregnant. I was stunned. A seventeen-year-old daughter was one thing. I wasn't looking to father a baby. Fortunately, Marie was 100% clear that she did not want another child. We both agreed not to have the baby. I was there with Marie for the procedure and it went smoothly.

After this, Marie decided she wanted to have her tubes tied. Unfortunately, the tubal ligation did not go as smoothly and her recovery was difficult. Marie was bed-ridden for a couple of weeks. She was so vulnerable that first week, both physically and emotionally, that she cried much of the time. I cared for her like a newborn child. She stayed in my room so I could be with her as much as possible while she was recovering.

I was so happy she felt safe and cared for with me. This was a new experience. Being there for Marie during these delicate procedures and feeling her frailty brought out the protector in me.

Marie wanted privacy when it came to the Mission. I aligned with her wishes and we took care to keep these events from getting out, particularly to Kalindi. Marie did not want our Master involved. If Kalindi were to hear, her focus would alight on Marie and both of us wanted to leave Kalindi in peace during her seclusion.

It was an all-consuming love. My heart was open again, yet something else was happening; something I had never noticed or felt before. Along with the love, Marie was able to match and even exceed my sexual energy and desire. She gave herself fully and completely. I was grateful Gourasana gave me Marie to fully experience my sexual self. I was intoxicated with her sweetness, passion, and raw sexuality. With her thick, flowing red hair, her sweet breasts and magnificent, delectable pussy, I could never, ever, have enough of her, and I never wanted our intimate time to end.

All this hormonal, pheromonal, and fanciful delight deepened my attachment. Marie quickly became the source of my love, pleasure, and fulfillment. I thought that, without her, I would not only lose the love but also the best sex I ever had. I was falling into the main trap of 'illusory love' – **convinced the source of my love and fulfillment was outside myself,** in this case, in a woman.

As I opened and felt this great love, simultaneously I felt attachment and neediness. This was a counterweight to the love, joy, and passion I was feeling. I had never really felt this kind of 'needy' before. Not to say I wasn't always needy; it just never registered like this on my screen. I suppose I was more aware and awake than before so the duality became more apparent.

Nor had I ever felt so much fear in a relationship. I wanted Marie for myself. I loved her independence and strength, yet was also frightened by it. She was deeper and stronger than I was. I knew I could not control her. She could leave me at any time. This fostered a deep insecurity in me. This insecurity fed an anxiety that became a hallmark of my first years with her.

I lived in duality. There was great fear, neediness and anxiety side-by-side with great love and sex. I was being pulled forward into places I had never gone before. I thought of Kalindi and could hear her saying, *"Mark, your path will take you through a maze of illusory love as you develop your awareness and desire for God."*

At first, it seemed like the only time this duality wasn't pulling at me arose during sex. Maybe that was yet another reason I loved and craved sex so much. Many years later, as I became more aware, I realized that even during our sex I was still afraid. Deep down, I knew the pleasure was temporary. It wouldn't last, and I would eventually return to my needy self.

Here is a letter I saved from Marie that captures the essence of our connection:

June 11, 1998

Honey, lover boy and man filling my wettest, wildest sexual desires …

I will hold you closely as I continue to open, stay open and feel the pain of the longing for true fulfillment in our Lord. The love I have with you is cracking open my being, blowing my mind and taking my breath away.

I love to hold you next to me, to feel your love all over me. Thank you, Mark, for staying by my side through my difficult times. I love, adore and admire you.

Here we go… Loving you endlessly, Marie

CHAPTER 13

CHOOSING GOD

*"Walking the spiritual path properly is a very subtle process;
it is not something to jump into naively.
There are numerous sidetracks which lead to a distorted,
ego-centric version of spirituality; we can deceive ourselves
into thinking we are developing spiritually, instead we are
strengthening our egocentricity through spiritual techniques."*

Chögyam Trungpa

*"The Spiritual Path is 25% the disciples' effort,
25% the guru's effort on his behalf, and 50% the grace of God.
"Don't forget, however," the Master warned,
**that the 25% that is your part represents 100%
of your own effort and sincerity."***

Paramahansa Yogananda

"God, Guru, and Self are the same."

Ramana Maharshi

From April until early July, I did not hear from Kalindi. During this period, I had time to reflect on my personal relationship with her. Towards the end of May, I sent her this letter:

Dear Kalindi La♪   *May 23, 1998*

I want to share my recent revelations and admissions about our time together. Early on, I fell in love with a woman. She was a female phenomenon, yet who I fell in love with was the most wonderful woman I had known. I was blown away by her. She talked to me a lot about freedom and truth and how being with her would never be "normal" or "ordinary." I understood as best I could. We spent time together as she went through the next phase of her own manifestation in God. We shared a lot and I gave everything that I could to her.

Eventually, this 'relationship' had to change, as it was getting in the way of my own freedom and my relationship to her as my Master. This broke my heart, more than I knew. Still, I loved her and gave her all I could as the relationship shifted and changed into the intimate friendship that it now is.

I loved being with the woman, giving to her, and this I could do. I knew how to give to a woman. When the Master was there, I was scared. I felt like I did not know how to give to a Master, and I wanted the Master to go away. I wanted the woman. Now, I embrace you as my Master and desire to give you whatever I can.

Mark

When I wrote to Kalindi, I had no expectation of a response. The writing itself helped me to feel her and stay connected to her. I wanted to continue sharing my love with her and expressing my appreciation and gratitude.

In early July, I received a card in the mail. I recognized it was from Kalindi La♪ and my heart leapt. I eagerly opened it and read it several times. It was a simple card in which I felt her endless love and care for me. Her first line, "Mark, my friend and disciple,"

In Gratitude for Friendship

In "God's Love" and God's Way

Marcus - my friend + disciple,

I thank you,
I think of you,
I say to you one thing :
NEVER GIVE UP!
NEVER

All my Love,
Kalindi La♪ Gourasana
June 30, 1998

clarified how she was currently thinking of me, which I was grateful for. Her encouragement to "Never Give Up! Never" let me know we were in it for the long haul.

I also noticed she had signed her name as Kalindi La♪ Gourasana – a new name I learned more about two months later.

Soon after my elation from receiving this note from Kalindi, I received other news that left me disheartened. Marie had been asked to move to Marin County for her job with the organization. Of course she said Yes. After only three months together, we would be living in different cities again.

Initially, I felt desperate and angry. Marie's commitment to her service trumped any feelings she had about moving away from me. I thought, *"It's happening just as it did with Kalindi. We grow close and then have to separate."*

Only this time I trusted that somehow it would be OK. By now, I had learned to have and feel my feelings, and then let them go. I told myself, *"San Francisco is only an hour and a half flight away.*

We can still see each other one or two weekends a month." So, I was acceptant, even as I mourned that the love of my life would be further away.

My choice to be on this spiritual path meant relationship would never be a top priority. With Marie, as it had been with Kalindi, I would always come after God, the Mission, her work, service, and her daughter. I had to surrender to being fifth or sixth. I understood this, and some part of me even appreciated that I couldn't make her the main focus of my life. Still, it wasn't easy. This reality continually humbled my ego, knowing I would never be number one for her.

Boxing Myself In

After another two weeks, I heard that Kalindi was planning to return to Marin in the middle of August. She had completed her seclusion and was 'hell-bent' on helping her serious disciples to move quickly towards Ultimate Freedom, Full Awareness, and Union with God.

I received a message from Kalindi asking if I wanted this type of rapid, break-free help and guidance. I recognized that if I said Yes, I would be giving up some choice to control my own life and make my own decisions. Whatever Kalindi guided or asked me to do, I would do. I was thinking, *"What if she told me not to laugh or smile for a year, or to give up sex, or not to drink or smoke, or only eat a certain kind of food, or not watch TV, and so on. Would I be OK with that?"* [1]

I was afraid of this type of guidance, despite knowing that it would relentlessly push me out of my comfort zone and deeper into my connection with God. I asked myself, *"Do I want this kind of rapid speed, or do I want to move at my own pace?"* I wanted my decision to be sincere. I was aware that saying Yes would be a choice to have no choice.

---

1 I had seen her give this kind of guidance to other disciples.

As I meditated and contemplated the request, I landed on how deeply I trusted Kalindi. In my heart, I knew that any serious guidance she would give me would be to help me have more of God's Love and become aware. While my ego was afraid, I wanted to go fast.

I sent this reply to Kalindi:

I am aware of the magnitude of this choice and, after careful consideration and meditation, I'm giving you my answer – Yes. It is my desire to break free in this lifetime and it is my desire to do this as soon as possible. I want your help and your guidance. I know that you are the link to Gourasana and I desire to offer myself to Him to be used for His Will.

I give you my full permission to guide me as necessary, to free me of all illusion. You have my complete trust to do whatever is needed.

In deepest sincerity and prayer, your disciple,

Mark

In mid-August, Kalindi asked for me and two other disciples to come to Maui and accompany her back to San Francisco. I was happy she was still interested to have me support her personally. I considered it a great honor.

After four months of additional seclusion, and knowing how Kalindi was always changing, I wondered who she would be when I saw her this time.

Before I left, I sent Kalindi this letter:

I have wondered if I should continue to write to you as a close, intimate friend. Yet, I cannot see why I would stop. It seems more off-base for me not to express and share this part of myself with you. It remains to be seen if we will spend time together as we used to.

Regardless, please know that I love you, I desire you and I will always be here for you. I have been touched by you and blessed by God. I hope we can still take walks together, watch videos or sit by the pool.

I look forward to seeing you and escorting you back home to Marin.

Your eternal friend,
Mark

When I arrived in Maui, I got a phone call from Karin to inform me about what had happened and who Kalindi was now. Karin told me, "Kalindi has undergone further extreme transformation. She has allowed more of Gourasana's Power and Presence to enter her, the same Power and Presence that consumed David Swanson." I listened intently, feeling what Karin was saying, although not fully understanding.[1]

Karin let me know that, "Kalindi looks and feels different, more masculine than before. This period of transformation has been difficult as she was emptied out and filled again and again. The process was physically exhausting and greatly taxed her nervous system. Sometimes she felt like she was having a heart attack. It took all her trust and faith to fully surrender to what was happening."

I was in awe, imagining what that may have been like for her. Karin continued, "After three grueling months, she is now experiencing a level of peace with more of Gourasana's Presence and Power inside of her. It is becoming easier for her body."

I was glad Kalindi was feeling peace and more ease. Then Karin cautioned me, "There is little of the 'woman part' left in Kalindi. You shouldn't expect anything sexual." I told Karin I understood, and we hung up.

---

1   Later on, Kalindi let us know Gourasana was doing this to help her with completing some of the foundational set-up work for His Mission for the next 2,000 years.

Conversations with Karin about Kalindi were always very straightforward and matter-of-fact. This was somewhat due to her German acculturation and the rest to her training from Kalindi to deliver information in a straightforward, simple, and clear way.

This set me up for the next challenge in our relationship: how was I to relate to the female phenomenon I had known, when there was less and less female and more and more phenomenon?

The next day, Kalindi sent over a beautiful picture of her and Marie. I was touched by this and felt Kalindi was showing me Marie's surrender and the devotion I should have in my relationship with her. It was a simple way of guiding my heart forward.

Kalindi and Marie 1997

La♪ Gourasana

I did not see Kalindi until the day of departure. I held the car door open for her as she walked towards the car wearing a casual pants suit and a hat. As she came closer, I noticed she looked different from the Kalindi I had left there months ago. She had straight hair! She had changed her signature curly hair! I wanted to say something complementary but the serious and sober mood from Kalindi and the others let me know this was a time of silence with no talking, frivolity, or pleasantries.

As we drove from Lahaina to Kahului airport, Kalindi remained silent. It was difficult for me not to say anything. I had so many questions I wanted to ask her. Still, I knew enough to remain silent unless she asked me something. In the meantime, I focused on driving.

About thirty minutes into the 45-minute ride, Kalindi turned and spoke to me slowly and deliberately, "I am changing my name to Kalindi La Gourasana. Taking His Holy name as my last name to indicate His Presence in this body." My eyes widened at the significance of what she was telling me. "I want His name to be heard constantly until He is known."

Kalindi La Gourasana 2005

I looked in the rear view mirror and saw Kendra and Karin smiling in recognition of what she had said. After a few moments, I nodded, acknowledging her new reality with all of my seriousness and depth. Kalindi seemed satisfied and turned back to look straight ahead. Things remained like that until we rolled up to the departure terminal.

It was a quiet and uneventful flight. After delivering Kalindi La Gourasana (KJG) to Ames, I went to stay with Marie at her new house in Marin where she lived with Mariah. When I arrived, Marie welcomed me into her bed and all was well.

That night, I wrote to KJG: *"What a fulfillment to feel you and Gourasana simultaneously today. I could feel the peace, calm and power of Gourasana very strongly today – His pure light and love that dispels the illusion. I am with you forever, and always by your side."*

Early the next day, Marie hopped out of bed to head over to Ames. She was helping to transition KJG and her team. All day Marie was busy with arranging flowers, being with KJG, sorting clothes in her closet, unpacking her stuff, and other activities.

I went over to Ames in the evening. As it got later, it became clear I was not going to see KJG, and Marie would be occupied for a while longer. As the evening went on, I was hoping to have personal time with Marie, yet that too was not meant to be. Feeling disappointed, I returned alone to Marie's that night.

The same thing happened the next day. With no end in sight, I swallowed my desire and hopes of having more personal time with either K♪G or Marie. Feeling more and more dissatisfied and rather empty, I left my Master and girlfriend to head back to San Diego. Just before leaving, I received this note from K♪G:

Dearest Mark, friend to Kalindi La♪ Gourasana,

Never, ever give up. Thank you for your love and care. I will call for you when it is accurate.

My Eternal Love,

Kalindi La♪ Gourasana

I was grateful for her note. Her line, "I will call for you when it is accurate" gave me a lifeline towards our next connection.

Material Self vs. True Self

After I returned to San Diego, I went to a meditation where they played the newest talk from K♪G called "Material Self versus True Self."[1] This talk helped me greatly. It clarified questions that I had about enlightenment, also known as full awareness, self-realization, and ultimate freedom.

I already knew that my spiritual transformation was not about becoming a better person in the material world (although that naturally happens) or having an 'enlightened ego.' I was endeavoring for full self-realization in God.

Still, the difference between a highly evolved ego and the True Self in God was never quite clear for me. I was learning that Self-realization connects me to the Truth from a known place inside myself. Being in the light of the truth develops a material self that is healed and released from negative thoughts, emotions, and energy. Becoming a superior man or woman, highly evolved, capable and compassionate, is often mi taken with full union with God. The main point was that this healed self was a goal along the way, not the destination. Here are the notes I took for myself while listening to this talk:

- My ego will never become enlightened, there is no such thing as an enlightened, false or illusory self. I will eventually shed my fear, anger, resentment and shame and become the highest possible human being I can (kind, respectful, loving, caring, etc.). However, this will be the fully developed material self, the illusory self without the trappings, not my True Self.[2]

- In the beginning, do not seek out the True Self, it will be the false self that's doing that. Even the journey to freedom can be fueled by the ego. That's not a problem, as long as you are aware of and recognize what is motivating you.[3]

- Just desire God and Truth. God and your Master will do the rest. My true being only wants to be in the arms of the Lord. I experienced this in my Intensives when I connected to the 'the true part of my being' that lives in God.

- Use my awareness to observe and watch the illusion and ego in action. My True Self will come forth in time, as the false self falls away. The part of ego (material self) needed to function and serve God will stay. It goes like this – **material self is ready, ego is in humility, then the True Self starts to manifest** and leads to breaking free.

- During my transformation, I may go through periods of time where it seems 'difficult to function' in the material world. I will come through these and always be able to do what is needed.[4]

---

1 Kalindi La Gourasana, *Material Self versus True Self* in Golden Information series of talks. San Diego: Miracle of Love, 1998

2 "The False Self means the identity we manufacture in order to find our place in the world – our jobs, our occupations, our religion, our culture, and our sources of status. False doesn't mean that it's bad; it simply means that it's external, passing, that it changes. Everyone has a False Self – you need it to function in the world." Robert Rohr, Immortal Diamond: *The Search for Our True Self,* 2013.

3 This is what I did for my first ten years. Around 2007, I started actively praying for my True Self to take over.

4 Indeed, during the hardest parts of my transformation (1999-2002), basic material functioning was difficult for me.

I was happy and relieved to hear all this. It helped me understand what I had been going through and the process I needed to incorporate into my life moving forward. At the time, I had not yet realized most of this, Although it did point me in the right direction. I had several more years of healing and illumination to go through to keep letting go of more of my illusory self.

What I did know was that this was not simply a path of light and love, but a very serious endeavor for Ultimate Freedom, Union with God, to return home to God. Kalindi would often say, "There will be no stone left unturned." Indeed, any time I thought I was arriving or had arrived, Kalindi would knock my ego down and put me back into humility. To this day, I continue to turn over stones at deeper depths, looking to see what lies below.

Who Is She Now?

In mid-October, KJG called for the Business Team to meet with her in Marin for the weekend. There were major changes happening in the organization around direction and timing, and KJG wanted everyone clear and aligned.

Kalindi had an amazing grasp of the structures of the organization and the details of virtually everything that was happening. She was connected to each person, project, and situation that was going on. She had the vision, the big picture, and comprehensive overview, and she was also willing and able to get into every detail – more so than any person I have ever known, including every CEO, vice president, board member, executive director, and so on.

Along with all that, she had a pure and clear consciousness. She had no hidden agenda, ill will or hatred towards anyone. She had no walls or limitations. Her capacity and memory was extraordinary, remembering specific events that happened for other people 15 years ago; knowing where everything was in her house, her automobile, and every file and bin in her storage. It was like she was using 50% or more of her brain and the rest of us were struggling along at 5 to 10%. To top it all off, she cared about everyone personally, and every action she took carried the love of God.

When I heard we were going to Marin to meet with K♪G, I was simultaneously thrilled and also filled with trepidation. I wondered if K♪G would think I was advancing quickly enough spiritually. I was stupefied and frightened that we would no longer have a personal relationship. Even so, I was delighted I would get to see Marie and was extremely eager to hold her again.

When we arrived, K♪G welcomed us and showed us to our rooms. When first in her presence, I noticed how K♪G moved differently, walking with less sway and more directness. She felt less feminine and even more masculine than two months ago. Her physical appearance had changed as she continued to manifest more power and presence of Gourasana.[1] To me, she felt less approachable and more intimidating. This left me feeling insecure and apprehensive as to what the nature of my relationship with her would be now.

As I was unpacking, Karin came and gave me a note from K♪G asking me to meet her in her quarters that afternoon. When I came into her quarters, K♪G looked relaxed sitting on the couch in her sitting room. She had her eyes closed. Quietly I sat cross-legged on the carpeted floor in front of her.

After a few minutes of silence, she said to me, "You can't figure God out." This had been a huge trap for me, always trying to make sense of everything – a futile effort in the realm of God and Spirit.

Kalindi and Gourasana 1991

---

1 Disciples of Neem Karoli Baba (Maharaji, Ram Dass' Guru), Swami Nityananda and Swami Muktananda have reported similar changes in their physical bodies in short periods of time.

Then she said, "I talked to you once before, and you could barely hear what I was saying."

I was thrown, suddenly aware that it was not Kalindi but Gourasana who was talking with me. I sat straighter and listened intently.

He asked, "Do you want to say anything to Kalindi?"

I thought for a moment, and said, "Kalindi, I miss you." I waited in silence, barely able to contain my feelings.

After a moment, He nodded, and then inquired, "Would you rather have Kalindi or Gourasana here?"

I thought, *"What a question!"* The truth was I wanted Kalindi, yet I didn't know if I should admit that.

Before I answered, and as if to handle my mind, Gourasana said, "When I am dominant in this body, Kalindi is completely in peace." I understood. The words made sense, yet my mind was tweaked. I was still new at being with Gourasana through Kalindi.

Then her expression and energy changed. It seemed as if Kalindi was back again. Her expression changed to a softer look, and her way of speaking and even the tone of her voice were different. I was relieved, while at the same time trying to assimilate what was happening in front of me.

To let me know she was still here, KJG spoke to me about our past together. This soothed me and I relaxed more. She showed me her hand, pointing to the opal ring I had given her the year before and whispered, "I wear this ring every day." As tears welled up in my eyes, my heart was breaking inside. I nodded with mutual regard.

After a few more minutes of silence, she asked me, "Do you remember when I came to the RV and got sick from drinking rum?" I nodded as I smiled. Then she looked at me with a curious expression and said, "I drank the rum and coke to get you unstuck."

That shocked me. I had not considered such a possibility before. *"She did that for me!"* I thought, *"to break my concepts about a Master drinking alcohol?"*

Before I had a chance to process that idea, she became very serious and said, "Don't have your businessman ego going on in your phone calls for the Mission."

Another blow that put me off balance! I knew what she was talking about. I thought, *"How does she know this? Is she reading my mind? Am I that much of an open book?"*

I was aware my businessman ego had many positive and negative qualities – charming, humorous, clever, and also manipulative, untrustworthy, and attached to results. When the businessman ego was around, I was not fully open, connected, or caring.

Then she gave me the following guidance, which I wrote in my spiral notebook:

1. Learn to be in the deepest part of your heart without ego.

2. You will never receive what you want from God if you approach this body in that way (I had casually started to lie down in front of her and quickly got back to my knees.)

3. You are scattered in your mind and often distracted. You need to learn to focus. Work on this while you are here. (This was so true. I could barely keep focused on any one thing for very long.)

4. Go inside to know what you're feeling that has you be tense (note to self: I am afraid of being wrong, of fucking up)!

Kalindi also told me it was essential for my spiritual movement and the well-being of my body to have one day of rest and quiet time to be alone with God. She suggested I could write love letters to God on that day, and not speak with anyone. She said it was okay to listen to music, but nothing too stimulating. She mentioned I could occasionally have a rest day together with Marie, but mostly to have these precious days with myself and God.

Then K♪G took my notebook and wrote:

Dont look at Me if you are not in the deepest part of your heart. Do not be afraid to cry, it cannot be avoided.
My Eternal Love + Embrace
K♪☺

I nodded gratefully and took my leave. I left feeling loved, known, blessed, and challenged. K♪G had let me know who she was and how I needed to be with her for my own spiritual salvation. I had to let go of being special. It was time to become an 'ordinary disciple.'

K♪G was delivering on my request and permission. She was giving me break-free guidance. I was grateful. In the midst of this gratitude, I was challenged to let go of Kalindi as I had known her. Yet, her continued manifestation into all of who God wanted her to be was way more important than any personal relationship I had wanted. Gourasana was there in her stead, and Gourasana confronted me. Seemingly, He had taken my God-like girlfriend from me.

Conscious Lifestyle

Later that day, K♪G met with the entire business team. She asked us what was going on in the organization with the volunteers and other people. We shared that the organization was overwhelmed, trying to keep up with everything she wanted us to accomplish.

Upon hearing this, K♪G told us, "Postpone anything that isn't absolutely essential. While you are here, we will talk about what is and isn't essential. Once it is prioritized, the rest can wait." This was a huge relief for everyone.

Then K♪G announced we would need to stay longer. Her goal was for everyone and everything to be clearly aligned. She said this might take a month or more. Getting started, she told us to unplug from our habitual work mode and let go of the sense of busyness. She guided us to disengage from the daily running of the organization. She said this was the only way to free ourselves up enough to create what was needed next. She told us to start by handling our personal affairs so that nothing superfluous pulled at our time away.

I was ecstatic to hear this news. For me, staying in Marin for a month with K♪G and Marie was much preferable to working back in San Diego. I would gleefully stay in Marin forever.

Next, K♪G took my notebook and wrote out a new schedule for us. She gave us the next four days to handle our lives and set up the other staff and volunteers in San Diego. After that, we would start meetings to sort out what was needed next.

Our daily lifestyle included exercise, blocks of time for work and phone calls, and time for quiet and reflection. It was a schedule for optimal performance and unending spiritual movement. K♪G was showing us how to let go of the illusion of overwhelm and merge our spiritual and material lives.[1]

She noted that the illusion would have us think that it was all work with no time for God, prayer, or meditation. She called these our foundations for staying deep. Given my weaknesses of busyness, laziness, and overwhelm, I welcomed this disciplined lifestyle.

Later that day, I received a brief note from K♪G:

"I am going to call you Marcus so you can feel my love for you, not the illusion of Mark."
You will make it!!! My Love, K♪G

Later she suggested I legally change my name to Marcus. She said this would be a true letting go of my identification with the ego personality of Mark. I really liked this change. My Mom had called me Marcus as a pet name when I was growing up. Mark was difficult for me to pronounce with my New York accent. I was eager to let go of my ego, so this felt like a win for the light![2]

---

1   This became the basis for the Spiritual Advancement Course, *The Divine Grace of Efficient Living & the Disciplined Lifestyle for Spiritual Transformation,* Miracle of Love, 1999

2   This ended Mark. Kalindi had used both Mark and Marcus until now. I had used Marcus when writing to her personally and Mark as a disciple. From this point forward, I was always Marcus. Although I took everything Kalindi asked or suggested very seriously; I did not legally change my name until I made my full name change in 2000 from Mark Elliot Brostoff to Marcus Bond.

Special Relationship

K♪G began the team meetings by expressing her extreme love and gratitude to everyone there. She continued sharing her love and drawing out our love by saying a prayer for each person in the room. She asked each person if they felt their prayer deeply and, if so, to sign the page in the booklet with their prayer and she would then pray over it for that person's freedom.

Then she gave each person a gift that personally touched them, something that had significant meaning for them in their spiritual lives. To one disciple she presented a beautifully framed letter she had written to Kalindi after her first Intensive; to another she gave prayer beads to wear on her wrist to remind her to pray.

With all this love in the space, she left us to get to work.

Later that day, while I was walking in the gardens on a break, K♪G approached me. I was open and receptive, waiting for her to say something, so I knew with whom I was interacting.

Very sweetly, she asked, "Would you like to stay in the RV while you're here?" I almost cried. I nodded, and said, "Thank you." I felt my heart opening from her unsolicited, personal care for me.

We stood together silently for a few minutes, as I waited to see what she would say next. Then she told me, "When you leave the RV in the morning, take what you need for the day. During the day, stay in the house and back yard area. Do not use the RV to hide."[1]

Then she suggested, "Maybe take on an austerity to take away some pleasure – like not using the hot tub." I nodded, and realized my soaking days were over for a while. Lastly, she reminded me, "Do not pop out of your depth. Talk less, listen more, and be silent if it is not necessary to speak."

I nodded with understanding, appreciation, and consent. As K♪G walked away, I felt loved, held, and guided. In addition, I felt her energy transmitted to me to help me with what she had suggested. Years later when K♪G gave me some extremely difficult guidance around eating and sex, she explained that a true

Master also transmits to the disciple the energy and trust needed to accomplish their guidance.

A couple of days later, during a brief interaction in the garden, K♪G asked me, "What do you feel about what has happened to this body?" I was unable to answer. I didn't know what to think about it. I was struggling with my ideas of Gourasana, and how much reverence I had for Him. She said, "I will ask you again in a week." Then, "You were a friend to Kalindi, you helped her get here, and now you must find your way to Me.[2] Then your life will be different because you will be different."

Kalindi told me she wanted Gourasana to be dominant in her and that was now happening. I understood she wanted this. It was an answer to her prayer to be filled by Him. In my soul, I could feel Gourasana, yet my soul was not yet dominant in me. My physical senses and mind were primarily dominant, and what I saw was a female body but with a strong, male energy and not just any male energy – The Lord's.

It was confusing for me. I was feeling the deepest love of God from Gourasana, and my human self wanted personal love with a woman who was no longer dominant in that body. My head was spinning from the ever-changing energy, information, and guidance now pouring into me. Still, I loved the intimacy I had shared with that God-woman.

I was still getting used to the idea of Kalindi being gone when, later that day, Karin came to me with a message, "Kalindi wants to have the next special relationship with you, but you must first let go of the past so it can happen."

I loved that, and understood what she meant. I didn't know how I was going to do it but I had to let go of what I had with Kalindi previously so that my next 'special relationship' with K♪G could develop – Gourasana and all. ♪

---

1   She knew me well. As events intensified, I wanted to hide in the RV!

2   Lord Gourasana

CHAPTER 14

SPIRITUAL TRANSMISSION

*"The guru intensifies experiences.
Right there in your consciousness all the time
is this being who is completely free,
loving you totally with the deepest compassion
for your situation.
The absurdity of your attachments in relation
to this incredibly wonderful being drives you to deal
with your petty stuff and get it out of the way.
In a sense, the guru uses your attachment to daily situations
to show your own delusional system.
The guru is constantly showing you where you're not,
your most secret places where you're holding on
to your stash of attachments."*

Ram Dass

The Road Home

During the second week of our business retreat, I was sitting on a cement bench in one of the gardens as Kalindi walked around the path with her sister. It was a pleasant, warm, and sunny day. Kalindi gestured for me to join them. They were discussing my role in the Mission. Her sister, who acted as an advisor to the organization, held the opinion that I should leave the business team, come off supported staff, and go back to work as a consultant or coach.

I wasn't surprised. I had known for months that Kalindi's sister wanted me off the business team. She thought I was incompetent and insufficiently committed. She had approached me in San Diego, saying that I did not put the organization first. I was too distracted by Marie and resisted working into the night. Simply put, my work ethic did not meet her standards.

She was right. My priority was being with Marie, particularly during her difficult times. Now, as I heard these charges being leveled against me, I froze.

Then came a moment I will never forget. Kalindi looked piercingly at her sister and said, "Are you crazy? He would get completely captured by the illusion if he went back out there. Can't you see that he's not strong enough to maintain his connection on his own?"

I was astonished by what Kalindi had said. I had never thought in those terms. *"She is probably right,"* I thought to myself. *"More than my position in the organization, her primary concern is keeping me safe from the illusion and that I succeed spiritually."*

This is how Kalindi was – not only with me, but with everyone. **Our spiritual growth was her number one priority always.**

I was grateful that she was watching out for me in this way. It's why I trusted her. She was resolute in her dedication to my freedom; I was resolute in my commitment to her. That is why I said Yes to the position with the center, because she asked me. That is why I did everything, because she either asked me or guided me to do it. I trusted her more than I trusted myself because **she knew my heart and certainly my soul better than I did.**

Kalindi turned to me, her eyes radiant with love and asked, "How would you like to be on my personal team and live here at Ames?" Oh my God! I couldn't believe it! It was everything I could have asked for – to be back together with Kalindi, and close to Marie again. I felt like running around the grounds, yelping in joy, "Kalindi saved me! Kalindi saved me!"

I was relieved to be released from the organizational constraints. I was happy to be part of such a committed organization, yet the work was tedious and stressful for me. My soul wanted to be with Kalindi, and my heart wanted to be with Marie. This was too good to be true.

Then Kalindi spoke the following points to me. I struggled to write her words down as she spoke:

- You know how to be around and care for this body;

- I am going to break you free;

- Give up the businessman ego;

- When Kalindi is sick, stay with her;

- Live at Ames in the RV;

- Help with safety but no night shifts because you will fall asleep;

- Arrange all travel for Kalindi.

I thanked Kalindi profusely, and skipped off in so much ecstasy that I could barely contain myself. I was off the business team and out of all the pressures of the financial and registration goals and I would be together with my sweetheart, Marie.

That night, before I went to sleep in the RV, I wrote Kalindi this card:

Beloved ❤ Kalindi La ♪ Gourasana ❤

From the first time that I personally contacted your body in the swimming pool, you have constantly awakened my heart and soul. Every part of me comes alive near you. I feel complete devotion and love for you. I loved and gave my all to Kalindi and now I will give it all to you.

I spill my heart open at your feet, Marcus

The following day I had some alone time with K♪G in her bedroom. She said, "You can love K♪G. Do you want to touch me? Do you want to care for this body?" I nodded enthusiastically.

She continued, "You have Marie now. Kalindi always told you, you would be with one of her leaders. Please help Marie with the logistics for the groups that are coming to be with K♪G (logistics was not one of Marie's strengths). Also, talk with Siegmar about gardening and what needs to be done around the property."

She went on, "Get very focused. Don't be spaced out. Don't get distracted by anything. Come all the way into K♪G and your jobs." Lastly, she said, "You and Marie can be together like Karin and Siegmar. They are both standing right beside me. Be with Marie, work together closely, and keep loving her."

I left flying high with what was being showered upon me! It was all happening. I could stay with Marie and be together again with my beloved Kalindi, albeit in her new manifestation as K♪G.

At this time, another extremely sweet gift was given to me by K♪G. When we were together the year before, I would occasionally make her a BLT (bacon, lettuce, and tomato sandwich). K♪G reminded me of that and asked if I would make her one each day and do it with all my love and devotion. Naturally, I said, "Yes."

Each day, Karin would come to me and say, "Okay, Marcus, Kalindi would like her BLT now."

Instantly, I would drop whatever I was doing and pour my heart into that sandwich. I carefully laid out all the ingredients: bread, butter, mayonnaise, lettuce, tomato, and bacon. I cooked the 3 strips of bacon until they were crisp – the way Kalindi liked them. I lightly toasted the bread, and put the right amount of mayonnaise on both slices. I added fresh sliced tomatoes, the lettuce, and the sandwich was done. Every morning I made this sandwich, giving it my full attention. It was so important to me that Kalindi liked it and, with every bite, felt my love for her.

Spiritual Movement

As the days passed, KJG's focus on the spiritual movement of the business team grew. Kalindi put them all living together in one big room in the middle of the house. She instructed them to stay in this room, coming out only to use the bathroom, shower, and eat. They were not to speak or interact with anyone else.

When outside, they were allowed to walk silently in the gardens. Kalindi had 'trapped' them, literally forcing them to go within. By clamping down on living situations, she pushed negative ego traits to the surface, forcing them to become more aware of the muck they waded in and the separation it caused. When she had them at the edge, Kalindi could help them let it go.

Kalindi sometimes woke them in the middle of the night to meditate or go on a prayer walk. Prayer-walking happened outside – walking silently in a circle with a fervent, heartfelt prayer leading you on. Prayer walks were a powerful way to build desire. In the middle of the night, it was quite chilly, and a perfect way to stay awake and be clear in their focus.

Kalindi announced to the business team that other small groups of disciples from San Diego would be coming to the house for week-long seminars with her. She told the members of the business team that they may be involved in some of the seminars. In the meantime, their main job was to complete their organizational work.

She kept them on their schedule and informed them she did not know when they would leave. Certainly not for Thanksgiving; and Christmas and New Year were questionable. She was helping them with letting go of their attachments to family, relationships, and comfort – to let go of what was keeping them separate from love.

At first, this kind of guidance was hard to swallow. Feelings of fear, guilt, shame, and obligation quickly rose to the surface. What would family, friends, lovers, husbands, and wives think? These usually paralyzing thoughts were dispelled when the relationships only deepened from the conversations they had with their family and spouses.

During this time, I participated in a couple of meetings with the business team to turn over my responsibilities. I spoke with my staff in San Diego by phone, and I was quickly replaced by the de facto leaders of each area. I was happy with my new respon-sibilities for Kalindi of safety, travel, and being a simple pool and garden guy. It was a great way to let go of my 'businessman' ego. I was basking in the glow of returning to Kalindi and having perso-nal time with Marie. KJG was full on with the business team and preparing for the next groups who were coming to Ames to receive her help. Marie was at Kalindi's side so we didn't have much time together. I cherished whatever time we did have.

When the first group arrived in November, Kalindi had the newcomers stay in the Cabana at the back of the property. The Cabana was built to sleep four people. Accommodating eight bodies was a stretch since this number required people to sleep on the floor – four abreast – using futons and sleeping bags. This was another spiritual movement 'tactic' used by Kalindi – to get people out of their comfort zones and privacy boundaries until there was no more separation because there was no physical space in which to contain it.

Within the first day or two of the new group's arrival, things immediately took a turn. As she had done with me and others, she had to help them know that Kalindi was no longer dominant in her body. Now it was Gourasana. With her straight hair, she looked more like Gourasana. Her lips were a different shape. Her eyes looked different and her forehead was longer. Her entire face and being looked different. Still, it was not easy for any of us to comprehend.

While we all heard what Kalindi was saying, and we could see it and feel it, none of us had any prior experience with someone changing to this degree where, literally, another energy inhabits someone you know. We knew it would take some time to adjust, to let it sink into our being, rewire our brains, and expand our awareness to this new reality.

To help us with this change, Kalindi started walking around with a large, cardboard-mounted photo of Gourasana in front of her face as a way to let us know who was in her body now. She asked all of us to feel Gourasana and be with her, the way we would if He was there in the flesh. This was a powerful reminder to see Gourasana there and listen to Kalindi speak from behind His photo.

Gourasana 1992

Another visual aid she provided us was that, when she wasn't sitting in her chair, she left the giant poster of Gourasana in her chair instead of the usual red rose from Kalindi. I would walk by the chair and it would register, *"Oh, there is Gourasana, not the rose of Kalindi."* These two actions were quite helpful in shifting my habitual mindset.

The next week another group of eight disciples arrived. Kalindi put them into two rooms of four each. Also, she asked the first group to stay another week. With the five business team members, this brought the total number of disciples at the house to twenty-one. Including Kalindi and her team, we had nearly thirty people staying at the house.

Ames was a large house with eight bedrooms, three living rooms, and a large kitchen. The garage was set up as a workout room with rubber mats, exercise equipment and weights – the whole nine yards. There was also the RV, and a small, one-person shack out back. With their bedrooms occupied by guests, Kalindi's team members slept on futons in the living room. Every bed, couch, and futon in the house was being used. Even with this large number of people, the sleeping logistics went amazingly smoothly.

The main problem was showers and bathrooms. There were only four and a half bathrooms on the property. Besides a shower schedule, Siegmar and Kendra were concerned about the plumbing – God forbid, one should back up! Needless to say, we kept a close eye on the toilets and drain systems.

The other logistical challenge was food. I was responsible for the care and feeding of all the guests. Each person handled breakfast and lunch on their own. Marie and I mobilized a team of volunteers to help with shopping, cooking, cleaning, finances, and so on. Initially, we prepared large soups and stews for dinner for everyone. As the number of people grew, we resorted to catering dinner each night from a local café, since we could not handle that much cooking on site.

Throughout the day, Kalindi would go into each room and help the people in different ways. I was busy doing safety shifts, logistics, and grounds' keeping so I didn't know what was happening in the different rooms. I saw people walking around quietly and going from place to place with Kalindi, Marie, and other spiritual leaders.

I made my daily BLT for Kalindi but otherwise spent no time with her. Each night I hoped to get some alone time with Marie; however, she was busy helping K♪G with the people, supporting K♪G, and holding people through fears or tears so for the most part that did not happen either.

Although I was not part of the larger scene of spiritual help that Kalindi was providing at that time, I was not neglected. Each night, when I came back to the RV, I found a new card. Each card had a quote from Gourasana or Kalindi on the front, and a short handwritten message inside. I often cried in gratitude from feeling her personal love and care through these cards.

Here are a few examples:

LOVE GOD

With All of Your Heart

K⁺ⓖ

1998

The only solution to the problem is to

Go Deep.

- Gourasana

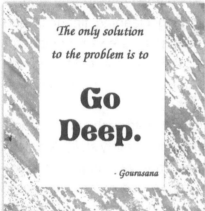

Go to the deepest part of your heart

K⁺ⓖ

Pray for the experience; pray that you will know the truth directly.

~ Gourasana

Your true self will take over to the degree that you let go of your illusory self. It is that simple.

~ Gourasana

Awakening

When I wasn't in the safety room or working the grounds, I had a vantage point in the living room where I could watch all the comings and goings of the different people. The living room had ceiling-to-floor glass windows, and church music was playing continuously. Whenever I had a few minutes, I would stand there to see what was going on.

I didn't really want to be involved; on the other hand, I did want to be in the energy and soak it all up. I watched attentively to see what was going on, while trying to not be seen as eaves-dropping. For me, it was a whole new world and a birds-eye view of a spiritual Master at work.

I did notice that there was a lot of activity from the room in the back of Kalindi's quarters. The room was attached to Kalindi's bedroom, dressing room, and living room, and had its own sliding glass door. I saw Kalindi, Marie, and a few others going in and out several times over a couple of days. Something was happening back there. No one would tell me what it was. When Siegmar brought several large rolls of aluminum foil to that back room, I decided to ask what was going on.

Siegmar said, "Kalindi is helping a disciple to awaken. She put him into the small room in the back. He's all by himself with a futon, a towel, and a few basic items. He's been meditating and praying night and day. She is helping his True Self emerge."

I noticed a tingling in my body. The hairs on the back of my neck were standing up. It sounded significant and wonderful, and Siegmar seemed comfortable with it. I asked about the aluminum foil.

He said, "Oh, that's to cover the windows and sliding glass door so that no daylight comes into the room."

"Why is that?" I asked.

He replied, "His eyes are sensitive to light. Kalindi wants nothing to be in the way of its emergence."

I was trembling with a mixture of excitement and trepidation. I related the light sensitivity to what had been happening to Kalindi. Lately she had taken to wearing sunglasses. I had heard that Gourasana used to wear sunglasses indoors as well. I didn't want to create a concept so I stored this information away, asking myself, *"Are spiritual eyes more light sensitive?"*

At first, what Siegmar described enthralled my soul. After a while it just scared me. This fear was similar to the fear I felt before entering my first Intensive, or that time when Kendra called to tell me I could move in with Kalindi. Clearly the fear came from my ego. It was afraid of losing control and each step towards its annihilation.

The next day I wanted to check out that room. While working in the gardens I maneuvered myself towards that room. From the outside, all I could see was aluminum foil! *"Rats, I thought, I want to know what was going on in there."* I could feel something building and percolating inside of me; I felt like I was going to explode.

The next day I was in the living room looking out towards the back room when the sliding glass door opened and out popped Kalindi, followed by Marie, Kendra, Siegmar, a few others and the disciple. They were all joyously dancing and singing, dressed in flamboyant outfits. Seemingly, the disciple had broken-through or awakened.

I was glued to the spot. Kalindi was leading the procession, and Marie was right behind her dressed in a blue bra and thong panties – a big yellow boa wrapped around her neck and flowing from her body. The disciple who had been in the room was walking serenely, like a young child, amongst the group. Kendra was blaring a trumpet, while joyous music played full-bore from the music system.

Just watching swept me up in this heavenly celebration. The energy gave me goose bumps. I was uplifted by the freedom they moved in. The cavalcade paraded across the lawn, then disappeared into the cabana, apparently to include those inside.

Now I was really curious. What had happened? That night in the RV, I asked Kendra if she could share with me about it. Immediately her eyes started to glow and her energy increased.

She said, "The True Self is a completely different being than the illusory self. It is pure love, strong and powerful, with no material attachments. It has its own personality and energy, and lives in God's will."

I asked Kendra what happened specifically with the disciple in the room.

She replied, "He went so deep. He had so much desire. Kalindi worked with him to let go of his material attachments to his family, self-image, money … to everything he thought he was." I sat waiting for more. She added, "When he hit up against his fear, KJG physically held and comforted him. He kept going until he was swept up in the 'break-free energy' that came through her. KJG looked as fierce as I have ever seen her. This energy was palpable – a powerful love to rip, shred, and destroy his illusion! It was scary for me."[1]

It sounded scary to me as well. But it also sounded like a siren's call ringing in my ears. Kendra continued, "As he received this energy, he started screaming. Then he began to vibrate rapidly and to chant 'OM' – more as a vibrational sound than a word. He got swept up in the energy and couldn't stop. She kept him going like that for three days. Last night we stayed up with him. As he let go, the energy ripped through until another being started to appear. His face and voice changed. There was so much love in the room. KJG was guiding the whole thing."

"He and KJG lay down on the floor together. It was around 7am. I could feel their union. KJG said that they would always be connected and he was to always stay with her. We slept a few hours and then Kalindi felt he was ready. His True Self was suf-

---

1 "All these experiences add up to a transmission, a deepening of the moment, into the very heart of Being, the eternal moment of God. This is a moment shared on many planes, a silent pause in a moving sea of love." Ram Dass, *Be Love Now*, 2010

ficiently grounded. He could walk out into the world. That's when we popped out of the room. That was the celebration you saw."

Wow! I was blown away. Although it came secondhand, I felt I was getting another view of the ways of a Master. I recognized the importance of her energy to my own freedom. I had heard Kalindi speak of break-free energy before. She called it, "Transformational energy, part of the special assistance coming from God and the Heavenly Host of True Beings." I wondered if that energy was involved when Gourasana had come into me so powerfully.

Feeling my own energy stirred up inside, I could barely sleep that night. Now I was driven to know more. The next day, while I emptied the dishwasher and cleaned the counter tops waiting to make Kalindi her BLT, Marie walked into the kitchen. I grabbed her, asking to know more.

She said, "The break-free energy that comes from Gourasana now lives in Kalindi. The energy has an extremely high vibrational speed. It can quickly move people through lifetimes of attachments. If you are able to let go, the energy will act like a powerful magnet drawing you closer to God's Love. It helps to manifest the True Self and greatly accelerates awareness."

I asked her how this happens.

She replied, "You can't have anything blocking your heart or mind. If you do, the energy will not come through. That's where Kalindi comes in. That's why she spent so much time with one disciple these last couple of days. She literally walked him through his fears and attachments. She knew something was stuck in his heart. It could be this life or a past life. She kept asking him, "What else? What else?" It was around his mother. Once he let go of that, Kalindi could connect to his innermost being and his True Self started to emerge."

I took a deep breath. Marie was talking about this as though we were having a normal, everyday conversation. I think it was normal for her. Until now, Marie and other members of the Core were the only ones who could relate to Kalindi at this level. They had all connected to their True Selves while Gourasana was still in the body. Their ongoing work was to continue to manifest more and more. Meanwhile, she stood there chatting with me. That's what I loved about this woman. Marie could fly with Kalindi and still be so down-to-earth with me.

Before leaving, she said, "A key element of this energy is speed and change. It takes so much willingness. Letting go is extremely important when you desire to be 'taken.' That's why you see Kalindi telling her disciples to do one thing and then immediately change it. Pick up that stick! Now drop it! It's a snake. It's a stick ... snake ... stick ... this ... that." She reached out to touch my heart. Adding, "And truly it is beyond the mind." Then she was gone.

I stood there in a state of amazement. I thought I understood what she was telling me. I had seen Kalindi guide her disciples in this way many times, instructing them to go in one direction, and then another, and another. Their egos would get visibly pissed off. Their bodies would complain. They would grow frustrated and confused. And still, she kept at them. Like a spiritual wasp, she stung them again and again. If the disciple surrendered, they ended up in an effortless flow with her – flowing through the here and now in the energy of God. If they resisted, they crashed into judgment, discouragement, and negativity.[1]

Marie popped her head back in and said, "If people listen and follow, Kalindi can take them into different places, sounds, and movements beyond the control of the mind, into a place where there's no time to be afraid, embarrassed, or worried about anything."

Now she trotted off for good. I was left feeling empowered, thinking, *"Wow, that sounds good to me."* I also wondered, *"Am I advanced enough for this kind of letting go, or too attached and afraid?"* I didn't have long to find out.

---

1 "A strong constitution is needed if you want to progress on the Path of Spiritual Perfection. This work will induce a progressive emptying of your personality and a combination of suffering, so you will 'lose yourself in every way'" Irina Tweedie, *Daughter of Fire,* 1995

Ready, Willing and Able?

I was cleaning leaves from the pool, feeling inspired by recent events. The more I pondered what was going on in the different rooms, the more I understood. And here I was, in the middle of these transformations with Kalindi holding me in her heart. I guess she was feeling me as well because, just then, Kalindi came out of the Cabana by herself. There had been a lot of strange noises emanating from the Cabana and, when she invited me to go back in with her, I felt so much trepidation.

To allay my fears, she said, "You don't have to do anything. I just want you to see what's happening." I nodded and followed her inside, completely unprepared for what I saw.

Some people were on the floor meditating and praying – that I understood. However, others were exhibiting different kinds of bizarre behaviors: one person was sitting on an upside down trash can playing the drums; another was preaching out loud in a corner to no one; another was making shrieking bird noises; while another was riding on top of someone else like a cowboy on a bucking bronco. It was a surreal scene like out of a cartoon show, with a sense of wildness, abandon, and freedom.

I felt constricted. As I continued to look around, I froze up even more. I looked for Kalindi. She was calmly sitting on a couch, perusing the scene. She beckoned me over to her. I sat in front of her, on my knees.

Kalindi asked, "Do you want to stay and be part of this group? Are you ready to face your fears about how you are, how you look and how you behave? Do you have the desire to find something deeper within?"

I had always said Yes to Kalindi, wanting to do everything she asked of me. But this felt like too much. I just wanted to get out of there.

I gathered my courage, looked her in the eye and said, "No, Kalindi, I'm not ready."

She smiled, took my hand, and said, "That is totally fine. Just go back outside and continue scooping leaves out of the pool." I slowly breathed out.

"While you are doing that, think about God and how much you love Him. Relax and enjoy yourself in your service to our Lord."

I was filled with gratitude. Kalindi understood me. She had such compassion. Happily, I skipped outside to return to my pool service.

Destiny Calling ... Again

That night, as I slept peacefully in the RV, someone came in to wake Kendra. Kalindi was having one of her middle-of-the-night 2am meditations with the business team. This was not unusual. It had happened before. Kendra was usually invited to participate. This time however, I was asked to join as well.

I was reluctant, preferring to sleep and, admittedly, quite afraid of what might take place in there. Yet I was also curious, so I hopped up and went with them.

When we entered the room where the business team worked and slept, it was dark, and they were all on the floor meditating. Everyone, including Kalindi, was wearing pajamas. People were on their knees, with their heads bowed in a prayerful position. Some rocked back and forth, others whispered under their breath; still others sat unmoving on the floor. Kendra and I joined them.

I tried to meditate and focus within, yet I was way too distracted. My mind was racing. I was thinking, *"Now I'm in it. What am I doing here? What does Kalindi want from me?"* I kept opening my eyes and scanning the room, *"Where was Kalindi? Is she moving about the room? Where is she?"*

I couldn't stop thinking about what I thought she thought of me. *"Is she judging me for my lack of depth? Am I doing it right? The others are doing it better than me. I am a shallow, miserable being with no right to even be here."* I wallowed in this mind-fuck, as I heard Kalindi's quiet voice encouraging and prodding others to go deeper, trust more, and let go.

Then she got louder and more intense. "Trust God," she said, "let Him take you," she implored. "Let Him move you. Give Him your heart!" I was swept up by her words; they carried so much energy and power.

She was guiding us to go deeper. This push-pull energy came out of her sometimes. She used it to pierce egos and illusions. I never liked this energy. It seemed to confront and even attack my sense of comfort and innate laziness. I liked life when it came soft and sweet. This intensity made me want to crawl into my shell, literally covering up my body for protection.

Mark
Your Job
is
to get
Kalindi to
chill-out
Gourasana

Then Kalindi kneeled down next to me and whispered, "Marcus, I am screaming and getting too intense. I'm not supposed to do this. He only wants peace for this body." Her soft voice and vulnerability melted all my resistance and I started to cry.

Kalindi put her hand on my back as she continued to whisper, "Remember He wrote to you, 'It is mandatory that Kalindi chill out!' You are supposed to help me. I need you to help me." This made

Kalindi and Mark 1996

me sob more deeply, both from her invoking the job given to me by Gourasana, and her personal cry for help.

Then in the faintest possible whisper, she repeated in my ear, "Marcus, Kalindi must chill out." I nodded my head up and down to let her know I understood. I cried the rest of the meditation, feeling smothered by my own self-absorption and how it kept me from helping or holding K♪G.

I re-awakened to how important I was to her and she was to me. She was giving me the key to my own movement. Destiny was once again calling me to focus on my Master's well-being and longevity.

I woke up the next morning, remembering the events of only a few hours before. I asked Kendra, "How am I supposed to help Kalindi chill out when she won't stop herself?"

Kendra acknowledged that it was not an easy thing Gourasana had asked me to do. As usual, she suggested I meditate and ask Gourasana how to best do this. I knew this was the way; it was what Gourasana had told me in His letter to me the year before. I nodded my agreement and we got ready for another day.

Caregiver

The next special relationship for me with KJG was to be her caregiver and chill-out buddy. Kalindi asked Ginny,[1] Marie, and Karin to train me as a caregiver during those times (as now) when she was 'in the break-free energy' and how to hold her as she came out of the energy after all the disciples left and the break-free mode ended.

Kalindi always entered the energy when she worked with disciples on a regular basis. From the desire of the disciple, His energy would come through her. The more open the disciple, the easier the energy flowed through her nervous system and body. The more closed or shut down the disciple, the harder it was on Kalindi and the disciple.

Normally, if Kalindi kept to a balanced, sensible schedule with enough rest and time away from disciples, she could stay in the energy for extended periods. But this was not normal, and

---

1   One of Kalindi's close caregivers who usually came whenever Kalindi's health or well-being was being challenged. She had been a caregiver for Gourasana for three years. Karin was Kalindi's primary caregiver most of the time. Marie was also well-trained and experienced to fill in when needed.

her caregivers were currently concerned for her. She was working strenuously and had been every day for weeks now.

I knew that being a caregiver for Kalindi was an extremely important role that was also extraordinarily vexing. In my heart, all I wanted to do was help in any way I could. I was ready to step up from basic things like food and drink to watching over her energy levels. I had never done this part alone. Karin or someone else was usually the responsible party. Yet I was willing to be trained. I cared so deeply about her energetic health and well-being.

Naturally, I was anxious. It was such a huge responsibility to care for my Master. What if I messed up? What if harm came to Kalindi? How could I live with myself if something like that happened? Despite my concerns, I dove into the training, mainly delivered by Ginny. Here are some of the notes I took during the first few days:

1. Kalindi needs to stop whatever she is doing by 8 pm. It takes 3 to 4 hours for her to come out of the energy and then fall asleep. She should be alone after 8 pm with little talking so that she can go to sleep with nothing on her mind.

2. Tell-tale signs of stress include: shortness of breath, whispering, trembling hands, raciness, headache, chest pain, or stomach pain.

3. You can ask if she is in discomfort. If you ask, she will tell you.

4. None of this is hard and fast.

5. I have to be flexible and tuned into her.

I thought, *"I'll be practical about this. If I see any symptoms, I'll ask her to stop. I'll say, 'Time to rest now, KJG, let's go to your room.'"*

Yet there was a mind tweak. Both Karin and Ginny conveyed it to me. Many times, Kalindi refused to listen. She kept going anyway. This happened most often when her caregiver was worried or afraid. At all times, she was a force to be reckoned with. It was like trying to contain a runaway train, except this was a bullet train that was on track. For Kalindi, the only reason to stop or slow down was because of the limitations of the physical body.

Kalindi's consciousness was programmed to help others. At the same time, she relied on our help for the health and longevity of her body. It was quite the challenge for all of us. To me, there was **a paradoxical thread** that ran through everything she said and did. For example, spiritual urgency was necessary to make it in this lifetime. Yet, calm and no urgency were important as well for spiritual and physical well-being.

I had to keep in mind that K♪G was connected to a much bigger picture. Her reality encompassed so much more than our awareness. Oftentimes, helping others simply trumped our physical concerns for her. If a caregiver was not deeply connected and humbly concerned, their suggestions or requests were simply brushed aside.

Fortunately, I was not thrown into the front lines immediately. K♪G had been working with people now for almost a month and, while not perfect, she somehow maintained a balance. Her health was OK. Still, my awareness now shifted. Instead of avoiding her meetings and work with others, instead of staying on the outside of things, I now inserted myself into the space so I could observe her well-being. Rather than being affected by what others were doing, now I focused on Kalindi.

Spiritual Energy Transmission

A week into this new regimen, Kalindi met with the business team and a group of those with whom she was working spiritually. We gathered in the living room. Fifteen people were present. Kalindi sat in her wingback chair. The disciples assembled on the floor in a semi-circle in front of her. I was off to the side. Karin sat on the floor next to her. Before we started, Kalindi had agreed to limit herself to five hours. Karin had permission to quietly let her know when that time limit approached.

It was 2 pm and the meeting started. Kalindi began by checking in with people to hear about their spiritual breakthroughs and organizational insights. Then she spoke, and disciples asked questions. This went on for two hours. It was a fairly peaceful and informative scene.

Things began to change when Kalindi responded to a disciple who got confused. Kalindi reiterated herself, explaining in several different ways. The disciple became more confused, and then fear set in. The disciple was no longer able to follow what she was saying. I had experienced this myself. Fear could make me deaf, dumb, and blind and then my self-judgement would start and I would become stuck.

Kalindi asked the disciple to come closer. She shimmied on her knees, until she was directly in front of Kalindi. She could barely look at Kalindi. Kalindi took her face in her hands and whispered in her ear. Immediately, the disciple burst into tears. Kalindi slipped out of her chair and got next to her on the floor. Their eyes connected and Kalindi started transmitting light energy into the disciple. The woman was screaming and thrashing around as wave after wave of energy poured through into her.

When the energy coming from Kalindi started to subside, the woman quieted down. Kalindi knelt over her, gently stroking her face. The disciple started repeating, "Thank you, God, Kalindi, Lord, Father. Thank you, thank you."

When Kalindi returned to her chair, she focused on her breathing to calm herself. Yet, rather than calm, Kalindi's vibration became higher and faster. Her head was shaking, and sound vibrations poured out of her taking all the disciples with her.

All the disciples were shaking and vibrating. Some harmonized with the sound while others were on their backs – their legs and arms moving rapidly. This was it. Kalindi's energy increased. Her hands moved out towards them, showering them in more of the energy.

I became alert. I looked at Karin. She was keeping a close eye on Kalindi. I felt pulled to be near Kalindi. It felt like I was being turned inside out from my navel. Some aspect of me was being ripped apart.

As a caregiver, my job was to go with her like a disciple would and, at the same time, stay focused and aware of the energy's effect on her physical well-being. This paradox was always challenging for me. I needed to keep watch over her but not get overly involved. I started praying, asking Gourasana to help me move with her while staying aware of Kalindi and her well-being.

After another ten to fifteen minutes, the energy subsided. Everyone was flat out on the floor. Some were sobbing, others were quiet. It looked like a bomb had gone off. Kalindi was, literally, the only one left standing.

Gently, she made her way around the room, checking in with each person, stroking them, whispering love and encouragement. As she spoke, people started crying again or vibrating. Through her transmission, KJG had deepened the moment for all of us and taken us into the very heart and eternal moment of God. I felt this as a moment shared on many planes – a silent pause in a moving sea of love.

After she had tou-
ched everyone, Kalindi
went back to her chair
and closed her eyes. I
closed my eyes, too,
not opening them until,
once again, I heard
her speaking. She said,
"The body can only
take so much of God's

Kalindi with disciples 1996

energy. Over time, your nervous system will adapt and you will handle more. Do not be afraid. It is love and ecstasy that awaits you." She closed her eyes again.

After another half hour, people started sitting up. Kalindi opened her eyes and cleared her throat to speak. When she did, the words came as a whisper. Everyone drew closer.

Again, I saw that Kalindi's hands were trembling.

I shot a look at Karin. Karin nodded. She had seen it too. By now, Kalindi was also rubbing her heart. This was yet another symptom of exertion. Karin whispered to Kalindi that she was nearing time. It had been four-and-a-half hours.

At first, Kalindi seemed annoyed, and Karin stood back. Then Kalindi's face changed. It was like she had re-entered this reality. Karin became her reference point. Karin nodded knowingly, and Kalindi got up to walk unsteadily out of the room, with Karin following behind.

I stayed where I was, blown away by what I had seen and felt. I was exhausted from being there. I had just witnessed a classic example of how the energy came through Kalindi and affected her physically. Karin had been magnificent and Kalindi had ended the session at just the right time.

I was becoming aware of an obvious and significant difference between Kalindi and everyone else. The illusion is a dense energy that works constantly to stop or slow our forward movement, much like a muddy field or powerful undertow. For myself and others, it takes constant effort to keep going. We strive to accelerate our soul's vibration to move further into spirit. For Kalindi, this energy was essentially unencumbered. Her only constraints came from her body. There was no fear, laziness, or resistance.

What Kalindi needed was massive discipline to slow down and sometimes stop the energy, despite being filled with His ever-increasing power and love. Kalindi lived in God's desire to help everyone, even to the detriment of her body. It required a delicate balance to control the enormous energy pulsing through her. ♪

In 1998, Kalindi La Gourasana
gave me this picture of her,
writing, "This is how I feel inside
all the time –
vibrating, always plugged in."
She wrote on the back,
"Remember who I am
and what is really happening."

CHAPTER 15

BREAKING FREE

*"What is your existence all about? What is the point?
There is only one thing for certain: that you exist to find the truth,
to find the light, to find the love, to find the Lord,
to return Home to the True Realm of Existence.
Whatever else you may believe or feel, the conclusion that your
existence here was never meant to be eternal is inescapable.
Your existence is designed to culminate in becoming aware.
So become aware."*

Gourasana

*"This is the great secret behind Spiritual Realization and
the functional reason for the Guru-devotee relationship.
Devotees don't gather around Gurus merely because the Guru
is a charismatic (but otherwise ordinary) human being.
They are attracted to the Guru because the Guru literally
transmits an extra-ordinary spiritual State, which they themselves
can realize over time, by **tuning in** on that transmission from the
Master over and over again."*

Adi Da

One morning, around 11:30, Karin came into the kitchen saying, "K♪G is missing!" Feeling alarmed, I asked, "What do you mean?"

"I went into her bedroom to check on her and she's not there!" We started running around the house and property. I looked in all the rooms, the gym, and the safety room. I asked Marie if she had seen her and she said No. I went into the safety room and no one was aware she had left her quarters. They all thought she was in the house. Now, Marie and I and two of the safety people were looking for her.

Then we saw Karin walking with her out of the cabana. She had been out there for four hours without her caregivers or safety people asking where she was. We had all assumed she was still in her bedroom. This was a breakdown for the team. We were supposed to always know Kalindi's whereabouts. Our procedures called for someone being with her at all times once she stepped outside her personal quarters – for her safety and our awareness.

Apparently, Kalindi had escaped, slipping into the cabana at 7:30am without anyone noticing. When Karin found her, Kalindi was smiling. She had pulled a fast one and knew it, having convinced the people in the cabana to keep her hidden.

Instead of being heavy or stern with Karin, Kalindi showered her with love for looking for her. She asked the safety people to learn from their failing to notice that she had come out of her quarters. K♪G asked, "So, will you increase your awareness? Will you stay alert, please? It takes focus and desire to keep up with me you know."

1998 was coming to a close. Kalindi had been working intensely with her disciples for two-and-a-half months. There was no end in sight. Through my caregiver's lens, I was concerned for her well-being. I checked in with Karin, Ginny, and Marie to hear their thoughts.

Karin said, "The energy keeps increasing. It's more and more difficult for her to breathe. She can barely talk even when she's not working with the disciples. The headaches are growing worse and she sometimes has heart pain, nausea, and intestinal problems. She really needs to rest."

Ginny added, "She is tired and that's good. Sometimes fatigue is the only way to get her to lay low and rest."

"So what are we going to do?" I asked.

Karin said, "I want to wait and see what happens next."

Ginny interrupted, "Well, I don't. I think it's time to talk to Kalindi for her own well-being. We have to intervene now."

They both looked at Marie. Marie asked me, "What do you think is the right course of action?" I didn't know what to say. We all looked at Ginny. She said, "OK, we'll wait but, if she doesn't improve, we will have to do something!" We all agreed.

Over the next period of time, we did our best to hold K♪G so her condition did not deteriorate. The worst part for us was that she did not seem to care. She had become single-focused. All she cared about was taking everyone deeper. She was relentless in her desire for people's freedom. When she was 'in the energy,' it overrode all her physical symptoms to the point where it did not seem to matter to her when she had to whisper, clutch at her heart, or had trouble breathing.

The holidays came and went. We entered a new year. Kalindi kept at it but now it was getting harder. She would not stay on schedule. Her meetings with the groups regularly went over the five-hour limit. Each day the fatigue became more pronounced. She became wan; her skin color was ashen. Whenever she removed her sunglasses, her eyes looked bloodshot from lack of sleep. It was horrible seeing her like this and I felt helpless to intervene.

Once again, the team of Ginny, Karin, Marie and I met. We all agreed it was time to talk with her. K♪G had to end her work with the groups and take a break. We decided that Karin and Ginny would talk with her. When they met, Kalindi was firm. She said, "I am not ready to take a break. The two energies (Kalindi and Gourasana) are still merging. It is not yet complete. The people's desire for God, for love, actually helps me in this process. Don't worry. Gourasana will not let this body be harmed."

Ginny tried to say more. KJG shushed her and continued, "Something final is happening. It is a kind of death. I'm letting go of Kalindi so that more of God will be available in and through this body. Like Kalindi has said many times in the past, the body is the last thing to let go at the time of death. Kalindi has been aware of death all of her life. She thinks of it every moment, knowing that disease can hit, that death can come at any time. This is not an exercise. This is reality and she is accepting it."

Neither woman knew what to say or do after that. Then Ginny said, "I'm going to call Dr. Tavakoli. I'm going to enlist his help."

Known to us as Dr. T, Kalindi met him a couple of years before when Kalindi walked into his urgent care clinic on Maui. Dr. Tavakoli is a sensitive man and a brilliant diagnostician. He listened intently and somehow understood the energy Kalindi was carrying and how it affected her body. Dr. T was genuinely fond of Kalindi and was honored to care for her. What they had between them went far beyond the normal doctor-patient relationship.

I listened to Ginny's call with him. Ginny repeated much of what we had been sharing with one another. She said, "Kalindi is very tired, yet cannot come down from the energy. Her stomach bothers her all the time now and she has a headache almost every day. Her nervous system seems maxed out and yet she won't stop. She told us the other day that there's something like another death going on inside – that Kalindi had to let go of even her body staying alive."

Dr. T remained silent. When he did not respond, Ginny added, "We feel it's time for her to have a break. We want her to rest before this intense energy harms her body. We want to get her away from her disciples. Maybe then the energy influx will cease."

Dr. T replied, "I have some vacation time. I'd be willing to come to California to see her."

Ginny was thrilled. She said, "Yes, that would be great! We can make arrangements for you to have a place to stay."

He responded, "I'll get a hotel nearby. I can be there in a week. In the meantime, take her to the lab, get some blood panels. That will help me to know how her endocrine system is doing."

The next week, Dr. T arrived as he had promised and came to Ames to see Kalindi. They walked together in the gardens. Kalindi was open with him. She knew they were connected and that he cared about what happened to her.

We were thrilled to have him there. She listened to him. When the results came back from the blood tests, he reported that her thyroid and cholesterol were worse. She would need to start taking medication, but otherwise Kalindi was okay. He suggested that she complete her work with her disciples and return to Hawaii for rest and recuperation. Once she was back on Maui, he would continue to monitor her.

Kalindi wanted one more week with the people. She would let Karin manage her schedule. If she got off schedule, Karin would call Dr. T and he would get Kalindi on the next plane to Hawaii. This was a turning point. Kalindi trusted and listened to what Dr. T had to say.[1] I immediately scheduled her flight for Maui to leave in ten days.[2] Kalindi personally made arrangements for where we would stay during our three weeks there.

A week went by and Kalindi felt that the people were sufficiently awake and open to return to the outside world without losing the deeper connections they had found. It was time to let them go. Even I could see the changes. It was in their faces, particularly their eyes, yet it showed up everywhere – even in the way they wore their clothes. Each disciple left, having received clear direction and guidance from Kalindi for their forward spiritual movement.

It was not easy for Kalindi to let go of them. She knew how powerful the illusion was and, if it was up to her, she would have them all living with her all the time.

After the disciples left, Kalindi arranged for a skeleton crew to remain and care for the house. Ginny went back to San Diego.

Karin, Siegmar, Valentine, and I prepared for her departure. I was happy Kalindi was going to Maui and I was going with her.

Marie was not going and I was sad to leave her. Things had been going well with us. Still, I was okay; it was only for three weeks and then we would be back together.

Rest and Recuperation

When we arrived on Maui, we moved into a beautiful, spacious estate outside Makena with several acres of oceanfront property, its own cove with a gazebo, a spacious lawn, and rows of tall palm trees. Removed from the world at-large, it was a stunningly quiet spot and ideal for relaxation.

The property was owned by a wealthy, marketing guru. He and his two daughters had participated in The Intensive a few years earlier. He was so grateful for what they received that he made his empty houses available when possible for Kalindi and The Lady when they needed rest and relaxation.

The house had a living room, dining room, five bedrooms, three bathrooms, and a large kitchen. Kalindi's room was at one end of the house, and the other bedrooms and kitchen were far enough away not to disturb her. The setup was ideal.

We were right where we needed to be. Kalindi was transitioning out of the intense energy that had consumed her in California. As she relaxed and came out of the energy, her body changed as well.

---

1 Dr. T loved Kalindi and her disciples. He recognized the value and importance of what she was doing for the world and therefore cared for her above and beyond the call of duty until her last moments in her body. However, Dr. T was never a disciple of Kalindi which helped when they had a difference of opinion or when she had to surrender to him. Kalindi felt he was fulfilling his destiny and work with God by looking out for her.

2 Maui was always Kalindi's favorite destination, not only for the fresh ocean air but that was where her personal physician Dr. Tavakoli lived and practiced. This gave him time to be with her and observe her on a regular basis. Although Dr. T would also come and see Kalindi in Marin, and in later years in Colorado, it was always best when they could spend time together on Maui and he could monitor her health and nervous system.

It was extraordinary the way Kalindi's body would change in a matter of hours or days. As Kalindi, oftentimes she seemed tiny, sweet, and feminine. She looked and felt diminutive, fragile and vulnerable, and I wanted to protect her. The soft, smooth quality of her skin and baby-like smell made her seem like a small child at times.

Other times, when Gourasana was more dominant, she seemed like a mountainous hulk, where her features changed and how heavy she felt shifted. Normally, I could lift her off the ground – yet one time, when she fell asleep on the couch, it took three of us to put her into bed. Sometimes her face would expand, as well as the immense expanse of her belly, taking on a Buddha-like quality, all of which were the effects of His Energy.

In California, she felt, walked, and dressed like Gourasana. She wore her hair straight, her body had thickened, and she loved to run her fingers through her hair. KJG would say, "This shows the love affair between Kalindi and Gourasana. I don't know who's doing it. Is it Kalindi or the other one? Either way, this union is a happening thing."

Kalindi 1997

In Maui, she looked more petite. She wore summer dresses and strolled across the lawn with her arms held softly behind her back. Karin and I kept an eye on her from inside the house and, as she relaxed, so did we. We did note one new mannerism. Kalindi appeared so deliberate in her actions, lifting one foot in front of the other in an unhurried, measured way. But other than that, she just seemed peaceful. I loved to watch her eat her lunch and snacks outside, and found myself sinking into a much-needed calm when she sat by herself in silence for hours.

Her interactions with us were light-hearted and peaceful. There was no heavy Master-Disciple energy. It brought with it a breath of fresh air. From my point of view she was doing the right thing – fitting in well with these peaceful surroundings.

In the meantime, The Lady was staying in Napili, about forty-five minutes away, with her caregivers, Andrea and Hana.[1, 2] As it turned out that day, The Lady had driven to a nearby cove in Kihei to snorkel. The Lady loved to snorkel, often for hours at a time. As I was putting away Kalindi's lunch, I saw The Lady, Andrea, and Hana appear, walking up from the cove. They had snorkeled for two hours along the coast to get to Kalindi.

It was quite a sight: The Lady and Andrea were both tall and slender in their snorkel gear, Hana was just the opposite – a five-foot bubble of blond curls and bouncing joy.

Kalindi was thrilled to see them. It was always glorious for her to be with someone whose consciousness was close to her own. The Lady was always quiet and demure when in the presence of her beloved Master. The two women treasured those times together when the heavy spiritual lifting was done and they could relax and enjoy one another. That day, they drank smoothies and ate tropical fruit, while chatting about this and that. To me it felt like all was right with the world.

By the end of the day, Kalindi was so relaxed and things were going so smoothly that it felt utterly normal for her to suggest that the men go on a camping trip. She proposed we take a week to explore a remote part of the island. At first we were concerned about her care. She told us not to worry because she had Karin, and The Lady and Hana were down the road. We all said OK and were honestly thrilled to have an adventure. Kalindi guided us in packing our 'Jungle Bags.' She set us up like Eagle Scouts. We were ready for all eventualities (snake bites included) and, by the time we got in the car, we were primed for our escapade.

---

1   The Lady would also come to Maui for rest and solitude in between Intensives.

2   Andrea was The Lady's main caregiver, similar to Karin for Kalindi. Hana, formerly known as Lynn or Mazzarati, was an original member of the Core. She had been my group leader in my first Intensive. I held onto her for trust and faith for the years before I found Kalindi.

Kalindi Calling

Siegmar and Marcus

Our destination was Kapao – a secluded area of rocky cliffs and untouched nature. We camped near a small chapel, out from which paths radiated into the jungle and down to the river where it merged with the ocean. I loved being with the guys. We danced in the waterfall during the day and fell asleep at night gazing up at the luminously clear star-filled skies.

At Kalindi's request, once each day, I went out to the Point in order to check for messages. Cell phones were somewhat new back then and cell towers were few and far between. So, on this unpopulated piece of land, we had virtually no reception. On the third evening, I found a spot on the Point where I caught a faint signal. There were 13 messages from Kalindi. I was utterly alarmed.

Several of her voicemails were unintelligible due to poor reception; nonetheless, the gist was unmistakably clear. She wanted me, and only me, to return immediately. She had left Makena and requested that I meet her in Kahana on the other side of the island.

Obviously her energy had changed. I was bummed. I was walking and talking aloud, saying, "Fuck, fuck, fuck, I just got here, damn it!" I considered ignoring her messages and even rehearsed the script I would use about there being no reception. It sounded good because it was utterly plausible. Yet I could not do it. I had to go. She needed me. There was no choice in the matter.

I said nothing to the guys that night, waiting instead until we had breakfast in the morning to inform them. I went out to the Point and called Karin to tell her I was coming.

The guys drove me out to the main road. I was going to have to hitch a ride, since we only had one car and the guys would need it to drive themselves and all our gear back to civilization. They left me in front of a remote outpost, a combined coffee shop/market/ post office-type place. I had a cup of coffee and dutifully went out to the road to 'thumb' a ride. I was kind of hoping no one would pick me up so I wouldn't have to leave.

The first car came by and didn't stop. Fifteen minutes later, a second car not only stopped but the two guys in their 30's were actually going to Kahana. *"This is a miracle,"* I thought, as I climbed into the back.

Once I got back into cell reception, I called Karin. She filled me in explaining that, shortly after we left for the jungle, Kalindi started doing some small projects around the house. At first, it was basic consciousness stuff, like deep cleaning, rearranging, and tidying. Karin was okay with her busyness knowing that Kalindi needed an outlet for the energy. She also knew it was important to catch her before the energy took over and the doing became too much to stop. As I listened to Karin, I had an eerie feeling something more was happening and Kalindi was just getting started.

My stomach dropped when Karin went on to say that four other leaders had flown in from the Mainland. Kalindi was concerned about their connections with God. She wanted them near for their own protection. Karin told me that Kalindi left Makena for her condo in Kahana because it was closer to town and easier to arrange accommodations for her disciples. This was troubling. We were supposed to leave Maui in ten days. Why were so many disciples coming?

It was afternoon by the time my ride dropped me off at the condo. I took a deep breath and walked through the door. The condo had a narrow entry way, then a small kitchen that opened into a large living area.

I didn't see Kalindi anywhere. The four newly arrived disciples were sitting on couches in the living room with their eyes closed. It looked like they were meditating, but I wasn't sure. To tell the truth, I wasn't sure about anything. I was certainly anxious and kept asking myself, *"What happened to rest and relaxation? Why was she doing this?"*

Kalindi emerged from the back bedroom. She looked angelic in a white, flowing summer dress. I was happy to see her. She smiled at me and said, "Welcome back, Marcus. Do you want to make me a BLT?" She had me at, "Welcome back, Marcus."

As I made her BLT, I gathered my thoughts. Things seemed quiet enough, "So what was the urgency for me to return," I wondered? I could hear Kalindi. She was sitting on the couch talking quietly to her disciples. When Karin walked into the kitchen, I grabbed her to find out more of what was happening.

She told me, "After her visit with The Lady and Hana, Kalindi's energy started to increase and, as it did, she became more easily agitated by our lack of consciousness. She gave us clear instructions about what to do and we did something else. She asked me to buy her one thing and I brought back something else. It was like we couldn't hear her clearly anymore. When this happened repeatedly, she told us to write everything down, exactly as she said it and then repeat it back to her. Somehow we still made mistakes and then she got heavy with us."

"So the R & R ended just like that?" I asked.

"Yes," Karin continued, "just like that." "She no longer had time or space for frivolity or casualness. She knew if those near her were messing up, not hearing or fulfilling her requests accurately, it was happening elsewhere in the organization and Mission. That's when Kalindi got on the phone and started calling people in San Diego."

"Kalindi had a call with the group from Ames and said they had all lost their connection. The Illusion had captured them right away after they had left her. She told them they had to live in the depth of their hearts and never come out of it. She had them all commit to helping each other."

"The next day, Kalindi called again and they hadn't shifted enough for her. Like us, for some reason, they couldn't follow her directions. She said the illusion was covering their minds and ears. Kalindi started feeling like she needed to talk to them every day. She was willing to sacrifice everything to help them break free. That's when she started telling them to get over here when she knew they all still needed further help."

When I heard that even more disciples were coming to Maui, it unnerved me. Yet I was grateful to at least understand why it was happening. I considered myself a good listener so, at some level, I thought I'd be all right, at least for the time being.

The next day, Kalindi asked me to go to the store and get her a particular type of body lotion. Then she asked me to write it down and repeat it back to her. This triggered me. It was a simple request that I didn't need to write down. I became arrogant. I knew what she had said and resented having to be lumped in with the others – writing it down and repeating it back to her.

I returned from the store and gave her the lotion. Kalindi looked at it and gasped! I'd bought the right brand, type, and size but it was scented lotion, not the unscented kind she had requested. I was aghast! So was she. I couldn't believe what I had done. I looked at my note. I had written "unscented" down. It was on the paper. Where had my mind been?

Had my arrogance blinded me? I couldn't understand. *Did I not care enough to get it right?* She cut me off mid-thought. Her voice was intense and at the same time pleading. She said, "Please, Marcus, you must wake up! Please expand your mind, expand your awareness!"

I understood her frustration with all of us. Our mistakes disturbed her. I knew she was alone in her full awareness and perfect consciousness. I was sorry to have let her down.

Simplicity

The Lady and Hana returned to San Diego for the next Intensive. Karin, Siegmar, and I were left with Kalindi in the condo. The other disciples were lodged nearby in an inexpensive motel. Without explanation, Kalindi said we would be staying longer. Her only comment was that she did not know how long we would be there. I was torn. Although happy to be with Kalindi, I had begun to ache from missing Marie.

Things calmed down over the next week. Kalindi had Siegmar go out looking for another house to rent. Now she wanted more disciples with her. Once contracts were signed, Kalindi invited another group of five disciples to fly over to Maui. She decided to vacate the condo for those arriving in a few days and move into the new house in Napili. Karin, Siegmar, and I took several days to clean and set up the condo. We cleared out cabinets and pantries. Everything unnecessary was culled, leaving only essential items. Kalindi wanted only one of each item – one mustard jar, one Ketchup, one salad dressing, one shampoo, and so on and so on.

She directed us to keep the sleeping situations geared to simplicity. She had us set 'bed rolls' on top of the already made beds so that her disciples could unroll their covers whenever they slept and then roll them back up when it was time to get back out of bed. This process took less than 30 seconds to complete.

These bed rolls defined Kalindi's mood. She had become disciplined and austere. In the days leading up to their arrival, she focused on us. We slept very little and worked long hours every day to have everything ready. It was not easy for me. I was reactive and resistant. I hated cleaning house. I wanted to escape. I wanted to sleep. I wanted to be alone and she was pushing me, she was pushing us, making us let go, and forcing us to think about others. Karin was great. She responded so well. Siegmar and I tended to fall down on the job. I was still holding back. I could push beyond my limits for Kalindi – but others? I was not so very inclined.

With anyone else, I would have protested and ultimately left. With Kalindi, that was impossible. I knew who she was. I felt too much love for her and through her from God. The only path left open for me was to push through my resistance. I had to face the hard times in order to find the good.

This was not the first time Kalindi had pushed me through fatigue and my body's need for sleep. The first time it happened I thought I hated her. It had been four in the morning. I had been standing close to her while she discussed a project with someone else. She turned to look at me and I knew she felt my hatred. The darkest part of my ego wanted to kill her. She said something – I can't remember what. Somehow my mind went blank and that helped me to not only disengage but to fall back into my heart.

The second time happened when I felt overwhelmed by exhaustion. It was a little easier, and I wasn't so distraught or so blinded by rage. And now, in Hawaii, while I resented the strain of being overworked, my own feelings were somehow distasteful to me. I knew I could keep going. She was my Master and that changed everything inside.

Around 2am on the night before her disciples arrived, Kalindi threw an impromptu mini-celebration for Karin, Siegmar, and me. We had followed her direction; we had done the hard work. The four of us sat on the kitchen floor. Kalindi gave each of us a stick of butter and some maple syrup. Her feast was to eat the butter with maple syrup on it! At first, it repulsed me. Who could like such a mixture? Karin dove in. She took a healthy bite and reported it was delicious. I gathered up my courage and took my own bite. She was right. It was quite delectable!

239

The Wrath of God

When the fresh recruits arrived the next day, I was relieved. Valentine returned with them. He was back as Kalindi's Secretary and Communicator. Other spiritual leaders could also offer support. While Kalindi could focus on their consciousness, they could also be available for other administrative duties. Things were looking up.

Kalindi warmly welcomed the five disciples at the condo. Immediately, she showed them the sleeping arrangements and set up of the house. She was deeply serious as she described what she wanted from them and from all of us – to live simply, austerely, and with no lack.

"Have what you need – nothing more, nothing less," she told us. We nodded our heads. At this point, she opened the kitchen pantry, showing us the basic staples – rice, pasta, beans, etc. She continued, "You are to eat only what is here. There is enough food in the pantry and refrigerator to last a week. Do not buy anything else or eat out at a restaurant. Do you understand?" Everyone nodded. Clearly Kalindi was bringing in new teachings for simple living and no waste. She had preached to us for years about gluttony and excess. Now she was having us live those teachings.

One disciple, looking in the pantry said, "Excuse me, Kalindi, I notice there is only wheat pasta ..." Before he had a chance to finish his sentence, Kalindi exploded like I had never seen before. Suddenly, it seemed like she was ten feet tall. A tremendous power and intensity emanated from her, and it felt like the all-powerful Lord of Lords was there. Her body trembled as she deliberately and slowly snapped out each word, "YOU-WILL-EAT-WHAT-IS-HERE-AND-NOTHING-ELSE. IS THAT CLEAR?"

We all leaned back, like willows blown in the wind. The disciple said, "Yes, Kalindi, I understand." Kalindi calmed but no one else did. Our collective hearts were racing. Later on, Kalindi explained, "That is the wrath of God energy. It comes from Gourasana and flays the ego. Please listen to me and do what I ask, so He does not have to bring that energy to bear again."

In response to another question about the difference between God's Wrath and human anger, KJG responded, "When you can get angry at someone you are separate from them, but God never throws anyone out of His heart."

After completing our tour of the pantry, we moved into the bedrooms. Kalindi explained the bed rolls, the night stands, and so on. Everyone was still shell-shocked from her "Wrath of God" energy. We were listening intently to what she said and nodding submissively. There were no more questions.

Kalindi entered the walk-in closet and showed her guests the empty hangers and shelves made available for clothes and other personal items. Kalindi and Valentine then had an enlightening exchange as described by Valentine:

"We were in the master bedroom, and she was showing me the closet, which was empty, and explaining how my clothes would be hanging in the closet."

She said something like, "Do you see the clothes?" while pointing to the empty closet.

"I looked, and obviously the closet was empty. It was a high pressure moment (given what had just happened) because she was wanting us to be right with her and to be moving along with her consciousness. I got the sense that if I said No, which was materially true, it would break the flow and not be the right answer. So I said Yes."

"What I remember is that she paused, and then she laughed and said something like – Yes, that's the right answer, Valentine."

"It was the right answer because even though there were no clothes in the closet, in her mind's eye she was seeing the clothes there – and by me saying Yes, I was able to jump the gap between what seemed to be materially true (no clothes) and into where she was looking from (where there were clothes)."

Kalindi then moved on to the bathroom and the rest of the house without incident.

Let Go, Give Up and Surrender

About a week later, Kalindi asked another six disciples to come to Maui. We put them in a nearby motel. We now had twenty people staying on the island. The Lady and her team of three were back from The Intensive and staying elsewhere on the island. When Kalindi asked them to join us at the condo, the total number burgeoned to twenty-five.

Kalindi now brought everyone together. She focused on following her instructions. She asked for full surrender and submission. She said it was time. We were to follow her instructions exactly. It did not matter what we thought or felt. Her energy was intense and serious. Gone was the sweetness I loved the most.

Willingly, we all agreed. Kalindi kept going. She started orchestrating everything we did. She told us where to sleep and what and when we would eat. She made sure we only drank water from our personal water bottles, and without making a sound. When someone slurped their water, Kalindi gazed at them as though caught in the act of a felony. She told us to bathe using one bucket of water. She asked us to be silent, except for necessary logistics, and told us we would sleep only when she said we could.

Nothing Kalindi asked of us was very difficult. Yet, during that day and into the next, I felt like a volcano inside. I surmised this was her point. Being stripped of free will, even willingly, was very difficult and I wanted to scream or cry most of the time. I thought, *"This must be what it's like in the military or prison."* My sense of freedom had been taken away. The one great difference being that I had chosen to have no choice.

The following day the intensity increased. Kalindi asked us to hold our arms up in the air to show our surrender to God. One of her disciples had recently done this for four hours and she had loved it. About twenty minutes later my shoulders started to ache and I wanted to let my arms drop. Kalindi maintained that I could go longer. She explained I could pass through the pain. Once again,

I was angry and felt like I was being mistreated. I did manage to go for another half hour until, when she wasn't looking, I gave up.

The following days pushed my buttons. I was used to constant change and had witnessed the wildness of break-free scenes – but always from a safe distance. Now, I was in it. She was pushing on all my limitations and resistance. No matter what else I had seen and experienced in the presence of Kalindi, nothing else came close to this. ♪

CHAPTER 16

TRUE SELF

*"When you discover your True Self, it's very easy to recognize the presence of God. When you're living out of your False Self, you tend to be more attracted to externals – external beliefs, external rituals – but you are never **really touched at any deep level because it's not really YOU that's making contact.** It's your temperament, your personality, your culture, all of which are okay, but your True Self is that part of you that already knows God, already loves God at some unconscious level. When you can connect with your True Self, the whole of spiritual life opens up."*

Robert Rohr

"Every act that comes from such (liberated) beings is optimum in all dimensions. It can't be anything else. The only reason they're in form is to alleviate suffering. Their acts, no matter how heartless or immoral they may seem from the outside, cannot deviate an iota from God's will, God's love. It's the nature of their being. That's who they are, a statement of that perfection. If there's no clinging, there's no way they can go against the will of God. They are the will of God."

Ram Dass

That night Kalindi asked everyone to return to their quarters and rest. When she offered me the opportunity to stay with the others at the motel, I jumped on it. I was eager to take a break. Kalindi had Karin, Siegmar, and other close disciples with her. She was well cared for.

Once back at the motel, I was looking forward to a good night's sleep. Before I had a chance to hit the pillow, we got a messagethat Kalindi wanted everyone to return to the condo at midnight.

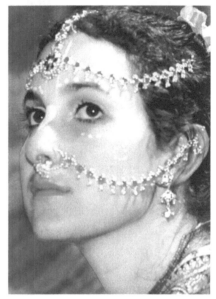

Carol around 18 yrs old

The Entry of the Lord

When we arrived back at the condo, KJG was in a lighter mood.

The disciples entered the smallish living room sitting on the tile floor, chairs and couches. Everyone quickly settled and KJG told us that Gourasana wanted to talk about David Swanson and his wife Carol.[1] Gourasana wanted to inspire us. Here are some of my notes from this talk:

Long before Kalindi appeared, Carol typically slept about four hours each night. She was both determined and devotional, waking each morning at 2am and going outside to begin a two-hour chanting meditation. She liked being awake out under the stars. She loved praying to God with her body in motion in the cool air. At 4am she joined others for a more formal meditation at the Temple. Carol was a Hare Krishna devotee.

---

1 David and Carol (her Krishna name was Champa) met in the Hare Krishna Movement in the 1980s.

Swami Prabhubada[1] was the Master of the Krishna Consciousness movement. He gave his followers guidance to chant 64 rounds on a 108 bead mala[2] in a single day. It takes eight hours to chant 64 rounds. No one could do it.

Prabhubada said, "If just one person can do this, they will truly find God, and the world will be different." David Swanson was the one who chanted 64 rounds. He did it while praying to a Krishna deity.[3] That's when Gourasana first came. He came out of that deity. He came full force without scaring David. It was the middle of the day. David was surprised when it happened. He fell to his knees crying, since he knew it was the Lord.

Ten years later, Gourasana returned with the Host of Light Beings. That was a more intense evening. David told Carol, "The one who came out of the Krishna deity ... this time he is here with a Host of Light Beings. He was standing in front of all these light beings and asked, 'May I use your body to help this world?'"

Carol was speechless.

The Heavenly Host of Light Beings, The True Selves

David continued, "The Light Beings were on the balcony, all over the balcony, and then I said Yes, how could I not?" David had agreed to let Gourasana enter his body. Then he was screaming and writhing on the floor. Carol wondered if he could handle the intense physical exertion.

After four hours of sitting and witnessing David's struggles, based on nothing but faith that the energy was benevolent and from God, she knelt down beside David and whispered "I know that you can stop this, if you want to."

He replied, "No, no it's everything I've been searching for."

*She returned to her place and sat back quietly **to watch the entry of Lord Gourasana into David.***

At a certain point his body grew still and he started to speak. His voice was garbled so she moved closer to listen. Gourasana spoke in a whisper, saying, **"There are so many of you – thousands praying to take a leap of consciousness, to break the cycle of birth and death. There are thousands ready to come Home – that is why we have come. When will you ... when will you let go, give up, and surrender?"** *He fell silent.*

They looked at one another and, after a period of silence, she helped him to his room, staying at his side until he slept.

KJG stopped and looked upon us. I felt this heavenly presence descend on the room. I was uplifted, elevated beyond my mind's comprehension. We sat in silence for what seemed an eternity.

It was almost four in the morning. I wondered if we would sleep after this. As though once again reading my mind, Kalindi moved us into tasks. As the sun rose, she reminded us that it was a brand-new day. She coaxed us through our weariness. She said, "Let go. Don't think about not having slept; just be aware that you are alive at the beginning of a new day."

My True Self Comes Through

Kalindi began to give guidance. She focused on her leaders, helping them to stay out of their heads as she worked to break their attachments to everything from food to sex, relationships, family and the rest of what binds us to life.

---

1 Bhaktivedanta Swami Prabhupada (September 1, 1896 – November 14, 1977) was the founder of the International Society for Krishna Consciousness (ISKCON), commonly known as the "Hare Krishna Movement." As the founder of ISKCON, he emerged as a major figure of the Western counterculture, initiating thousands of young Americans. Despite attacks from anti-cult groups, he received a favorable welcome from many religious scholars who praised his translations. After his death in 1977, ISKCON continued to grow and is still respected today in India.

2 A mala in Hinduism and Sikhism are a string of prayer beads.

3 Gourasana first appeared to David in 1981 as a benevolent presence appearing as a pure golden light and coming out of a Krishna deity statue that David had brought back from India. The Lady currently has this statue on her bedroom altar.

I was happy to be there in the background. Still, I kept one eye on Kalindi to stay out of her line of fire. The last thing I wanted was my attachment to Marie to come up. Then it happened. Out of nowhere, Kalindi turned towards me to ask if I was attached to Marie. Immediately I fell into deep fear. *"Was she going to ask me to let go of her?"* I knew my attachment was slowing me down, yet I wanted it anyway. Kalindi saw my horror and said, "Don't worry, Marcus, it's not what you think."

Kalindi and The Lady were now sitting on the couch. KJG asked me to get Jim on the phone, which I did. Then I sat on the floor in front of Kalindi, holding the handset with the speaker-phone on. All of the other disciples gathered around. Everyone was tuned in.

KJG asked me to repeat every word she said to me directly to Jim. Kalindi started talking to Jim about illusory love and other spiritual traps that exist in man/woman relations. I focused on repeating verbatim everything Kalindi said, exactly as she said it, without paying attention to the content or meaning.

I felt like a conduit for Kalindi's energy. It poured through me to Jim. It filled my consciousness. I disassociated from my ego self. Kalindi's exact words came out of my mouth. She shared with Jim about my fears of losing Marie, that I was afraid of pain and ran from feelings of loneliness.

The more I parroted what she said, the more my sense of self disappeared. The time came when I felt empty – a clear vessel for Kalindi to come through to Jim. I was not tracking the conversation. I didn't really know what was happening; I was just doing what Kalindi had asked me to do.

Then Kalindi asked me to hang up the phone and stand up. I did as she requested and a presence came through me. It spoke loudly, and in a deep, clear voice said, "Ha illusion, you have lost another one." I felt myself shaking. This force, this presence, was different from that of Gourasana where He had taken over my body. Instead, this powerful spiritual Presence and energy was **emanating from me.**

Kalindi recognized my True Self right away. She pointed towards me and spoke to The Lady, "Look, Lady, do you see?" The two of them were in ecstasy for me.

Kalindi immediately asked me to gather a small group of men together and lead them in singing, "Bad to the Bone."[1] My True Self stayed as we grooved in a small circle. Truly, I was in some realm beyond space and time. Nothing else happened beyond what I was doing. There was no mind chatter – just love, joy, peace, compassion, and presence. There was no past and no future, no mind, no thoughts, no anything. **The eternal present was all there was.**

I sat down and took a moment. The world around me came back into focus. Time slowed down. Everyone seemed to be moving in slow motion. Kalindi was telling this one to sit still and that one to walk a certain way, while a third was directed to hide under a table.

Kalindi was directing the movie and the actors. It was her movie, except she was not one of the actors. It seemed like she had the script or was being guided by the One who wrote the script for this play of getting free. Everything KJG said and did with each person was bringing them closer in their process of liberation.

Usually, I was too involved in the movie itself to remember it was a movie. From my illusory being perspective, what I usually saw were other illusory beings. With my new perspective, I saw other True Selves, other beings of light. I imagined this was what Kalindi saw all the time.

With my new found vision, I could clearly delineate between darkness and light. Kalindi's individual instructions to each disciple guided them into the light. It was a masterful chess game played out with human beings right in front of me. Truly, it was an illuminating experience.

---

1 George Thorogood and the Delaware Destroyers, *Bad to the Bone*, EMI, 1981

Everything a Master does in relation to other souls is part of that process of liberation. You might not even notice a Master in the street, unless it is helpful to your spiritual growth. Even when you're sitting in the back row or seeming to be ignored, that is the optimum thing for you at that moment.

Sadly, after a few minutes of this spiritual view, someone asked me a question, my mind engaged and, given my inexperience with this state, my True Self receded.

Fighting the Illusion[1]

The rest of that day and night was a blur for me. I re-entered my normal state of consciousness but it wasn't the same. I'd experienced something I'd never experienced before. A new part of me had **seen the light of day.** I felt so alive and at the same time detached, more like a witness than an actor involved in what was happening. Kalindi's guidance was leading me towards the realizations I sought and craved.

The next day, more spectacular events occurred. They began to unfold with Kalindi in the front bedroom with Ginny and another leader. Ginny came out to find me. The room had a large bed, a nightstand, some chairs, and a dresser, with an ensuite bathroom. Kalindi was on her knees on the bed, wearing pajamas. She was shooting an invisible gun towards the top right corner of the room.

While in full action, she asked, "Do you see the illusion in the corner, can you see it?"

No one responded. My altered vision was gone. I could see nothing but wall. Kalindi was engaged in a fierce battle, yet she alone saw the enemy. Then she stopped shooting. She was sweating profusely.

She said, "I am fighting a life-and-death battle with the darkness." Even though less than 24 hours earlier I, too, had seen this dark force, now that we were back in normal physical reality, it was only because I knew her that I didn't dub her a crazy woman.

She talked about Gourasana. She told us that more and more of His power and light, along with the ever-increasing Host of Light Beings, was entering this plane. Simultaneously, the darkness fought to keep the light out.[2]

Then Kalindi told us the darkness was going to scare us into leaving her alone in the room. She pleaded with Ginny, "Please, do what you must but don't leave me and don't listen to the darkness." I was agog. *Was she being possessed? Was the Illusion attempting to take her over? What was actually going on?*

One thing I knew for sure: whatever Kalindi warned us about always happened. She would tell us the illusion would try to convince us of something and, as she spoke, her face would change, her body contorted, and it appeared as if the illusion had seized hold of her. This dark being would tell Ginny to get something. She would order us about. We would ignore these requests and after a while Kalindi would return, cautioning us against the next attack, and warning us about the darkness.

Then, out of the blue, Gourasana came through. He looked at me and said, "Kiss me if you want to be with Kalindi in that way again." I kissed Him. And with that kiss, Kalindi lay back in Ginny's arms, exhausted.

True Realm Shower

Before I could comprehend what had happened, Kalindi climbed off the bed, went out to the living room and asked everybody to come into the front bedroom. In no time, she had jammed

---

1 Illusion aka Māyā in Hindu philosophies is a spiritual concept that connotes, "That which exists, but is constantly changing and thus is spiritually unreal" and the "Power or the principle that conceals the true character of spiritual reality." Ramachandra Dattatrya Ranade, *The constructive survey of Upanishadic philosophy,* Bharatiya Vidya Bhavan, 1926.

2 "The highest spiritual states are not possible without the Divine itself entering into conditional existence (via an Incarnation) and creating a "hole in the universe" that bridges the otherwise insurmountable "barrier" between conditional existence and Unconditional Existence." Adi Da, *The Knee of Listening,* 2004

15 disciples into her tiny bathroom. She turned on the water and took the flexible hose shower head and started spraying water all over everyone.

Kalindi was shouting joyously, **"The Light has prevailed! The Light has prevailed!"** She was in ecstasy, lit up beyond anything I'd ever seen before. Then I felt it myself. A wave of ecstasy rolled over me. It was joyous! Kalindi was invoking the True Realm. She was shouting, "It is True Realm rejoicing time!" Kalindi climbed into the shower. The water looked like colored rain drops.

Then I noticed the pooling water flowing into the bedroom. I ran into the bedroom. Siegmar checked on the electrical outlets. We put down towels to hold the flood back and I jumped back into the celebration. There was so much joy and ecstasy.

This moment marked the culmination of weeks of intense focus, surrender, and willingness. It took some time for Siegmar and me to mop up all the water. After we finished, we wandered outside and sat on the ocean wall together, acknowledging how **crazy, incredible, and wonderful it was.**

That's when the next extraordinary event occurred.

Freedom Walk

Siegmar and I watched as Kalindi walked out of the house naked. The Lady followed her with a bathrobe, attempting to get her to put it on. KJG was not interested. She walked intently and freely through the complex. Siegmar jumped up and ran towards her.

As caregivers and helpers we tried not to panic when KJG did outrageous things. Still, she often had to remind us who she was, helping us to remember that He knew what she was doing.

Kalindi stopped as Siegmar approached. She studied his disapproving face and asked him, "Do you know who I am?"

He replied, "Yes."

"Who am I?" she asked.

"Gourasana" he said.

"Will you follow me?"

"Yes," Siegmar replied.

"Ok, let's go."

Satisfied, KJG walked past the pool and headed toward the street.

A few of us ran after her looking to keep her out of any trouble. Little did we know that trouble was what Kalindi wanted. I caught up to her as she turned onto the road headed towards people and cars. There she was, our Master walking down the road **clothed in nothing more than trust and faith.** I was concerned about her safety and the law, and she was as free as a bird.

Siegmar got into the mood and asked, "Should I undress too?"

She replied, "No" and kept going.

By now there were several other disciples walking with her, and behind her. Two cars passed by – one of them filled with gawking men, the other driven by a frowning older woman. Kalindi turned to Siegmar and said, "The police will come. I want there to be a report that says Kalindi La Gourasana walked naked in the street on this day in Maui." Then much to his surprise, she turned to another disciple next to her and asked her to call the police!

I was walking behind her in the company of a few other disciples. Kalindi told us to feel the freedom of who we truly are in God's Love and Protection. I felt a lightness I'd never known before. At some deep level, it felt like how God wanted it to be.

I felt so free of fear. I was in her wake, untethered by my usual worry or concern. My mind was used to telling me I was doing something wrong and something bad was going to happen. Kalindi walked before me in His Glory. She was living as He intended us to be in His creation. This was why I loved being with Kalindi. She inhabited this 'illusion-free' zone, this bubble of pure love.

Kalindi turned back. We returned to the condo. As Kalindi reached the house, a police car showed up. She calmly sat down on the steps of the townhouse and told us to scatter. She chose to be alone when she talked to the police.

I went around back and jumped into the ocean. I felt so free. I remember swimming in the warm, blue water. I knew I was not my body. Somehow, my body and spirit felt entirely distinct. Such a wonderful experience! What a deep realization – **I am not this body!** It was crystal clear. I was an eternal soul. One day my body would die, this life would be over, but my soul would live on.

When I returned to the condo, Kalindi was in the living room and the police were leaving. I asked what had happened. Someone who had stayed nearby told me that, when the police approached, Kalindi asked them, "Can you help me, please? All of these people have crowded into my house and they won't leave."

The police officer replied, "Okay, ma'am, but first will you please put some clothes on?" KJG did as requested, donning a bathrobe. Then, she asked that they file a report and be sure to include her full name – Kalindi La Gourasana. The officer filled out the report and left.

The Light has Prevailed

As dusk descended, we slowly regrouped inside the condo. After all this, even more power and energy came into Kalindi. I could see it in her eyes and in the ferociousness of her gaze.

She began to station people all over the condo. She told them not to move. Some sat on the couch. The rest were spread out between the two bedrooms. When she found me, I was out in the parking lot. She told me to sit by a tree.

For 45 minutes, I didn't move a muscle. It was getting dark and I decided that my role as a caregiver trumped her instructions this time. I needed to go inside and see what she was doing.

As I entered the house, KJG was in the back bedroom with The Lady, Karin, and some others. She came out with The Lady in tow. Kalindi was fully dressed in a pants suit and a scarf. Her hair was long and wavy. She moved towards the front door and as she passed by me, the most powerful energy I had felt to date was streaming out of her eyes. She exuded force and presence. I stepped aside. As The Lady and Kalindi walked out the door, someone told me they were on their way to see Dr. Tavakoli.

Kalindi La Gourasana 1998

While Kalindi was stationing people, Karin with support from The Lady, had called Dr. Tavakoli and told him what was happening. The Lady knew that Kalindi needed help to manage the influx of energy. No one knew how to establish the physical effects on her body. Dr. Tavakoli understood the link between the energy and the effects of the energy in the physical body. He was one of the few who could talk her out of these episodes.

Kalindi and The Lady got into the back seat of the car with Siegmar driving. It took 45 minutes to cross the island to Dr. Tavakoli's urgent care office in Kihei. As a caregiver, I was pulled to stay close to Kalindi. I grabbed another disciple and we followed in a second car.

By the time we arrived at Dr. T's office, he had already seen Kalindi and given her a sedative. They left in company with The Lady and Siegmar and headed to a hotel. We followed after.

Dr. T, The Lady, and Kalindi remained one step ahead of us. They'd already gone up to her room when we caught up with Siegmar in the lobby. He reported that Dr. T suggested she stay away from her disciples. He believed further interactions would bring more power that would overload her nervous system when she had few reserves and needed rest. Kalindi was not happy. She did not want to stop. Even so, she surrendered.

Dr. T re-entered the lobby. He had given her more sedatives to make sure she slept until the morning.[1] Karin, Siegmar

---

1 His "should" was based on times he had given Kalindi sedatives or sleeping pills that should have knocked out a 120-pound woman for quite some time. Instead, she was barely fazed and would keep going.

and I got a room next to Kalindi's. We would be there when she woke.

The next day when the three of us went to see her, we were expecting KJG to be wiped out, sleepy and in her pajamas. Karin knocked, the door opened, and there she was – dressed and irrepressible.

She was hopping around the room, smiling and announcing, "The Light has prevailed. His promise is fulfilled. You who were with me have experienced Home." She added, "You still must walk your own path, but you've experienced Home and the True Realm. Your souls are like mirrors, they must be wiped clean. It is your job, as you move forward to keep polishing the mirror."[1]

Kalindi's Rules of Love

All the disciples who'd been asked to come to the island had now left, leaving only her personal team behind. The medical plan was for Kalindi to stay at the Hotel for three weeks. Physically drained and depleted, we knew that as Kalindi came out of the energy, her body would more acutely feel the exhaustion.

Before leaving His body, Gourasana had left behind a set of rules for Kalindi's well-being. These "Rules of Love" were hers and her caregivers' Bible for ways to keep her body strong and healthy while carrying the presence of God. Gourasana wanted Kalindi to have a long and productive life. He knew what this energy could do to the nervous system and organs. He knew she would need a disciplined and controlled lifestyle.

It was challenging for Kalindi to follow her rules. For a long time, I didn't understand. I thought, "If she is a Yogi and has so much control, why doesn't she just follow her rules?" Over time, I could see not only my concepts about this but also realistic reasons why it was so difficult.

The Energy of God, and particularly the energy of Kalindi, was one of movement and change, change and movement. It flowed freely from the Source into her. It came unhindered. She was fully receptive, unencumbered and always asking to be filled more. She had no desire or attachment for the status quo. There was no resistance. There was no time. She lived in the moment. It was always Now, Now, Now. Sometimes it felt like everything needed to happen at once.

One of Gourasana's first rules in His rules for Kalindi concerned *no urgency*. It addressed the dilemma of merging spiritual and material realities when bringing the Energy of God into a human body. Caring for her required continual discipline from all of us. It was not easy to support her as the energy and power receded and the time of recuperation began.

Caregiving for Kalindi was all about her rules. But now, after what had just happened, we needed to step up our support of her adherence to them. She told us to study Gourasana's Rules of Love until we had them memorized. The rules covered some 10 pages so we had our work cut out for us. Key sections included:

Kalindi's Morning Program

- Morning meditation is essential as it sets the stage for the day.

- To sit in meditation without thinking is ideal.

- Allow the meditation to be a free-flowing movement of consciousness.

- Always keep the mind under control.

- Ask God to help you.

- When important ideas come, write them down. One or two sentences. No details.

---

1 "Illumination happens when we polish the mirror of the heart with daily practice – and see beyond the illusion of our transient thoughts and emotions to the vast and luminous landscape of our true nature." Ram Dass, "Polishing the Mirror"

Keep Kalindi's space calm and under control

Kalindi's day should be as peaceful and undisturbed as possible. At times, solitude is essential.

- There should be no excitement around Kalindi.

- Kalindi's team and entourage should refrain from looking into her eyes.

- Her exercise time must be peaceful and undisturbed.

- No matter what happens around you, remain calm and focused on the love and care of Kalindi.

There were pages of rules but these few were now indispensable.

Our two rooms shared an adjoining door. Karin had easy access to Kalindi and spent varying amounts of time with her each day. I joined when asked. Together we assisted Kalindi to rest, recuperate, and integrate. Siegmar was our link to the outside world. He made runs to Kahana, bringing back supplies and other necessaries.

Karin and I practiced Gourasana's Rules of Love. We made sure her environment was 'disturbance free,' preventing anything that would trigger her energy.

For the first week, K♪G was quiet. She followed the rules. We created a schedule. Karin would be with her in the morning, giving me time for a quick swim or snorkel in the ocean. Then I joined Kalindi. We watched a lot of movies and ordered room service.

It was a peaceful time. When I went through the adjoining door into her room, I left my personality at the door. **We did not**

have to speak to connect, the connection was already there. I did not have to speak to have love, the love was already there. **She was love,** she was connection. It was calm and peaceful to not speak and just be. In the end there was very little to say anyway, so I just loved her.

It's Just the Love

The routine lasted until the end of the week. K♪G was showering. Karin was out and I was in the sitting area waiting to go for a walk with Kalindi. I heard the shower turn off and a few minutes later she called me in. It was a large bathroom with two sinks, an oversized tub, and wall-to-wall mirror. K♪G was naked. She asked me to put some lotion on her back. As I was finishing, she asked, "Would you like to feel how Gourasana kisses?"

I was stunned. "Of course," I said.

She turned towards me and said, "Okay, here is a Kalindi kiss." We kissed for a few moments. It was sweet. The taste of her mouth and tongue were warm and familiar.

Then she said, "And this is how Gourasana kisses." It was a very different feeling – stronger, with more of an open mouth, and no tongue.

Kalindi turned back to putting on her makeup as though nothing had happened. I returned to the living room, fell on the couch and cried. It was another mind tweak – *Him, her? Both? What was going on!*

The next day, the three of us were in her room when Kalindi gave me some valuable guidance. We were lightly talking about nothing of consequence when she said, "Marcus, stop trying to be humble. **It is false humility.** You are trying to act in ways you think humility looks like. It is play-acting. Your face and eyes look weird and you become unnatural."

I took her message in. I waited some time and then asked if she could talk about humility and what I knew and didn't know.

She answered, "Just be real. Be normal. When I address your ego, let it go. Your ego can't hide. It just gets weird."

She added, "Stop trying to act like you know something when you don't. **You know what you know and that's it.** Everything else you don't know. Humility does not mean you don't know anything at all. It means that you know what you know, and that's it. When I talk about what you know, I don't mean what you think you know, I only mean that what you have experienced or realized within. These are real. When you speak from there, people feel it since it is real."

This guidance helped me in the years to come as I endeavored to speak what I knew and maintain an open and humble stance around everything else. It helped me to hear others more openly and to realize that there are so many perspectives to everything.

A few days later, Kalindi and I were walking through the hotel lobby. It was extremely hot. I was wearing a tank top and small, loose fitting shorts with no underwear. As we walked, I noticed I had an erection which clearly stuck out without underwear. Kalindi noticed and said to me, **"Don't worry, Marcus, it's just the love!"**

I blushed and was relieved at the same time.

Then, in a most endearing voice, she added, "And when you are with me, please wear underpants."

Kalindi truly loved me. I felt so cared for. She didn't mind my guilt and shame. She looked at it and shrugged. It had no true value for her. Sometimes she took it seriously and sometimes she was hilarious, able to juxtapose the childlike with the cosmic and all-powerful. Kalindi was a chameleon; like any good Buddha, she could go from belly laughing to deadly serious in the twinkle of an eye. ♪

CHAPTER 17

CRY OF THE SOUL

"How can one enjoy something in the state of fear?
Only a wedding with your own freedom, your own Self,
is a wedding which will see no separation.
Very few people will celebrate such a wedding.
And this wedding can only take place
after the cremation of the world of objects.
Then the Lord will dance on the rubble
of the destroyed world. Then samsara (worldly illusion) is over.
Then all is over and the Self is realized."

Papaji

"... Humanity completely misunderstands God. ...
The world could change overnight if we accurately
comprehended what God is, what God wants,
who we are in relation to that, and to each other."

Neale Donald Walsch

By the beginning of the second week, our rest period had ended and the energy had returned. Kalindi was now creating notebooks for her leaders in which she wanted them to track the spiritual progress of those in the Mission that they helped. Karin and I tried to discourage this. Kalindi promised to stay calm and peaceful. We relented.

Siegmar brought in the supplies and the four of us created "Leader Notebooks." We used 3-ring binders that KJG personalized by creating meaningful collages for each leader using cut-outs from magazines. We made twelve of them. There were sections for guidance, breakthroughs, obstacles, challenges, and the like.

We were done in a week. Kalindi's sister was coming. I was scheduled for time-off. It had been weeks since I'd had time to myself. I went back to the condo, packed my bag with sun lotion and snorkel gear, and filled the cooler with food and drink. I was headed for Hana on the northeastern corner of the island, two-and-a-half hours away.

My last stop was in the small town of Makawao where I gassed up and bought final supplies. With 5 minutes to go before I lost cell reception, my phone rang. I hesitated to answer it. When I did, it was KJG.

A deep and firm voice said, "This is me, Lord Gourasana. I am leading a seminar here at the hotel. Please return and come to Kalindi's room." The phone went silent. I couldn't believe it. The Lord was calling me and I didn't want to go. It took a lot to turn the car around and head back to the hotel.

Stay With Me

When I arrived, the seminar was in full swing. KJG was on the couch with Valentine on one side and Ginny on the other. I went off to the side to ask Karin what had happened.

Karin replied, "Right after you left, her energy picked up again. She said she needed Ginny and Valentine to help her with her schedules and memos. When I protested and tried to slow her down, she promised to remain calm. But how could she? Gourasana's energy was increasing in her again. It was time to resume training the caregivers on how to be with KJG."

I nodded, feeling deeply for Karin. It was nearly impossible to manage KJG. I asked what the seminar was about.

Karin went on, "Staying present and connected with Kalindi." She flipped open a small notepad and read, "We are to focus on what she is doing and nothing else. This means no distractions, no falling behind, and no going ahead."

Staying focused with no distractions was an ongoing discipline for me. I was easily distracted, not only by my thoughts but by external glitter, making it difficult to move in a straight line. An hour earlier I had been ready to relax at the beach and now I was being called back to do exactly the opposite. I gazed at Kalindi and remembered one of my first sincere prayers. I chose this one from The Lady because of my easily distractible nature:

> My dear Lord,
> Please keep me humble,
> Take away all distractions,
> Leave me standing in Your Will.

My desire to be anywhere else fell away. My mind quieted. I stopped wondering why she was doing what she was doing. Asking questions, needing to make sense and figure it out, always guaranteed that I would fall behind, and she wanted me to stay with her.

In my meditations, when I would get deep enough and feel my connection with God, as I would drift off, I would hear a whisper from within saying, *"Stay with Me."* It became one of my ongoing awareness practices to attempt to **'Stay with Him'** for as long as I could.

264

My goal was to decrease the frequency and amount of time I was not with Him. No wonder Gourasana called me back. I needed help in this area. Staying focused without spacing out requires disciplined awareness. I was forced to constantly catch myself because, if I didn't, I drifted off.

As usual, KJG was using her daily life to train us. Ginny had made handwritten schedules for Kalindi for the next two weeks. Kalindi asked me to sit next to her, on her right, and type these schedules into my computer. Ginny was on her left writing meal plans.

While Kalindi spoke to Ginny about the meal plan, I stopped typing as my attention went to what she was saying. Kalindi noticed and said, "Marcus, you can read, you can type, and still stay connected to me. If you are deep enough and connected to Him within yourself, you will automatically be connected to me, regardless of what you or I am doing."

Wow! I loved that! I started practicing what she said and it was true. I was learning it was about my depth and focus within, not what my mind was active with. My awareness could pull me deeper into that place while I did whatever I was doing.

A door had opened. It was happening. I felt a new possibility emerge. I was eager to keep going. I kept practicing this relaxed awareness, depth, and focus while Kalindi was training Valentine to stay connected with her, while he was typing the memos she was dictating to him at 100 words per minute. I was able to do it. I typed my schedules, listened to Kalindi speak to Valentine, and stayed connected with her the whole time.

Talk about a breakthrough or developing a deeper awareness. This was real time practical experience of situating myself in a deeper, more connected place within that allowed me to calm and focus my mind. I was able to begin directing my awareness, focus, and attention. Major changes were going on inside of me. I was grateful.

Attachment, Neediness and Sex

After the seminar, Kalindi asked several leaders to come to Maui to be with her and learn about the notebooks. Marie was one the first she called. Although Marie and I talked on the phone as often as possible, we'd not seen each other for nearly 5 months. Now that she was arriving on the island, I could hardly wait to see her. I was with Kalindi spiritually, but every part of my body wanted Marie.

She arrived mid-day. When she entered the room, there were eight of us already there, working to improve the notebooks. Kalindi had each person engaged in different tasks, some in teams, some working alone, and a couple sitting with Kalindi on the big bed.

Kalindi put Marie to work on the floor team. The project continued into the night. As the work wound down, my desire to be with Marie increased. It took all my discipline to stay focused as one by one the other leaders left for their rooms. In short order, only Kalindi, Karin, Marie, and I remained. Thinking I could leave Kalindi with Karin, I attempted to excuse myself so Marie and I could go. My plan didn't work.

Kalindi said, "Marcus, you are not with me." She was right. I was not. Then she added, "It is okay to be with Marie. You two should go have a night together." Then her voice became serious. "And also know you are in dangerous territory spiritually." I looked at her blank-faced. She said, "You want Marie more than God." Kalindi had me. She was dead on. I did not know what to say as Marie and I left her room.

For many years, Kalindi would say this to me, and for many years it was true. It was my main illusion – seeking fulfillment from a woman. In 1999, I clearly wanted sex and women more than God. In 2005, this was still the case. In 2007, Kalindi said it still was not clear which I would choose. It was not until 2012 that I had let go enough of my attachment to women and illusory love that I could clearly and authentically say that I desired God more.

Another woman might have shaken off what Kalindi said. Certainly I was ready to, but not Marie. Our night alone was a disaster. Marie heard what Kalindi said. She wanted no part in colluding with my illusion. She wanted my freedom. Focus on Kalindi was crucial for that. She even suggested that we not spend the night together.

I freaked! I needed her love and was dying for sex. Neediness enveloped me. I grabbed at her and whined about poor me. She partially relented. I could stay with her, but there would be no sex.

The room had a large bathtub. I persuaded Marie to bathe with me. We faced one another from opposite sides of the tub. It all felt so awkward. I was desperate. She was leaving the next day. We had to get physical. That's how I shared love. It was my medium. Left untouched, I felt unloved. Marie was resolute. She was not going there. With all the tension, we barely slept. Come morning, we were both tired and our relationship was strained.

Marie was scheduled to fly out at noon that day. Thirty minutes before she was to leave for the airport, Kalindi asked both of us to come to her room. She asked how our time together had been. I was speechless. Marie said, "To be honest, it was difficult. All I could feel was his attachment and need for sex. I love him, yet I'm prepared to sacrifice our relationship if necessary for his freedom." She looked at me. I was aghast.

Kalindi said, "Continue."

Marie said, "I feel I distract him from you and God and that is not okay with me."

I was deflated. *"Why was Marie saying these things? Even though they were true, she shouldn't be talking this way."* My stomach fell to the floor. I knew the gig was up.

Sure enough, Kalindi suggested we let go of each other for six months. Marie agreed and started for the door.

I panicked. My mind went into over-drive, *"She can't go like this, I can't lose Marie! I can't take it!"* screamed the thoughts in my head. Regardless of my soul's desire for God and connection with Kalindi, **Marie was my drug of choice.** I had to hold on to her.

I chased Marie down the hallway, jumping into the elevator as the door closed. I begged and pleaded. Marie would hear none of it. She was determined. There was no way I could sway her, especially in my frantic clinginess.

I followed her through the lobby and out to the curb. I felt embarrassed and humiliated. I acted like that scared little boy who screamed for his big brother to come inside and open a can of tuna fish for him. Marie did not even give me a kiss good-bye. She got into the car and sped off to the airport.

I was left at the curb not knowing what to do with myself. The fear and pain were too much. My mind was swirling. I thought of going to the other side of the island just to get away. Before I could take action, Kalindi called and asked me to return to her room.

When I arrived, she was in bed in her pajamas. She lifted up the blanket and asked if I wanted to get in with her. I said Yes and she enveloped me in her arms. Then she said, "You can be with me again if you want. It will be all right."

I couldn't believe it. Kalindi was sharing her love with me again! After we made love, I felt warm and safe, and for a brief time as though all was well again.

Illusory love preyed on my desire for Real Love. Real love, i.e., God's Love, is untainted by fear or conditions or time. That is what makes it real. It is love with freedom in it. It is unconditional, constant, and eternal. As Kalindi wrote in her *Illusory Love* work-book, "Illusory love binds you, Love of God frees you."[1]

In my relationship with Marie, I was hooked. I felt I could not live without her. I thought that I **needed her and only her.** When she gave me her love I was temporarily fulfilled, albeit with anxiety and fear, knowing it could disappear at any moment.

I had already experienced in San Diego and Marin when she would withdraw, sometimes for days. This freaked me out and triggered my fears and insecurities. I would call her ex-boyfriends to help me cope. "Did she do this with you? How do I handle this?" I would ask. Yes, she had. Their words provided some comfort for my mind, but I still suffered emotionally during those times. If I didn't know where she was or what she was doing, I would call or page her. **I was insanely jealous.** I wanted to own and control her, as futile as it was.

In my twenties and thirties, I didn't know Real Love existed. Even though my soul wanted Divine Love, I settled for illusory love. Somehow Kalindi knew this. God's Love is what she shared with me and drew out of me. Over time, I became acutely aware of the difference between illusory love and Divine Love. Years later, once I had realized all the suffering that accompanied illusory love, it still took me several more years to begin to walk away from it.

The Cry of the Soul

All that day, Kalindi could feel I was in pain. In the past when she had found me hurting, I would feel enveloped by her tremendous compassion. She could so massively soothe me. This time, it was different. I was broken. I told her about my feelings with Marie, that I'd already lived five months without her, that she was 'the one' and I didn't know how to make it through another six months of separation. I started crying.

This time, instead of comfort, Kalindi guided me within down through my sadness into the pain below. I closed my eyes. The hurt was so acute. I started wailing. The sound turned into a piercing cry. It felt like I was burning up. I sweated profusely. Kalindi knelt beside me with her hand on my back as I lay on the bathroom floor, guiding me to trust and go further into the pain.

Kalindi asked me to go through the pain of losing Marie. She said I had a chance to really go deep. As she said this, the bottom fell away. I dropped into a yearning I'd never felt before. The pain became excruciating. I was in the dark of me, alone, scared, and lost.

---

1   Kalindi, *Illusory Love Binds You, Love of God Frees you,* Miracle of Love, 1998

I lay curled up like an embryo, tears rolling out of my eyes. Kalindi's voice was reassuring. She said, "Marcus, this is *The Cry of the Soul.*"[1]

"It is what your attachments, busyness, walls, and distractions cover up. It is the pain of your separation from God. It is the sound of that separation and your soul's longing for Home."

Kalindi called The Lady. She was in San Diego leading an Intensive. It didn't matter. Kalindi needed to talk to her. When The Lady came to the phone, Kalindi said, "Hi Lady, Marcus is on my bathroom floor, crying from the depths of his soul. He thought it was about letting go of Marie, but now he is crying for God."

Kalindi put the phone close to me and continued, "Do you hear?"

"Yes," The Lady replied.

"There is no sentiment, is there?" Kalindi went on.

"No boo-hoo at all," The Lady said.

"You know this depth well, Lady. Please guide the participants there," Kalindi said.

"Yes, I will. Thank you, Kalindi," The Lady said.

They got off the phone. Kalindi pulled me into her lap and stroked me. I grew quiet. She said, "Marcus, you know how I like to use the transformations of those around me to illustrate core teachings?"

I whimpered a Yes.

She continued, "There are always new ways to help and when someone has a breakthrough, it delights me to get the word out to The Lady or other leaders. Marie will be pleased to learn you've had this breakthrough but you cannot be the one to tell her."

She looked at me speculatively and added, "I'm going to make a talk about this so it is available to the congregation." She was on her feet now. Before walking out of the room she turned back and said, "Go back to your room and get in bed. Take the rest of the day to be gentle with yourself."

The next day, one of Kalindi's closest leaders helped me go further into the cry of the soul. She told me to focus on the pain to take me deeper. She told me the pain was the driving force into my longing and love with God. Once I'd found my depth and was in that space, I could pray for God's Love to fill me.

I was desperate for God's Love so I immediately did what she said. I was using my feeling for Marie as a way for God to fill me with His light. I was turning my loss and pain into His love. I had always tried to avoid pain and Band-Aid it as quickly as I could. Now I was facing it and using it to **heal my wounded heart** and bring me closer to God.

Dark Weeks of the Soul

I was on my way. I'd finally cracked in the way Kalindi had wanted eighteen months earlier at Ames. I knew that spiritual progress was being made and I was grateful. Unfortunately, the intense feelings of loss made it difficult to control my mind. I was endlessly tormenting myself with vivid images and loops of dialogue around Marie and sex, and rehashing horrible scenes I imagined of her being with someone else. Adding insult to injury, I was tortured by memories of Helle and how she cheated and lied to me. I could not turn it off.

I was in a daze the morning we checked out of the Grand Wailea Hotel and returned to the Kahana Condo. I sat in the backseat of the car with the leader who'd recently helped me. Kalindi was up front with Siegmar driving. I felt so separate and alone. My walls of denial were seriously damaged. While they had not yet fallen down, there was enough of a crack for the light to come in. Pain and love were coming together at this point. While my heartbreak was painful, the joy of love and getting free was very great too. This was allowing me to shift my perspective from 'pain is not productive,' to 'all I want is freedom and love and pain is the way to it.'

---

1 Kalindi La Gourasana, *Cry of the Soul* in *Golden Information* series of talks. Miracle of Love, 1998

Still, I was giving up something so connected to the root of my worldly identity that it felt like a death. I thought to myself, *"I'm going through some of the same things people go through when they are physically dying, like avoidance, anger, and resentment. I'm feeling so alone because my superficial way of connecting is dying."*

Here I was in the car with my dear friend Siegmar and two of the most loving women I knew, and all I felt was separation. There was nothing I could do but tolerate my passage and surrender to the situation. I'd taken the next steps. Something new was going on – the possibility of the lightness of a new state of being.

Unfortunately, for the next three weeks, my mind subjected me to the most severe torment I'd experienced since the bouts of depression back in college. I could not get Marie out of my head. Variations on a theme of negative scenarios played over and over in my head. They ganged up on me. I couldn't stop them. I'd already lost her and would never see her again. She would fuck every other man I knew. I would never taste that incredible love. I wanted her so much. **It was all I could do to get through the day.**

Meanwhile, KJG and I were 'intimate' again, although it was very different this time around. She had changed so much. There was nothing romantic about our time together. We were more like personal and intimate friends with a twinkle of a possibility of sex. During our morning walks together, she'd say, "We could have sex tonight if you want."

Invariably I'd respond, "Yes, I'd love that."

We would even go into her room and set up the space with condoms, lubricant, towels and the like, yet never used them. Mostly we were intimate in thought only. Energetically, so much was happening to Kalindi. Still, I felt blessed to be near her and have so much personal exchange. It was wonderful to have Kalindi relate to me in this way. It truly helped me to let go of my attachments to Marie.

Kalindi decided to get a small dog. I've never been a dog lover but when Kalindi returned home with a small Pomeranian named Hercules, I fell in love. Hercules was cute and full of himself. It gave me joy to care for him.

In less than a month, Kalindi decided it was too much work to take care of a dog. We needed to give him away. I started to cry. Kalindi looked at me and asked "What's the matter, Marcus?"

I replied, **"Everything I love disappears."**

She said, "He will go to a loving home. There will be many children for him to play with."

I said through my tears, "I know he'll be okay, but **I don't want to love any more,** it only leads to pain." Kalindi smiled her knowing look that let me know she understood what I was going through.

What comforted me most during this time was my love, service, and devotion for Kalindi. I stayed close to her and, although my heart was shattered, I felt safe around her. At the end of the night, she would get into bed. I would turn off the lights and kneel next to her bed. She would give me one of her hands to massage and I would sing my eternal love song to her that came from the deepest part of my heart:

"Kalindi, Kalindi, Kalindi, I love you, I love you, sweet Kalindi ♪; Kalindi, Kalindi, Kalindi, ♪ I love you, I love you, my Kalindi♪."

Usually, she fell asleep in the time it took to massage both hands. Once Kalindi was asleep, I would stealthily leave the room, knowing she was in His arms.

After about three weeks, I remember saying to myself, "Enough, Marcus, enough! You have to stop now." I willed myself to detach from these thoughts. Thankfully, the severe mental anguish began to recede. This detachment began to bring some peace with it.

Transcending Sex

One week later, in the middle of the afternoon, Kalindi was in her chair, in her pajamas, while I was on the floor leaning up against her bed. She started talking about what was happening inside of her. She mused over the different energies now housed inside her body. It was June 6, 1999. She asked me to write down the main points:

- Gourasana is the Presence and the Power.

- Kalindi is His energy and movement.

- Kalindi moves Him, she dresses Him and allows Him to do everything.

- Kalindi's energy is pure creation and it wants to go, go, go.

- Gourasana tries to slow her down.

- If you have a problem with Kalindi going too fast or doing too much, call on Gourasana. He will talk to her.

- He is always here. He is on the team.

This helped me better my understanding of Gourasana (and The Host) as a Presence of the Source. Kalindi's body was the receptacle of their energy in the material world. This made sense to me. It was bizarre, yet I could grasp it.

I also kept it in the back of my mind that, if I needed help, I could call on Gourasana. He was in charge. I liked having Him on the team. It was comforting to know He was available to help if we needed Him.

I was becoming more comfortable being with KJG and Gourasana in the same body. I was aware that Gourasana had first been in a male body and now was in a female body. In a quiet moment, I saw I had a unique chance to ask something I had often wondered about.

I asked KJG, **"Is it better to be in a male body or a female body?"**

Gourasana was the first to speak. He said, "It is much preferable to be in a female body."

Hmmm, I thought. Then I asked, "Why is that?"

He replied, "Because **the sex drive in a male body** will just about drive you crazy."

Wow! This is what I had always thought. While I was still pondering His answer, Kalindi's soft voice added, "This is why it is so hard for men to break free. They have to overcome the sex drive without repression so they can transcend it."

I also better grasped why Kalindi seemed to know so much more about men. She got us. She understood our physicality and fears.

She was fascinated by our need to provide and the pride and power that fed the ego. Strong men flocked around Kalindi because they felt loved, held, and understood by her. She appreciated so many different kinds of men for bringing their masculine energy to God. She was a powerful space for powerful men.

For the next fourteen years, I worked on my sex drive. My mojo had many stages and phases – from **repression, torment and suffering** to control, choice and, finally, letting go. Starting in 2013 and for the next eighteen months, I lived in a kind of detached bliss, without the drive and craziness that I must have a woman and/or sex. All my sexual desire dissipated while remaining open. I was able to relate to women I found attractive in a calmer, more real way. By mid-2014, my sexual desire reawakened, without so much of the lust, torment, and emotional suffering.

Nowhere to Hide

I'd not talked to Marie in nearly a month. I wasn't so disturbed anymore. One day Kalindi came to me and said, "It would be fine for you to be in contact with Marie again."

While I was happy to hear that, I was not quick to take action. I liked the connection I was finding in myself. Marie no longer swirled around inside my head. I was not eager to risk that torment again. I talked with Karin and Ginny about it and decided to wait. For the next two weeks, I checked in with myself daily, until one day I felt I was ready to make the call.

I'd made a list of things I wanted to share with her. I jotted down several changes going on for me. I wanted to relate to her from a depth of love, with words of truth.

When she picked up the phone, I became cautious. We found our way into a new awareness. I even recognized some of my hooks and neediness. In the main, I felt I did well. It was wonderful to talk with her again. She let me be vulnerable and understood everything I said. I avoided any talk of the 'future.' I wasn't strong enough to go there yet. In the back of my mind, I was praying we'd be lovers, so I had some hope for that going on.

The next day, Kalindi asked about Marie. I told her that we had spoken and about our conversation. Kalindi sensed something. She asked Karin to call The Lady. I didn't know it, but Kalindi did – Marie was in San Diego with The Lady.

Kalindi and I were on a day bed in the front room of her house. Everyone was on speaker phone. Kalindi asked Marie to sit on The Lady's lap. Kalindi put her arms around me. With both us being held in pure love by our two Masters, Kalindi asked Marie and I to tell the truth with each other.

After a few minutes of our sharing with each other as best we could, Kalindi jumped in, "Marie, do you feel Marcus has let go all the way?" Marie replied, "I'm not sure, but I think something's still there."

Kalindi asked me.

I said, "All I know is that I love her and want her. If I'm holding on to something, I don't know what it is," I lied. I didn't want to say what I was hiding.

Kalindi said, "Well, you're holding on. We can all feel it, you included. So what is it?"

I didn't want to but in all that love my ego gave way and I spoke out loud the words I did not want to say, "If I get nothing else, I'm holding onto the hope that Marie and I can be together again sexually."

Kalindi said, "Yes, **hope.** That is usually the last thing that needs to be let go. Hope binds you to an imaginary future."

The Lady chimed in her assent.

Marie agreed, saying, "I'm sorry, Marcus."

There was silence on their end of the line as Kalindi and I waited.

Then, as if on cue, Marie said, "Marcus, you know we will never be together again sexually. You have to let that in." The words came like a body blow. This was exactly what I did not want to hear. Nor did I want to have to face the issues of my lust, jealousy, and ownership.

I didn't know if I could give lust up – it was EVERYTHING to me. My identity, who I thought I was, was very much tied into sexual escapades. I was all the time thinking about who I would have sex with if not Marie. "Would Ginny have sex with me? Would Karin? Would anyone?" I seriously thought I needed sex or I would die.

Now on the phone with Marie, I was experiencing her love of God eclipse any personal love she had for me.

Kalindi said, "OK, Marcus, now it begins. It's time to go even deeper. It's time to do the deeper work of getting free."

I was cornered. I had nowhere to hide except in meditation. It was like the only place I could hide was inside my own screaming. It was agony. It was all I could do to get through each day.

Dissolution of my ego identification ... surrendering the little self to the One ... anguish and desperation ... I could hardly tolerate it. This terrible slog through which I had to keep going was awful.[1]

God, how the sex drive ran me! The attachment felt so dense, like something beyond me that was virtually unbreakable. I identified with sex. It was the way I felt loved. I thought, *"If you loved me, you would have sex with me. Just have sex with me. That's all you have to do. That's all I want. Why not?"*

In the midst of my dire straits, deep in meditation, I heard from within, *"Don't worry, Marcus, you'll have everything with Kalindi."*

I thought, *"Yes, ultimately this is true, yet we'll never have the sexual connection I had with Marie."*

That night, I slept in Kalindi's walk-through closet in her bedroom. The next morning, when Kalindi awoke, she went to the bathroom and brushed her teeth. On her way back, she lay down next to me. We started kissing and then – Surprise! – we had the best and wildest sex we ever had. It was exactly what I needed. That inner voice was right – I can have everything with Kalindi. Once again she was giving me the love, trust, and faith I needed to keep going. ♪

---

1 This process continued for me virtually non-stop for the next three years.

CHAPTER 18

SURRENDER

*"All serious spiritual paths encompass extreme levels of
surrender and letting go of ego pursuits:
... those who live the life of
complete renunciation of falsehood, lies, hatred, anger,
greed and lust; and who, to accomplish all this,
do no lustful actions, do no harm to anyone,
do no backbiting, do not seek material possessions or power,
who accept no homage, neither covet honor
nor shun disgrace, and fear no one and nothing;
by those who rely wholly and solely on God,
and who love God purely for the sake of loving;
who believe in the lovers of God and
in the reality of Manifestation,
and yet do not expect any spiritual or material reward;
who do not let go the hand of Truth."*

Meher Baba

Kalindi's Prison of Love

We entered a time during which Kalindi held all of us tightly. She kept us on a disciplined schedule and focused lifestyle. My days began at 8am. It took two hours to prepare for Kalindi's emergence between 10 and 11am. Once she was awake, it was non-stop for the next 12 to 15 hours. Sometimes the days seemed like an endless marathon and at other times it was ecstasy. Either way, it was all about letting go. Anything could happen.

She might start out wanting to discuss ideas and information she had received while sleeping. Those ideas might turn into a new spiritual program and then we'd be discussing how it fit in with what was currently happening, and who were the right people, and what was the right timing.

Sometimes we just jumped into projects. She'd make changes to the inner workings of the organization – from sharpening communication processes to grievance policies. She was at her best when devising a caring and compassionate spiritual program for a disciple in need.

Kalindi guided the spiritual direction of the world-wide congregation. Many of her disciples received a monthly focus. She regularly met with The Lady and other spiritual leaders to discuss all aspects of the health and welfare of the Mission.

She communicated directly with organizational leaders to see if they were on track with the goals and direction she had given them. Kalindi looked for right consciousness and humility in her leaders. She was quick to point out illusions and correct behavior if there was any hierarchy, strife or separation going on.

It was difficult to keep any significant illusion from Kalindi. She was like a bloodhound. She constantly shifted the people through leadership positions to keep them from becoming identified with their position. Kalindi would literally spend hours on the phone helping leaders to stay connected to God's love as they ran the day-to-day business of the Mission.

During this time, whatever Kalindi was doing, Karin and I did it too. We went where she went, ate what she ate, and stayed at her side.

This was a major letting go for me. To stay in the house without going out, how could anyone do that? We were on Maui. I loved to swim and eat tacos, and go out at night for a drink and meet other people. But that was not happening ... not this time. This time I was giving up my will and surrendering to His Will, and that did not allow for beach time.

I dubbed our living space, "Kalindi's Prison of Love." I'd entered this space willingly, walked through the door, and then the door closed behind me. Now Kalindi showed me what God's prison was like versus the prison of my own thoughts, expectations, and insatiable desires; the prison of my mind's concepts, judgments, and beliefs; constantly hoping and trying to get some form of fun, satisfaction, recognition, pleasure, and relief from life, women, drugs, or whatever.

There were austerities in Kalindi's prison. She pointed out the need to control the sense pleasures. She knew I was run by my desires for food, sex, sleep, comfort, touch, and lots of free time. I'd dabbled in austerities like these before, but usually only one at a time. Now KJG was having me live without any of them. I felt like I was going to burst, even as I did my best to succeed.

In KJG's presence, I was enveloped in her love and light and it was easier to control my desire for sense gratification. I experienced a peace from being around her vibrational field. When I was in her presence, I experienced an ecstasy and a depth of love where I didn't need much. Simply opening myself to that love was more blissful than any sensual need.

I was satisfied to eat whatever food she did and keep her hours. I didn't need to chatter. After a while, even my need to feel special began to dissolve in the ocean of her love. Simply opening myself to that love was more blissful than any ego gratification.

I focused on her and my connection to her within me. All I did was be there and love her. Kalindi saw the change in me. She said, **"There's nothing missing with God.** He doesn't want you to suffer. He wants you to have what you need – with no lack and no excess, nothing more and nothing less. It is that simple."

And it was simple so long as I was with her. But when I was on my own, it was a different story. No matter how determined I was, I still longed for sex, the ocean, and free time. When temptation arose, it was hard to control. I'd be celibate for a few weeks and then I'd surrender to desire. I'd smuggle in chocolate to eat before I went to bed. If I ever went out on an errand by myself, I would stop at McDonald's near the ocean and eat a Big Mac and drink in the view before rushing back, knowing I'd be questioned if I took too long.

Here I was, two-and-a-half years after moving into Ames, willing to submit to Kalindi **in ways that changed all of me.** I'd already given up my material possessions and personal time. Somehow the act of letting go came more easily. Interestingly enough, nothing of importance ever went missing. I had everything I needed and more.

One of Gourasana's main teachings for those seeking to break the cycle of birth and death was to give up life as they would have it and live life as God would have it. For sure, I was getting a big dose of this one. Giving up my life as I would have it, day in and day out, was a most profound decision. I chose to surrender in obedience to God's Love.

Kalindi asked me to sleep on the floor outside her bedroom door. She said this made her feel safer energetically. I did it without comment. I didn't know if it was for her, for me, or for both of us. Questions of that sort didn't seem to matter anymore. Kalindi made requests that allowed us to act on our devotion and love for her and thereby move closer to God.

It was during this time that I decided to **give up any resistance** to Kalindi guiding every aspect of my life. As I did this, I shifted into a newfound peace and ease. Kalindi became my benevolent guide and the stress of my own decision-making disappeared. It was like I was on this endless retreat, during which all of my needs were met so that I could receive maximum benefit. Kalindi cared only for my highest good. It was a blessing to live in her will.

I was being transformed by doing what I was told. It was taking me deeper. I was becoming more present.

This level of surrender always takes me deeper. When I deviate from it, I suffer more. Surrender takes choice. It is an initial decision, as well as an ongoing moment-by-moment choice. Conscious surrender, conscious letting go, and total acceptance of what is, are some of the greatest tools I know.

I was beginning to give up needing to be somebody. My self-importance got no confirmation, and I was the only one who even noticed. After a while, my need to feel special began to dissolve in the ocean of her love.

Then it came to me. I was serving God's plan by submitting to Kalindi so that she might better help the world. Already she was directly and significantly helping thousands of people shift their consciousness towards love and God. What better place could I hope to be? What greater thing could anyone be part of. This conclusion added to the peace, simplicity, and purpose I was finding.

Running Away

Although it often seemed like not much was happening around KJG, a lot was going on for everyone. Most of what was happening was internal, and the tip of it was external. Even while going about simple daily chores, the changes beneath the surface felt like the movement of tectonic plates, or some form of neuro-logical rewiring, as K♪G reshaped us on subtle, cellular levels.

At this point, the care team was maxed out. K♪G had been working heavily with us. Our egos had been battered – just being near K♪G intensified the simplest life experience. She was so present, always right there in our conscious field. I had learned how to be aware of where she was all the time.

She was such a completely free being; loving us totally with the deepest compassion for our predicament. It literally felt absurd to hold onto our attachments when in company with this incredibly wise and wonderful being. And yet it was exhausting to constantly deal with our petty stuff. Kalindi would not back off. She used our attachments in daily situations to show us our own delusional systems.

Kalindi worked directly with our ego attachments, pushing on our tendency to make everything personal. She did this by making us responsible for the mistakes of others when they caused disturbance to her. It was around this issue that I broke.

After a couple of days of being blamed for what Ginny or Karin did wrong, I was livid. It happened around K♪G's breakfast. I'd been with her the night before. Before going to sleep, she told me what she wanted for breakfast. When I came out of her room, I saw Ginny in the kitchen. Ginny was responsible for K♪G's food, so I told her what she wanted for breakfast.

It was my job to remove Kalindi's breakfast tray. Before I went in, Ginny told me she had given Kalindi the wrong breakfast.

"What!" I said. "How could that happen?"

"I don't know," she replied. "I thought I made her what you told me." Ginny was obviously irritated. She had also been getting pushed and prodded by K♪G. All she could manage to say was, "You better go in there."

When I came into her room, Kalindi launched into a tirade, "What do I need to do to get what I ask for? Did you tell her what I wanted?" I nodded. "Why can't she follow instructions?" Her voice was so penetrating.[1]

I felt like I was being blamed for Ginny's mistake. I tried to explain that I had nothing to do with preparing the breakfast. That didn't matter to Kalindi; a disturbance was a disturbance and I was part of the problem.

When I left her room, I was fuming! I could not take anymore. I thought, "Why is KJG doing this?" I gave the tray to Ginny and told her, "I can't take it. I'm getting out of here!"

Ginny looked dumbfounded. She asked, "Really! You're leaving?"

I felt justified. I wasn't the first to feel this way. There had been others who'd been pushed to the brink and left when they felt too confronted.

I was freaking out. I couldn't make sense of things. My mind was whirling. I thought I was going crazy. I looked at Ginny and walked out the door.

Beyond My Mind

I drove to the top of a nearby hill and decided to call Marie. She could help me. Marie had been through this kind of thing. She had lived with Kalindi and Gourasana in the early days of this phenomenon. Somehow she had made it through. I told her everything that had transpired. After about a half hour of venting my complaints, fears, and negative feelings, I began to see what was going on.

KJG had pushed me to the brink of what I thought was sanity. This so-called sanity was made up of my mental models, belief systems, and world views. It was driven by my mind's desire to 'figure things out.' I needed to have the **world make sense.** I started to realize these were the walls of the fortress I had built to keep my ego safe.

I said to Marie, "If I don't let go of my mind, I may go insane." Marie understood. She asked me, "Which will you choose?" It no longer mattered that I thought I was my mind. Even if I didn't understand, I could still let it go, despite the fear that I might cease to exist or at least be unable to function.

Kalindi had prepared us for this. Not only would we continue to exist, she promised we would function at **an even higher level than before.** In fact, what 'ceases to exist' is what's false and illusory. I was not my mind. I was so much more. Kalindi taught that the more one's mind and material self come under control, the more I let go of 'who I think I am' and allow my True Being to manifest, the freer my life would become.

I thought for a brief moment and told her, "I have enough trust and faith. I know that **God lives beyond the mind** so I choose to let go."[2]

Having said that, I instinctively blinked and, feeling like a genie had granted a wish, **the walls of my prison disappeared.** The tightness in my head relaxed. My energy moved freely again. My mind and its thoughts stopped evaluating and blocking. Everything was flowing.

This began a new chapter for me. I began to practice letting go of 'rational' thought and to trust my heart and soul more. The more I let go, the less I felt pressured by my mind and ego. The taskmaster and warden were no longer so crucial to the next steps on my journey. Taming my mind reduced my suffering and torment. Now that I had let go, I could thank Marie and return to Kalindi, resolved to move forward in service, love, and transformation.

---

1   When I asked Kalindi about being angry with someone because of something they did or did not do, she said, "You can be angry, just don't throw them out of your heart." That was the difference between her anger and ours. She never for a moment was separate or had a flicker of forgetfulness of God. At the same time, she was fully human, flaws and all.

2   I knew it was essential to go beyond the mind to get free. It was the essence of every path to freedom – be it Zen, Taoism, Hinduism, Buddhism, Sufism, etc. I had read about it in books from Gurdjieff to Krishnamurti to Ramakrishna. I also knew it was not an easy task.

That was the only time I ran away from Kalindi. Others came and went but I stayed and stayed. Sometimes I'd fantasize about escaping: disappearing after a friend's wedding in Seattle; holing up on one of the other Hawaiian Islands; or finding oblivion some-place where no one knew me.

It was ridiculous. There weren't any chains or locks on my doors. *"Who was trying to escape? Was I to going to leave Love behind for the trappings of illusory world pleasures?"*

I couldn't go back to the very place I had broken free of. I knew where to find God. I was shedding my identification with my ego and its fears. I was surrendering to love.

From my soul's vantage point, I was coming Home. The boundaries of separation were fading. I was shifting from ego to soul. I loved Gourasana, I loved Kalindi, and I loved Marie.

What I hungered for was more intimacy. I desired to merge with Divine Love. I sought union in myself, with others, and with God. This desire had become like a snowball rolling downhill. The velocity of my transformation was increasing. I could not jump off. If I stayed it could be fatal to my ego. At the same time, the ride itself could be fatal too. It was like I was surfing waves that alternately deposited me on sand and then smashed me to pulp on the rocks.

Kalindi was as powerful as the ocean. I was being pummeled until I became part of the wave. This was the process I was in. Every part of me that was separate was being ground down and pulverized. There were moments when I looked around for a way back into the world, but what I saw only made me more desperate to continue my journey into Self-awareness and ever-increasing love with God.

Family

The next area I was to let go of was family. Uncle Lew was turning 80 years old and plans were afoot to get together in San Francisco. Everyone was going to be there – my father and stepmother, sisters and brother, Aunt and Uncle, cousins, nieces, and nephews. I felt this was a good time to see them all. Maybe I would bring Marie.

While I had become a disciple of Kalindi and chosen a serious spiritual path, several of my family members gave years of service and commitment to other transformational organizations. Uncle Lew and Aunt Francine had been on staff for est, which required long hours and a deep commitment to the work and transformation at hand. My stepmom, Judy, was currently a Seminar Leader for Landmark Education, so they understood transformation, sacrifice, and commitment to one's calling.

I had not seen much of my family in the past two years, though I had stayed in touch by phone. As understanding and supportive as they were, our lack of physical time together challenged their views. They generally believed that love required at least occasional proximity. Because of this, I felt our relationships were strained. I was looking forward to having time together as a way to heal any separation.

The days before my trip were difficult for Kalindi. She was going through major adjustments as more of Gourasana's energy came in. She was fragile and vulnerable. Before making plans, I'd checked with her and the team. All had signed off on my going. I booked the flight from Maui to San Francisco. It was set. It was okay. My family was thrilled I was coming.

The day before I was scheduled to leave, Kalindi and I were working on a project in her bedroom when she looked at me endearingly and said, "Marcus, I don't know if this is a good time for you to leave. I need you now."

My heart sank and my mind began racing. I was completely torn between care of my Master and obligations to my family.

Kalindi sat quietly as I went through several different scenarios in my head. *"I knew this would happen! I can't say I'm not coming, not now, not the night before!"* But then, *"Maybe it's okay not to go, maybe I'm just scared about disappointing them."*

I closed my eyes to calm myself. As soon as I did, I knew I couldn't leave Kalindi if she needed me. I opened my eyes, looked at her, and said, "Okay, I'll stay."

This was a major confrontation of my feeling of guilt and obligation with my family on my Dad's side. My Mom was more relaxed about these things. For me, family attachment was about doing what they wanted and not pissing them off. I also felt victimized, since they would make plans without asking me and then expect me to show up. I felt I had to acquiesce so as not to evoke their anger and judgment.[1]

I called my Dad to let him know I would not be joining them. I explained as best I could. He was upset, yet he understood and handled it quite well. On the other hand, my stepmom, Judy, was extremely angry with me. We talked for a long time. I felt judged by her. I had to say something. I gathered my strength and pushed back. Fortunately, after all of the transformative work she had done, Judy ultimately heard me and apologized. We wound up in a good place.

Uncle Lew was compassionate to the end. He told me he understood and thanked me for loving and caring for Kalindi so much. My other family members simply expressed their disappointment at not seeing me.

This was the next big step for me in letting go of guilt and obligation. The pull of family can be a mighty test. Even the avoidance of family can be an attachment. Over the years, we all managed to stay in touch and I did visit them whenever I could. When I did see them, it was challenging to stay in my depth and not fall back into my old, superficial ways.

While I was not there as often as they'd like, they came to know and appreciate my desire for personal, meaningful, one-on-one time when I was there. In the last years, they have seen and felt the changes in my heart and consciousness. They have accepted my path and we lovingly acknowledge our different world views. I am thankful and grateful for such an extraordinary family.

The Lady

In July of 1999, given all my heartbreak and depth of letting go, Kalindi suggested I connect more deeply with The Lady. The Lady embodies The Mother energy. I always feel tremendous love and compassion from her.

The Lady knew David and Carol six months before Gourasana came that first night in October of 1987. She was one of the Core and is Kalindi's first disciple. Originally known as Gayle, Gourasana referred to her as "The Lady."

She is an example of prayerful purity. She began leading The Intensive in 1993. Over the years she has created a substantial quantity of beautiful prayers and love poems to The Lord. No

The Lady 2012

matter her role, The Lady was universally loved within the Mission.

Most disciples staffed The Intensive month after month and became very close to The Lady in this way. My path had taken me straight to Kalindi, leaving me without much direct contact with The Lady.

I decided to write to The Lady about my days with Kalindi. I knew she loved hearing everything she could about Kalindi. Here are some excerpts from the letters I wrote to The Lady during this time:

Dear Lady,

I am "MG in a box" and K♪G is my love. I love being so intimate with her, she is so beautiful and extraordinary in every way.

Today Kalindi took us on a wild ride. She told us what she

---

1 A couple of years later I spoke to my dad about this. I asked him to keep inviting me, but with no expectation I would come. This way, if I did come it could be a pleasant surprise.

wanted to accomplish for the day. Then she said, "Please listen to me, so we can move through the day, His Way, all together, calmly and swiftly. Please do exactly what I say, when I say to do it."

So much happened during the day – cleaning, moving furniture and rearranging. It seemed like we moved mountains. At the end of the night she was pleased with what we accomplished.

Lady love, I am in ecstasy inside as I fulfill who I am for her – MG in a box! She finally told me what it meant – My Guy in a box. I am here for her totally in every way. The love I am sharing with her is overwhelming – sharing with her and sharing with Him – both Lord Gourasana and Sweet Kalindi!

Eternal Love and Gratitude,

Marcus (MG in a box)

Meanwhile, the team was maxed out. We'd been going at a high rate for months now, riding large waves and all the dips in between. Sometimes, after being smashed on shore, none of us were sure we would get up again.

Then, like the tide, Kalindi would come along, pick us up, and take us back out to sea where we'd be tossed and tumbled once more. Pain and pleasure came in equal measure. The pain was excruciating and sometimes exquisite, and the bliss of freedom was intoxicating.

The knowledge that we were breaking habits and leaving behind our limiting conditioning, made riding Kalindi's waves onto these newly-discovered shores all part of God's Freedom Ride on His Eternal Sea of Love.

Gourasana said, "You have got to know exactly how much you can take." He was talking about spiritual movement. Kalindi knew we were close to the edge. Although we were her committed saints who had dedicated our lives to her, she knew dedication was not enough once physical exhaustion took over.

Quote from The Lady,   8/15/97

"Ever longing in the Soul
Ever suffering in the body
Ever pain in the senses
Those who have utterly given
themselves to GOD, know
well what I mean"

The Lady spoke that & said it
makes her laugh because it is
so True -

Contemplate it when
you find your mind wandering

Youre on you way out of
this material world!

K♪G "Quote from The Lady"

We had been operating as caregivers, secretaries, communicators, cooks, and bottle washers. There was never enough time. We would meditate and let go and still we could not fully get free from our egos and the tendency to be victims filled with complaints, judgments, and blame. Kalindi would feel this in us. It was horrible for her. She was so wide-open and extremely sensitive.

Kalindi needed help, someone other than herself, to direct and guide the Team. She arranged a call for the team with The Lady. The Lady understood our situation. She had gone through the rigors of transformation with Gourasana. Her path had been one of purification by fire.

She spoke about being in the fire. She knew the only part of us that wouldn't be consumed by the flames is the part that is in God. Everything else must go. She reminded us that Ultimate Freedom stripped us of our attachments to everything, including our thoughts and senses. It all had to go.

She told us to keep in mind who we were helping and caring for. As she said this, I saw Kalindi in the True Realm of Love beckoning and pulling us towards her. Then The Lady spoke to the heart of the matter, and said, "Who are you in illusion to blame Kalindi for anything?"

This really struck me. I saw myself stuck here in the dark tar of illusion. I realized KJG was pulling me out with all her might. How could I judge and blame her for how she was saving me? I'd been acting like a spoiled child. As I took this in, I made a personal vow to never again blame or judge Kalindi for anything. That night I wrote to The Lady:

Beloved Lady,   *August 5, 1999*

It was a gift to hear you today. In the last week, my ego has been confronted beyond what I could have imagined and it has often felt intolerable. I feel there is nothing left to hang on to – no logic, reason or sense at all – only complete trust and faith in God and Kalindi. It has been hard to love her and trust her sometimes during all this. On the call with you, I saw my tendency to be a victim or resist the help I have asked her for. So now, I will let go and say goodbye to being a resisting victim – gone, goodbye, poof, no more.

Love, Marcus

Love God, Yourself, Others

The Lady was coming to Maui in a couple of weeks. Kalindi was hard at work preparing a rental house in the community near where we lived. She began by having the house emptied of furniture and professionally cleaned. Karin and I joined Kalindi when she went over to check out the job before having the furniture brought back in.

Kalindi looked at the floor, and said, "This is unacceptable."

The large white tiles may have been cleaned but there were still grey areas and sections stained yellow. Almost simultaneously, Karin and I said, "These tiles are old. This might be as good as it gets."

Kalindi was unwilling to accept this. She told us, "Please go and get the squeeze bottles of soft scrub with lemon fresh bleach. You'll find them in my house. I will work on each tile. I will clean them one at a time until they are pure white again."

When I returned with the equipment, Kalindi got down on her knees and started scrubbing the first tile, singing, "Lady/Lady, Lady/Lady, Lady/Lady, I love you, I love you Lady La, Lady La, Lady La." I thought, *"It is **so humbling to watch Kalindi** on her hands and knees scrubbing each tile so diligently."*

K♪G kept at it for fifteen minutes. By then, the tile was sparkling white. It looked brand-new. We were humbled and amazed. Only then did she ask if we wanted to help her. There were about 50 more tiles that needed cleaning. Of course we said, "Yes."

She told us, "If you pour your heart and devotion into each tile for The Lady, it certainly will come clean."

We worked together. After a few hours, Kalindi asked us to sit close to her on the floor. She sat in the middle, with Karin on her right and me on her left. She asked if we knew about Jesus' teaching to love God, love yourself, and love each other? We said Yes. Then she asked if we had experienced this love in what we were doing? We both confessed we had not.

K♪G took my hand and put it on her chest, and said, "Feel your love for me and God."

I did.

Then she took my hand and put it on my chest, and asked, "Can you feel your love for yourself?"

I said, "Yes."

Finally she took my hand and put it on Karin's thigh, and asked, "Can you feel the same love for Karin?"

"Yes."

In this moment, the love I felt for Karin, Kalindi, myself, and God was the same.

This was Kalindi's point. To fully affirm it, she repeated the same exercise with Karin. Karin also felt her love in the same all-encompassing way. With Kalindi infusing us, this was an amazingly powerful experience of the true nature of God's Love. As always, the trick now was to carry this love forward within ourselves.

Then K♪G said she was going to baptize us. Karin and I looked at each other, wondering what she meant. Kalindi took the soft scrub and poured some over our heads *in the name of the Father, the Son and the Holy Spirit* – another Holy mind tweak, heart wide-open, feeling love and the spirit of Jesus, with Soft Scrub now dripping down our necks.

We worked on the house for days until not only the tiles but every nook and corner was a masterpiece of cleanliness that sparkled with God-consciousness in every way – a fresh, bright, shiny, living space for The Lady.

When The Lady first entered that house, I was grateful to be there. Kalindi gave The Lady a tour. Karin and I trailed behind. When she got to her bedroom, I explained to The Lady how the alarm clock by her nightstand worked. It was the first time I'd ever personally spoken to The Lady. She listened carefully. When I was done she looked at me, and said, "Thank you." Those two words, the tone of her voice, the simplicity of her sound, made my heart melt.

Advanced Retreat

Kalindi decided to arrange seminars and retreats for her advanced disciples in September and October on Maui. To do this, she needed a site that could hold 20 to 30 people. She called Joe Sugarman.

Joe owned several properties around Maui. Kalindi wanted to use one or two of them for these upcoming events. There was a sweet history of Joe letting The Lady stay at his retreat house in Hana and we had used his Makena property a few months ago.

Joe's compound on the beach was huge. The main house was impressive and the grounds were luxurious. Behind the main house stood a two story, five-bedroom guest house with a huge living room and kitchen area.

Kalindi met with Joe alone. I waited outside. When she returned, Kalindi was very happy. She brought with her a piece of paper with dates on it. She reported that everything had been worked out. The Mission could use the guest house and his property in Makena for the weeks she wanted.

Having secured the sites, Kalindi started inviting many of the same disciples who were present several months before during the break-free scenes on Maui.

When the first twelve disciples arrived from California, Kalindi got them situated in their rooms and set up a schedule. Everyone followed her directions. All of us thoroughly enjoyed being with her.

As part of her team, Karin and I moved through each day at her side. We were part of everything that happened – the lectures, exercise, shopping, etc. while, at the same time, paying attention to her health, food, drinks, belongings, communications, and appointments. As usual, things started slowly and calmly. With each day more energy came in and the events became more intense.

After a week, Kalindi was asking for dead seriousness and 100% laser-beam focus and attention. She asked Karin and me to anticipate her needs and even what her next move would be. This was virtually impossible since she barely knew what she was going to do from one moment to the next. And yet, there we were, utterly focused and intent on serving.

It reached a point where she would sip water from her mug, stretch her arm out to the side, and expect us to be there taking the mug from her. If we weren't where we needed to be, she would drop the mug. Karin and I did well enough. We were tuned into her. All went well until one time when I was behind her chair and something distracted me as she put her arm out with the mug. I lunged for it but was too late; the mug fell and its contents spilled onto the floor.

Kalindi turned to the group, and said, "Do you see? He wasn't there. That lack of focus could have you miss your next opportunity with God."

This was humiliating for me. Then it got worse, as each person in the group started admonishing me for not taking care of Kalindi!

I'm sure they were trying to help, intending to ensure that Kalindi was not disturbed again. Nevertheless, as each person spoke, I grew more and more agitated.

In no time I was filled with angry thoughts. *"They have no idea what we've been through in the last six months. Yes, they could be proper disciples but only for a few weeks, then they go home again leaving us behind. We are here the whole time."*

When yet another person started in on what sounded like another sanctimonious rant, I snapped. **"How dare you! How dare any of you say anything?** Do you have any idea what we have been through?"

I threw my Mont Blanc pencil with such force that it stuck into the wall. Everyone, including Kalindi, was taken aback. The room fell silent. My outburst had shocked and perhaps humbled them. We were all waiting to see what KJG would do.

Before KJG did anything, another disciple started to admonish me. Before she got two words out of her mouth, KJG slowly stood up and with the full force and presence of Lord Gourasana, said, "BE QUIET!"

Then He spoke, "How dare any of you say anything to Marcus. He has stayed with me through my most difficult times. None of you can say that!"

Everyone was now cowed. In silence, they acknowledged her and bowed to the Presence that had come into the room. As I pulled my pencil out from the wall, I realized we had all learned a powerful lesson in humility and compassion. ♪

CHAPTER 19

FAITH

*"But how steep is the path that leads to this realization,
to this supreme experience.
We have to be progressively emptied,
to lose ourselves in every way and made into nothing,
to be filled with thy divine love,
with the purity of thy love, O' God!"*

Irina Tweedie

The Master's Grace

K♪G walked away from her chair and into her bedroom. Karin followed her. I stayed in the living room with Siegmar. My pencil had nearly hit him in the head. Everyone was talking about what had just happened. I had 'lost it,' and while it was an extreme lack of control, no one was hurt. I felt released and freed up. I had got something out of me, and already something new was coming in.

A few minutes later, Karin came out to ask me to come be with Kalindi. When I entered the room, Kalindi was sitting in her chair, looking sober. I knelt on the floor in front of her, with my head at her feet.

Kalindi gently tapped my head as a signal for me to lift my head up. As I did I was pulled to look in her eyes. Normally, I was reluctant to look into Kalindi's eyes. I never wanted to pull on her. This time was different. With a slight nod of her head, she let me know all was okay.

Kalindi La Gourasana 1998

I looked directly into her eyes, they were wide and vast. I was transported directly into a space that looked like the middle of the universe with God's eyes superimposed on it. Everything else had vanished.

From looking in her eyes, KJG had taken me into God's Realm. I was fully conscious and aware. I experienced this reality as a silent space in the midst of a vast infinite space. I was suddenly in the middle of 'The All That Is.' Nothing and Everything were there simultaneously. It was a taste of Eternity.

KJG closed her eyes. Like that, my consciousness returned to normal. I was kneeling in front of her. I was amazed. In Kalindi's eyes and the realm she inhabited, all my boundaries had dissolved. I tried to speak. Kalindi motioned with her finger to stay silent, knowing that speaking at that time would trivialize the moment.

KJG was a Spiritual Transmission Master. Having realized the great Spiritual State, she was capable of transmitting that state to her disciples if they were ready for it. Through God's Grace and my Master's effort, my soul's awakening was quickened.

Kalindi was always cultivating my spiritual heart and helping me to tame my mind. The transmissions and experiences she blessed me with were all for the purpose of validating and bringing forward my deeper self.

Furthermore, KJG strengthened my faith. She knew it was about faith. Experiences, even spiritual experiences, come and go. All of my experiences with Gourasana, with God, with Kalindi were just that, momentary experiences, yet the sum of them gave me more willingness to trust and keep going.

The next day, KJG was working with the group in the living room when she turned to me. I was standing under the ceiling fan when she said, "I have placed your energetic ego in the palm of your right hand."

I looked at the palm of my right hand and didn't see anything.

Then she said, "Close your hand into a fist and hold it tightly." Completely believing and trusting KJG, I closed my hand so tightly I was squinting. She told me she was helping to dissolve my ego while I held it in my hand. She told me to keep my hand closed tight and stay under the fan, to not move until she said it was okay. I would have stood under that fan forever if that would have completely dissolved my ego.

Yesterday I'd seen eternity. Now it no longer mattered that I didn't comprehend what she was doing. She was doing it for me. She was doing it for all of us. I trusted her completely. She was removing darkness for me. She was bringing me closer to the light.

Jesus, Kalindi and The Cross

A few days later, while Kalindi was imparting a consciousness teaching, I noticed I was feeling maxed out. What I'd taken in during the last few days was cooking inside. I felt full; I couldn't hear or take in anymore; just being in the room made me feel like I was going to blow up.

Kalindi looked at me and said, "Marcus, do you need to take a break?"

I said, "Yes, Kalindi."

She replied, "Why don't you grab your stuff and go stay at the retreat house for a few days."

I nodded and quickly left the room to pack my bag.

While packing, I reflected on the question I'd been contemplating for a week: *"Does God know everything? Does He know what I'm thinking or feeling all the time?"*

I was walking out the door when Kalindi called my name from the top of the stairs. I hesitated and thought, *"Oh no, she's changed her mind. She's not going to let me leave."*

She said, "Marcus, you know that God knows everything, don't you?"

Her words hit me like a truck. I couldn't believe it ... she was reading my thoughts. I was mad. I looked at her, turned away, and walked out the door.

I drove to a nice restaurant to eat, drink, and unwind. Then, for the first time in my life, I decided to go to a movie by myself.

I saw "The Sixth Sense" with Bruce Willis. It was a great movie. After it was over, I stopped in the bathroom on my way out.

I met a man in the bathroom and, for some reason, asked him what he'd seen. He said, "Stigmata. It's about the wounds of Christ." That struck me. I had to see for myself so I went in to the room where the film was playing again.

On the screen as I walked in was a woman receiving the 'Stigmata.' She was bleeding from her wrists and forehead. I was spellbound. At some point, I realized I was making the sign of the cross with my hand in front of my chest. I was confounded. I'd never done that before and yet the motion was so very natural.

When the movie ended, I got down on my knees. I felt so humbled and reverent. The theater emptied out and I forced myself to get up and leave. I wanted to prostrate myself in front of the Hawaiian theater employees, and then I thought better of it.

Something was happening to me. On the drive to the retreat site, I put on church music instead of the usual rock 'n' roll. I was feeling Jesus. It began as the energy of Jesus – love, compassion, and forgiveness – and then I felt Gourasana. I could feel the two of them together. Then I had the thought, *"I wonder if Kalindi knows I'm having this experience?"*

As I approached the retreat site, I was hoping somebody was up. I was feeling a bit shaky and wanted to talk with somebody. It was going on midnight and all the lights in the house were off, all except for one in the living room.

When I came in, another disciple got up from where he'd been sitting on the floor with his back against the wall. He approached me with one hand behind him. When he got close, he brought his hand forward and said, "Kalindi asked me to give you this." Inexplicably, in his hand **was a cross!**

I fell on the floor at his feet, weeping in disbelief, overwhelmed by God's Love and Omniscience.

After a few minutes, I asked, "How did this happen?"

He replied, "Kalindi called about an hour ago and asked if you were here. When I said No," she said, "OK, when he gets here, please, can you give him a cross?"

"I told her we didn't have a cross at the house," and then she said, "OK, go outside, find two twigs and tie them together with a blade of grass or a long reed. Give him that cross when he walks in the door."

"I have been waiting for you ever since."

This miraculous, inexplicable event greatly **increased my faith.** God was awakening me and strengthening my faith beyond anything I believed. This faith was so much greater than any belief

The Actual Cross

I could have had. **Faith is what was left as my beliefs were being blown to hell.**

It wasn't until the Seminar was over that Kalindi had me return to the guest house. When I arrived, she was in her bedroom putting on make-up. When I thanked her for the cross, she didn't react. So, I asked, "Why did you do that? Why did you call him to give me a cross?"

She looked at me matter-of-factly and said, "I am a child of Faith. I heard from within, *Call so-and-so to give Marcus a cross!* So I did."

She continued, "I regularly receive information from Gourasana. He gives me many different things to say and do. Often, I don't know why. But I act on it anyway. I do it with 100% trust and faith. That's why I call myself 'The Voice of the Incarnation.'"

It was then that I realized K♪G doesn't know everything, but God does. God told Kalindi what He needed her to know and she listened and acted. This was her personal example of how she moved and guided her disciples into more trust and faith.

Leaving Kalindi

It was September 1999. Most disciples had left the island. Our numbers were back to only her personal team. We moved over to the Makena retreat site. For a week or so things lightened up and the hours got filled with Kalindi's other favorite pursuit – shopping.

Kalindi loved the open-air market in Kihei. She'd go on buying sprees, stockpiling gifts for friends and disciples. Everyone at the market loved her. She used money as an exchange of energy and love. She was so unique in dress and manner … and then there was her entourage trailing behind.[1]

Those days and times were special for everyone involved. Kalindi had such presence. People adored her and she adored them. The atmosphere created made every day, mundane things like price, quantities available, and how best to gift wrap seem memorable.

---

1 Kalindi never went anywhere alone. We would not let her. Occasionally it would just be her and one other person, like Karin or me. Usually there were three or four of us with her. There was an energy surrounding all of us in public. Who's that woman with these people following her around and attending to her with such care and grace?

Most of what she bought we kept but sometimes I'd be sent back the next day with some doll, toy, or piece of jewelry. The merchants never argued. They'd been touched by Kalindi and I was welcomed as someone who served royalty. Some asked questions; they wanted to know who she was.

When I said, "She is a spiritual leader guiding her disciples on a path home to God." They would nod their heads in recognition and I would nod in agreement.

Kalindi was becoming well-known, especially on Maui. A lot of people didn't know who she was but that she was somebody was undeniable. She caused a stir when running errands or traveling on the island. Part of our job became keeping the scene around her as nonchalant as possible.

Kalindi wanted Maui to be a place where she retreated without fanfare or recognition. Whenever she felt her anonymity disturbed, she would start wearing hats, wigs, and sunglasses to disguise herself. She even created an alias for herself, Kaydee Robinson.

This became the name she used in public for her nail, hair, and waxing appointments. She asked me to supply her with some ID for this name. I got her a Maui residence card and a credit card from my account in the name Kaydee Robinson. She had a lot of fun with it and so did we.

The following week, K♪G called me into her room. As I entered her familiar space, I felt the now-welcoming feeling of Gourasana's energy. I kneeled in front of her. She was filled with His Presence. I sat quietly, eyes closed, head down. Then she said, "You are going back to San Diego to be on The Lady's team."

I was dumbfounded. I'd never thought of leaving Kalindi.

Cautiously, I raised my head to look at her. She was looking directly at me. She was serious. I was in shock.

Finally I said, "Yes, Kalindi, if that's what you want."

K♪G quickly said, "Gourasana wants it for you."

That struck my soul. I knew there was nothing else to be said. I left her, went outside, and noticed I was hardly breathing. I felt I'd been punched in the stomach.

The idea of not being with Kalindi was horrible and downright scary. Yet I was also relieved. I thought, *"Being at a distance would remove me from the constant bombardment of energy that emanates from Kalindi. Maybe this could be the right thing for me. Maybe this is why Gourasana is making this change for me."* After all, I had been on a nonstop ride with her for a year.

I also knew that K♪G had said people were leaving before. Mostly it never happened. This time I wanted it to. I needed time off. Maybe because Gourasana had spoken, it would be different now. I was thinking, *"Maybe Gourasana's sending me to The Lady out of love and care. He's giving me a break, making sure I don't go beyond my limit."*

Later that day, Karin told me she was also being sent back to Marin! She'd been going virtually nonstop for four years so, if anyone needed a break, it was her. *"This is very interesting,"* I thought. I was pondering what Gourasana was up to – a new line of thinking for me.

Although everything K♪G said didn't necessarily happen, she meant everything she said when she said it. Because of this, whatever she did say produced tremendous movement. When she changed her mind, it was because of the movement. Someone had let go. Some other piece of the puzzle had shifted. The energy was flowing in a new direction. A large portion of my personal movement took place during moments like these.

The next day, K♪G told Karin and I to take three weeks to turn our jobs over to Siegmar and Angel[1], then we would leave. The change became more real. Siegmar and Angel were wondering how they would handle all of it.

---

1 Angel, aka Ken Kettler, had known Gourasana personally while He was in the body and was part of Kalindi's personal team during this time.

I thought, *"Maybe it's my desire that's creating this situation. Maybe I'm the one in charge. Or is it more likely God's will and my true will are the same? Maybe my soul is working together with Gourasana?"*

Meanwhile, the team was wondering who would fill our spots.

Marcus and Karin

Marie and Karin

The next day, K♪G announced she had asked Marie to come over to replace Karin and me both. This sealed the deal. Marie was coming. My brain went haywire.

Marie and I had been talking on the phone. Our status with one another was unclear. Other than that disastrous night and morning in May, I hadn't seen her for seven months. My physical oasis had been nowhere to be found. Now she was coming and nothing else mattered.

I was overwhelmed by a flood of feeling. I wanted to crawl up inside of Marie and curl up in her womb to be loved and nurtured physically. After all, I was still desperately in love with her.

Marie arrived one week before I was scheduled to leave. I was with Kalindi at Makena, while Marie went directly to the other side of the island to get things set up for Kalindi's return to Napili.

As soon as I had a chance, I called Marie and asked if she wanted to drive around the island with me.

She said, "Yes."

I was thrilled! I picked her up and we drove along the North-west coast of Maui to Kahului and back. We had the whole day and stopped at different beaches and coves, sharing how it had been for each of us over the last months. It was glorious. Love and desire were thick in the air and I was hungry for sex. I could spend the night. I didn't have to return to Makena until morning.

However, when we got back to the condo, Marie set us up to sleep in different rooms. I was deeply disappointed.

I couldn't sleep. I went to Marie's room. She smiled and welcomed me into her bed. Hallelujah! I was happy and grateful. We were together. It was physical again. It had been a long road. I had truly let go of it ever happening as best I could. But when it did … wow! … reconnecting was heavenly.

We spent every moment of free time we had together. It was better than ever. As the days counted down to when I would leave for San Diego, I got seriously conflicted! The thought of leaving Marie was absolutely gut-wrenching but I knew I couldn't stay.

The night before I left, I sat with K♪G in her bedroom at Makena. She was calm, quiet, and vulnerable. She looked at me, and in a sad, sweet voice said, "Oh, Marcus, I wish you weren't going."

My first thought was, *"What? You're the one who told me to go!"* Then I remembered this was sweet Kalindi, not Gourasana. She didn't want her friend to leave. It was Gourasana dictating this change.

I told Kalindi I was sad too. We gazed into one another's eyes for a long time. I kissed her and without any words of good bye, left her bedroom.

On November 16, 1999, Karin and I flew together to San Francisco. Like me, she was conflicted. We were committed to K♪G and we both needed a break. During that flight, we swore on our hearts we would never leave Kalindi. Soon enough we were silent and I wrote my letter of departure to K♪G:

♪*Kalindi, Kalindi, Kalindi* ♪ *My sweet Kalindi,* ♪ *Kalindi La Gourasana*♪,

I already miss watching you as you move around this earth in complete faith, love and surrender. I miss your sweet smile and precious touch. You are everything to me, Kalindi.

Your love, your voice, your gaze, your eyes, your touch, your truth, your movement, your guidance, your direction, your care, your laugh, and your vulnerability. I put all of my heart and soul in your hands. My heart is your heart. I live and breathe only for you.

Kalindi, you have filled me with so much love and ecstasy. You have given and shown me how to lead a God-conscious existence. I will do all I can, to share all you have given me.

It is my desire to live at your feet always. It is my desire to always be with you. I am here with you, Kalindi. My time here is for you. I love you and only you. From you, all things come.

Please God, let me be with her! I live and breathe for her.

In endless love and gratitude, Marcus.

The Lady and San Diego

When I arrived in San Francisco, I went back to Ames. I'd been gone nine months and now I returned to pack my belongings, the sum of which fit into my Toyota Camry. That done, I drove to San Diego. I was to live in The Lady's 'team house' in Jamul, east of San Diego.

The Lady and her team operated 180° opposite from Kalindi. The Lady was meticulous; her schedule was consistent. She followed it exactly. She told her team what she was going to do and we prepared as required.

Kalindi, on the other hand, was always telling us what she was going to do and then doing something else. Change, uncertainty, and intensity were hallmarks of Kalindi. I had to constantly let go to keep up with her.

With The Lady, there was a different letting go that was more like a surrender into quiet intensity. The Lady was reserved. KJG was flamboyantly spontaneous and you never knew what she would do or say. She always wanted people close – even during her solitude.

The Lady lived alone, with her team nearby. She did not spend much time with her team. Member interactions with her were about logistics and work. I experienced a few of these, and saw The Lady was all business.

I liked the structured, predictable environment that existed around The Lady. After so much uninterrupted change, I enjoyed the stability and the way we followed her written procedures.

Everyone had a personal schedule. These were posted each day. There were times for exercise, breakfast, lunch, and dinner. We knew when to sleep and when to wake. There were even break times included. Each week, we had a specified day off. This was a new reality for me. I'd gone from almost never having a day off to having time to visit with my family.

The change was everywhere. For example, Kalindi kept the windows and blinds down most of the time, with the air-conditioning running 24/7. The Lady loved fresh air and sunlight. She turned on the AC only when the temperature went over 100 degrees. Even on the coldest nights, she keeps her bedroom window open and slept under a warm comforter.

Kalindi kept her lights on; The Lady preferred hers to be off. Kalindi loved to sample all kinds of food; The Lady was an ascetic with a simple diet and high consciousness about conserving energy and recycling. Kalindi had no interest in these things. Conceptually, I'd thought fully-awake Masters lived in similar manners – so much for that concept!

I was adjusting myself to my new situation when I received an unexpected phone call from Kalindi. I answered with a mixture of joy and trepidation.

K♪G asked how I was doing. I told her I was settling into my new situation. I wondered why she was calling, *"Was she going to take me off The Lady's Team?"*

Then she asked, "Marcus, do you want to stay in San Diego with The Lady or would you like to come back to Maui to be with Marie and I?"

Whoa! I was not prepared for this!

I became frantic, fraught with uncertainty. I hardly knew what to say. Being with Kalindi and Marie meant everything to me, but could I handle that movement and intensity? No, I could not. It was too much. I took a deep breath and said, "I need to stay here with The Lady, Kalindi."

There it was. I couldn't believe I had just said that.

Kalindi replied, "Okay, Marcus, I love you. We'll talk soon."

I put the phone down. I felt empty and despondent. I'd never really said No to K♪G before. I was so grateful for all she had given me but I could not go back to Maui. I just couldn't do it. The thought of it left me feeling dizzy. Meanwhile, being on The Lady's team felt like Sanity 101.

I looked at my schedule and it was time for pool cleaning at The Lady's house. I had to move on.

The Lady's focus never left The Intensive. Each month her life was pre-Intensive, Intensive, and post-Intensive. The Lady prepared meticulously when she was getting ready for an Intensive. She wrote down what she was going to say and continually upgraded her manual and prayers. She oversaw the huge staff of volunteers and held together all the spiritual and material aspects of the powerful, life changing Intensive.

My job was to take care of The Lady's personal logistics both inside and outside of The Intensive. I was in training and there was a lot for me to learn quickly.

On December 9, 1999, I wrote this letter to The Lady:

Dear Lady,

Lady, Lady, Lady – I love you! I want to help you so much. I want to care for your material existence here. Together with the rest of your team, I want all aspects of your life held so well that you only need to have the minimal amount of attention on it. So you may be everything that you are for the people of the world.

Thank you for your care with me, I feel it very much. I am well and happy about being here. I am blessed by Our Lord and Father with so many things and He gives me everything I need. Please let me help you, please let me give to you as much as I can. It is why I am here, it is my true joy and it is why Kalindi has sent me to you.

Giving is my salvation and true desire.

Love, Marcus

My integration into the team fit The Lady's profile to a T. I was immersed in logistics. It was all about training. I was given a schedule and attended orientations and management meetings. I had to be on my toes. It should have been wonderful, but it wasn't.

I was not able to fulfill my tasks very well. Kalindi had filled me to the brim. I could not take in any more. On top of that, I was in this ego death phase, barely able to perform basic functions. The suffering was so apparent to me now – both mine and others. You could relate it to someone who is seriously depressed. I wasn't depressed but I was going through so much fear and anxiety that I was a practical mess.

In order to make sense of things, I tried my best to patch some presentable aspect of who I thought I might still be. My mind swirled with anxiety. My body felt taut with the stress. I could not control the fear. My suffering greatly affected my performance.

Never Give Up

Kalindi had turned me inside out and I'd yet to come through the other side. I was letting go of who I thought I was and not yet standing strong in my True Self. My transformation was in a world of betwixt and between.

Denial and avoidance were melting away. I was acutely aware of my attachments and the suffering they caused. Yet, I was not willing or able to let them go. Letting go of my illusory self felt similar to the process people go through when physically dying. I was awash in fear, anger, and resentment. *"What is happening to me?"* and *"Can I bear this?"* were two of my common thoughts. I had to see if I could tolerate this seemingly unbearable process of ego dissolution.

Truth be told, I was barely making it through each day. I was so locked up in my fears and emotions that I couldn't even tell anyone what was going on inside of me. I was that trapped. I was too embarrassed. Strictly following my schedule and effectively carrying out my duties were beyond my capacities. I had trouble writing a memo to The Lady about what the air-conditioning technician said. I could barely help, when asked, with her Mom's finances. For a man who prided himself on his proficiency, this was humiliating. I was in a full-blown crisis of confidence.

These were the middle years of my path. They were the hardest and most tormenting. I was fully in the throes of my dark years of the soul where I had to make it through each day without enough light. I only had my desire for love, Home, trust and faith to hold onto.

Even so, I did my best to accept my situation, that is, when I wasn't in resistance. There were times when the intensity of my suffering simply overwhelmed my coping mechanisms. The Lady sensed all this and was gentle and kind with me.

One day, I was cleaning the pool at The Lady's house. I was being dutiful, performing my task, and inside feeling completely empty, alone and in despair. I started begging God, asking to feel love again, aching with need for Marie, desperate for any lightness of being to return.

Then The Lady walked by the pool. Without any words or even a glance shared, she said, "My dear Marcus, the path requires much tolerance and perseverance along the way. The most important thing is to never give up!" She walked on, as quietly as she had come. It was as if she knew my suffering personally.

I was alone again and yet my heart felt uplifted. I held onto what she said. Tolerance, perseverance, and **never ever give up!** *"Yes, that's it, I thought. I can do that."* Indeed, her words rang true then, and during so many other difficult times along my path.

I began to feel that KJG knew this was where I was supposed to be spiritually. I had developed a lot of spiritual fiber during my time with her. Perhaps she had sent me to The Lady for protection and to receive some of the calming grace for which she is known. This led me to believe that while I was there to serve, I was the one truly receiving the benefit.

My first Intensive with The Lady was Dec. 1999. Towards the end of that Intensive, I wrote to The Lady:

It helps so much to feel the constant and unconditional love I receive from you. It is not easy for me now, as I stumble through the many layers of hurt, pain and fear. Nonetheless, shutting down or holding back is no longer an option for me. I continually pray for Him to use me for His Purposes and Divine plan.

It is a privilege for me to be with you and the people in this Intensive. I am learning so much from all of them. I was dancing in my heart as you spoke of Kalindi and the beings of light dancing in the room. Thank you for bringing Kalindi's presence so strongly into this Intensive. My soul cries out for her continually and tears stream down my cheeks from your invocation of her.

Also Lady, your words of sweet love, devotion and surrender for Our Lord touch me so deeply. The way that you speak from the deepest part of your soul ignites my passion and desire for Him even more.

Eternal Love,

Marcus

Despite my own suffering, helping in The Intensive was wonderful for me. It was a chance to get out of myself and focus on The Lady and the participants. The combination of prayer and service quieted me down. Feeling the participants open to the light greatly inspired me.

After The Intensive, I wrote a critical letter to Kalindi that altered the course of my next future:

Sweet Kalindi,

I pray you are well. I pray that you have what you need. Leaving your physical presence has not been easy for me. I feel like I have been shot out of a rocket ship, orbited the solar system and returned to earth, having to relearn how to function here with new awareness.

I often think I made a mistake when you asked me to return and I declined. I should be by your side. You are so deep inside of me. You have always pointed me towards God, Father, Lord. There is nowhere else to go.

I have been with The Lady personally three times now. Each time I experience her incredible purity and depth of love for God. When I am with her, I see how much purity and consciousness I have yet to acquire. When I clean the pool for her, it reminds me of scrubbing the tile floor at number 44 when you baptized us with soft scrub.

From day one, I have felt nothing but trust with you and a knowing beyond anything of this place, that you love me uncondi-

*tionally. I can never thank you enough for this gift. It is what con-
tinually frees me from the illusion, which would have me believe
otherwise. No, God loves me, Kalindi loves me and I love myself.*

*I do not know how I endure being away from you. Every
day I feel you and every day I want to reach out to you. My heart
is filled with you, my memories of you are endless and our future
goes on forever.*

MG in a box,

Your Marcus[1]

Master Calling

A few days Later, I received a call from Kalindi. She asked
me again if I wanted to come back to Maui and be with her and
Marie. My heart smiled and my soul rose up. Now, I was ready. I
immediately said, "Yes."

Kalindi replied, "I'm pleased." Then she added, "Take the
time needed to inform The Lady and her team. Turn over your
jobs and functions responsibly."

I thanked her, and said I would get there ASAP.

This was the beginning of a new dynamic. Although we were
no longer lovers, she wanted me to stay connected and always be
on call. When she needed me, I would come, no questions asked.
And I did. For the remainder of her life (the next 10 years), Kalindi
frequently called on me and I always said Yes.

I returned to Maui on December 30, 1999, one day before
the new millennium. From first breath, I felt I was home. This was
where I belonged.

Without unpacking, and at her request, I went to see Kalindi.
When I arrived, she was sitting in her chair in the back bedroom of
the Kahana condo. I knelt in front of her, waiting for her to speak.

---

1   MG in a box when first revealed to me by Kalindi stood for "My Guy in a Box."
Later on during the last Makena break free scene, Kalindi said it stood for "Marcus of
Gourasana."

Without hesitation, K♪G said, "Marcus, I want to let you know about the current landscape here." I nodded. She continued, "Your time with me will be temporary. Soon, you and Marie will return to San Diego to be on The Lady's Team."

This was unexpected. In one sentence, my dream of being with Kalindi was shattered and my desire to be with Marie was fulfilled. Before I had a chance to process it, she continued, "Also, I am now intimate with Christoph."

I already knew this, yet it was important for Kalindi to tell me herself. Christoph was a disciple who'd been on The Lady's Team for several years. Christoph was a wonderful man – open, intelligent, and a world-class cook. He had a confident, calming presence, and would be an excellent companion.

Kalindi asked Christoph to join us. The two of us knelt at her feet. She said, "Please be in harmony. Do not compete with one another. Let go of your male egos."

In Kalindi's presence, this was easy for me to do. Whereas normally I experienced myself as separate, being in K♪G's presence dissolved such boundaries. With her I experienced our beings as shared. K♪G always brought me as far as I could go into that state – merging my consciousness into her love, soothing me when I held back out of fear, dissolving this fear and guiding me to go ever deeper.

Giving up positions and ego-based bickering became surrendering to a higher purpose. It was clear that supporting Kalindi was more important than petty differences. I opened my eyes and looked at Christoph. We looked at each other and then turned and nodded our heads to Kalindi.

Then Kalindi said, "You can both love and give to me in the unique ways you do. Are you willing to do that?"

Without hesitation, we both nodded our heads and said, "Yes, Kalindi."

So that was it. From that moment on, I easily fell right into that mode of friendship and partnership with Christoph for the three years he was with Kalindi.

Later that night, I mentioned to Marie my disappointment that I would be leaving Kalindi again. I said, "I feel at home with Kalindi and being on her team. She is my spiritual sustenance. I love being with her." Marie silently nodded with compassion in her eyes. She knew there were no words to console or soothe my soul.

Marie and I had stayed in touch and she was eagerly waiting for me. When I arrived, we took up right from where we left off in November. It was a breath of fresh air for me to be physically with Marie. I was still completely in love with her; she was 'The One.' She was everything I wanted in a woman. Her loving presence nurtured me, and temporarily filled the hole and eased the pain inside.

The next day, I was thunderstruck when Marie shared with me that, while I was gone, she had been sharing herself with Siegmar. Siegmar and Karin were no longer together, and now Siegmar and Marie had a sexual connection. This was extremely painful to me. Marie promised that she would stop. But the damage was done.

My ego came into play. I was hurt and threatened and consumed with jealousy, regardless of the fact that I also had dates while in San Diego. I became insecure and kept a close watch on her, particularly when Siegmar was around. Despite my jealousy, Marie didn't judge me or make me wrong.

The next month was some of our sweetest and deepest time together as Marie expressed in her card to me:

"I love all of you Marcus, every part, piece and shred. I am happy you love me and are my dear, dear friend and lover. It's true, it's all of His perfection taking place. The realm of the impossible is becoming possible because of His love for us and our desire for Him."

"I'm so grateful to be part of your life at this most precious time as K♪G takes you into the love of God and your True Self. We have gloriously big jobs to ensure she can do her job and that we take care of her. How absolutely, wonderfully, phenomenal! Amazing Grace… How sweet it is!"

My mind and my heart soaked up Marie's words and her sweet love. Still, in my illusory state of being unlovable, sex was what provided the assurance I needed. My illusory thinking was, "If she is having sex with me, she must love me" or "As long as we're having sex, I'm OK." Sex was the only relief, although temporary, to my 'she could leave me at any time' beliefs.

Given my fear and uncertainty, I needed the sex with her to feel wanted. I felt safe and alive during our sex. I loved being in bed with her and wanted to stay there all the time. My need for love and safety fueled my sexual desire. Love and sex were wired up inside of me as the same thing. My bottomless pit of unworthiness made my sexual desire as insatiable as my fears were endless.

New Millennium

That night was New Year's Eve. We were at K♪G's working on projects while the Millennium celebrations played on TV in the background. I thought my time with K♪G the night before had gone well, however I was mistaken.

K♪G told me that after our initial talk together with Christoph, I had lost my depth and was too casual with her. It was never OK to be casual around Kalindi and she gave me the following guidance:

Help for My Consciousness and Being with The Lady,
Dec. 31, 1999:

- Your being of illusion came in when we were laughing
together. You got too excited and left your depth.
Even now you are spacing out.

- You get lax around Kalindi. You will not be able to be like this
around The Lady. She will not tolerate it.

- You must address this part of your consciousness and gain
awareness. Do not become discouraged. It is far out what is
happening with you – your surrender and determination.
So do not lose that.

- Please let what I am saying penetrate you. It is now up
to your desire. Start a new diary and write down what is
happening with you now.

Her guidance was right on. My consciousness had slipped
and I allowed myself to be too casual around her. I had to shape
up. I prayed, "Please God, help me to stay in humble surrender,
to always remember who Kalindi is and why I am here." ♪

CHAPTER 20

DEVOTION

*"True happiness will only come from true awareness.
Again, it is where you focus your attention. If you focus it on
becoming happy, then you are missing the point.
You must focus it on becoming aware, and do whatever is
necessary to become aware. And sometimes what you need
to do will be very difficult, and for many, shocking,
but you must be brave and support each other."*

Gourasana

*"It is hard work to remain in contact with your True Self.
That's why daily prayer is important. Somehow we have
to reestablish our foundational ground over and over because
we lose it every day. We get caught up in letters, emails,
what people want, who I need to be, the little dance I have to
do today for this person or that person. It may be necessary,
but if you are living in that world, that revolving hall of mirrors,
you get so enchanted with these reflections of what
everybody thinks you are or wants you to be that you forget
or never discover who you really are before you did anything
right or anything wrong, before you had your name,
your reputation, your education, your family, your culture."*

Robert Rohr

Open Heart

As February came around, Marie and I returned to San Diego. We lived together in a sweet room at The Lady's house. I was so delighted being together with Marie in this situation. I enjoyed being together in service for The Lady. I appreciated that The Lady felt comfortable enough to let us live in her home.[1]

Of course, it was not all a bowl of cherries with Marie and I; there were also some thorns on the rose. As Kalindi would say, "This world is sweet rice with sand mixed in."

I also suffered. I was fully bound by the duality of love and attachment. I was acutely needy. I was in fear of being shut out and pushed away. At any time, Kalindi, The Lady or Marie might once again suggest that we halt the relationship.

The attachment to my unworthiness kept me in terror and anxiety. It also led me to hide what I felt from others. I was still so identified with my ego self that I could not admit to the panic and distress.

A close friend who sensed what was happening, begged me to get help. There had to be someone in the Mission with whom I felt safe. I trusted no one, and so I remained this miserable, polluted, wretched being, walled away underground, and inside my man-made cocoon of suffering.

I was caught in illusory love. Kalindi knew. She had warned me about this trap. Nothing had worked so this time she gave both of us the chance to go through it together. Normally, it does not best serve anyone to be oppressed by such fear, attachment, and neediness. Usually people fall in love, become attached in both real and deceptive ways, and then hold on to the wealth and poverty of the relationship.

At the same time, I worried that my neediness and attachment would smother Marie, and that I would be the one who pushed

---

1   The Lady would occasionally have 1 or 2 of her caregivers live with her. At this time, a couple living with her and her caregiver was unusual.

her away. It was difficult to give her the independence and space she required to lead her own life. I wanted her attention, love and body oftentimes more than she could give.

Sometime around Valentine's Day, Marie wrote to me about my fear and neediness:

… I want you to take this as help, love and encouragement for our friendship, commitment, desire and support for each other. I am the way I am with you sometimes because your neediness is up (I don't expect it to be gone). I feel you pulling on me and I feel your fear in our space.

I feel weird kissing you at times, when I feel it's coming from need rather than pleasure, enjoyment or a sharing of our love. I have to watch my own fear or judgment about this. I'm not leaving our relationship, I just want to keep it as simple as possible. I don't want to build a more complicated situation than what is truly there and genuine. I know you are a man who desires and wants the truth.

I need to address it with you as soon as I feel your neediness or ego, just so you don't feel me go in the other direction and don't know why. I am trying to get to this place in myself as you know.

I heard her. I realized I had a history of being this way. In previous relationships I stayed separate, protecting my heart by remaining guarded and shut down. This choice kept me in denial and helped me to avoid emotions that invariably led to shame, guilt, and neediness. Yes, I'd opened up somewhat with Lauren, yet in the main I preferred being withdrawn.

With all the emotional release and heart-opening work I'd done, I was now able to share my heart more fully. Unfortunately, a byproduct of my practice was the emergence of this wellspring of neediness that lurked inside my newly-found heart.

My higher intelligence knew that achieving Ultimate Freedom necessitated facing my neediness all the way. In my mind, it seemed so deeply ingrained that significant change was impossible. I knew I wanted a woman as a mate and companion with whom to share my spiritual path but, when I got close to her, Marie became my path. I knew my neediness left me unavailable to God, and God was my true priority. *How could I open my heart without losing myself?*

Sensing my suffering, The Lady did what she could to comfort me. She gave me a beautiful, bejeweled journal with the following inscription inside:

My dear Marcus,

This book belongs to passion's love for Him and only Him; For your treasured and sometimes anguished heart's communion with Him; For your soul to be released free and finally Home through the doorway of Death; Because you Never Gave Up as you traveled the transformational path of life through illusory obstacles desiring to find only Him; To live fully your final lifetime surrendering and serving only Him.

God is good, God is merciful, God reveals Himself.

Thy Will and Love,

The Lady ♪

I was so grateful and moved to feel The Lady's love and care for me from the highest. Her compassion soothed me and her words lifted me higher. Just knowing that she knew and cared for me filled me with the strength and desire to keep going.

Retreat 2000

It was the beginning of March and the annual retreat was coming up. As usual, Kalindi was filling with an influx of power and energy that she would transmit at the Retreat. I heard from Karin (she had returned to Maui when Marie and I left) that the energy was indeed ramping up. I wanted to send love and comfort to Kalindi, so I wrote her this letter:

Beloved Kalindi La Gourasana,

I feel you inside of me more every day. I am grateful to you for taking me towards His Love. I am in The Intensive with The Lady, helping her and the team as I can. I relish hearing the pure truth that comes from The Lady. I am able to hear her now more than ever. I am grateful for this time to go deep into my heart, longing and desire to be with the Lord.

My current prayer is for more humility, purity and surrender. I am feeling Lord Jesus very much as my teacher and friend. I feel him right with me, always holding me in his heart, giving me courage and strength to live in the truth.

Kalindi, I am here for you, in humility, prayer and deep reverence for who you are. Tears roll down my cheeks in love and devotion for you.

I thank you, I love you.

Always yours, Marcus

Kalindi returned to San Diego a week before the Retreat started. This was to be a full-on Kalindi event – she was going to attend every day. There were massive preparations. Four hundred people would be coming. There was much to coordinate with all the activities Kalindi had planned.

A few days before the Retreat began, and much to my surprise, Kalindi called to ask if I wanted to serve as her team manager. She said, "Marcus, I feel you are the one to make sure everything runs smoothly around me." And then she added, "There can be no disturbance around Kalindi. You will have three chances to succeed. If you fall short, you will crash, and immediately be taken off supported staff."

That hit me right between the eyes. I thought, *"K♪G wants to get my attention; she's never threatened me with consequences before."*

Kalindi inhabited a space filled with moving parts. She was constantly changing everything. To manage her team was one of the most difficult positions in the entire organization. Practically speaking, disturbances were inevitable. I would have to be at the top of my game. Given my present state, I could so easily fail.

Lastly, Kalindi added, like a slap in the face, "If you do not succeed, you can keep going with your spiritual work, but will no longer be supported financially. You will have to get a job. Either way she said, Never Give Up."

"Do you want to do this?" I could barely breathe and already she was asking for an answer.

Without hesitation, I said, "Yes, yes, yes." In my heart of hearts, I knew I'd have said or done anything to return to Kalindi. I was being taken back and I was truly grateful.

"All right, Marcus," she said and then added, "I am also bringing Marie back onto my team."

I was overjoyed! In that moment, I'd forgotten Marie (a miracle in itself). Now God and Kalindi were giving me another chance to have it all. I was determined to give it my best shot.

The interim team manager contacted me to attend a meeting with Kalindi the next day. She talked about how critical this position was and that KJG was serious about me having three chances. We discussed my responsibilities. Though frightened and unsure, I was eager to take it all in. I assured her that I would do my best (without touching on the fear and anxiety I had about it).

When I arrived at KJG's house, I thought I'd gotten the time wrong. The meeting had already begun. Kalindi was going over the different positions and responsibilities.

As soon as I sat down, Kalindi looked at me and said, "Marcus, it hurt me when you left." Whoa! I was stunned. What was she referencing? She must have seen my look of confusion because she added, "Once you got together with Marie, in your heart, you left me." With that, Kalindi turned her attention back to the meeting.

My heart sank. I thought, *"Oh my God, I hurt Kalindi"* and, *"Did I really leave her?"* I must have done but I didn't realize it at the time. That was the level of unconsciousness I lived in then, and now I knew it was true.

Bad to the Bone

Kalindi was preparing full-force for the Retreat. Marie or Ginny were constantly with her, looking out for her well-being. I loved being back on Kalindi's team. This time I didn't stay in the house with her or Marie; instead, I had a room in the team house about twenty minutes away.

One night, I came over around 2am to be with Marie. My plan had been to leave before Kalindi was up, usually sometime before 11. I snuck in, not knowing if it was all right. After sex, we fell asleep in her single bed and then around 6am, Kalindi appeared at the door.

Marie and I both jumped up. I was sure Kalindi was upset with me. As usual, she was in a whole other place. Instead she said, "Oh Marcus, good you're here. Let's get going, we have a lot to accomplish today."

No one could predict how Kalindi would be. She was letting go all the time, changing constantly and always new. While challenging, her let-go presence and newly realized states were refreshing, freeing, and enlivening.

Our annual Retreats have always been considered the highlight event of the year. They were always special. There was usually a large and diverse crowd, ranging from those who had just done The Intensive to others, like Marie, who'd been on the path since the beginning. The purpose of the Retreat was to increase everyone's connection to God. New teachings and programs were introduced. It was the one annual event that would bring everyone together with both Kalindi and The Lady.

The Retreat was in its third day before I was able to participate in ways other than as staff. Kalindi was delivering a new

328

teaching about spiritual life and exercise. She emphasized the importance of exercise to a healthy spiritual life.[1]

Then Kalindi shifted into a different mode. She raised her arms over her head and began to wave them back and forth, transmitting a rhythmic wave of joyful, enlivening energy that exhilarated all those in the room. I loved it when she did this. Hundreds of my brothers and sisters in God were grooving in her energy.

The Lady was on stage with Kalindi. As I looked at them, my perception shifted. Suddenly it seemed like they were in a different dimension – one with a higher vibration. As I focused my perception, an ecstatic wave of love seemed to permeate the room and I could barely see the stage any longer. KJG and The Lady appeared to be floating above the ground. I shook my head attempting to clarify what I was seeing ... all to no avail.

Was I hallucinating? Had some kind of spiritual eye opened? I aligned myself to this energetic vision and the higher vibration that came with it. I sensed I'd entered God's Kingdom of Lords, Angels, and Saints. I remained in this state for several minutes and then, in the blink an eye, everything returned to normal and Kalindi was again sitting in her chair.

On the break, I had time to journal about my experience. I was elated and ready for more. Then someone asked me to come to a room off to the side of the main hall. KJG was already there with a group of 15 to 20 disciples.

KJG was handing out gifts of appreciation. She had one for me. When she looked at me, she sensed something. Instead of beckoning me to come forward to receive my gift, she said, "Marcus, sing your song for us!"

Kalindi had found out that when I let go while singing *Bad to the Bone*,[2] my True Self would slip out. Often, when Kalindi asked me

---

1 Reasons to exercise from Kalindi: 1) To live healthier, 2) To prepare yourself for deeper spiritual transformation, and 3) To have enough strength and endurance to make it through what you have to make it through – mentally, physically, and spiritually.

2 The music I led the men with during my first True Self experience, see chapter 16. George Thorogood and the Delaware Destroyers, *Bad to the Bone*, EMI, 1981

to do this with other people around, I'd freeze up, making it a painful and disappointing episode for everyone. This time, I just let loose and belted it out freely and strongly. I felt energized. Kalindi was smiling. She waved me towards her. I received my gift – two Chinese singing balls inside a beautiful felt box. I was grateful and, at the same time, knew that something was brewing deep inside of me.

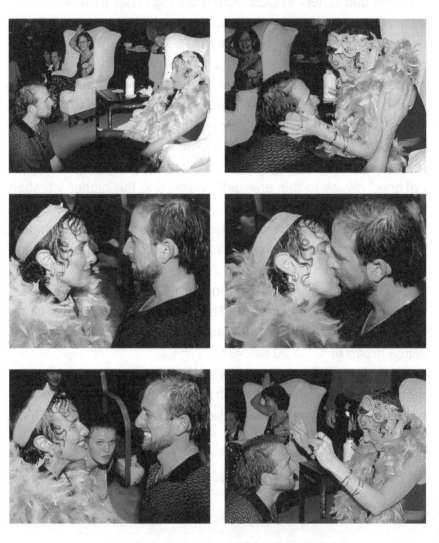

Kalindi La Gourasana and Marcus Retreat 2000

Kalindi Loves My True Self

Several different times in the past, Kalindi had mentioned a premonition she'd had – she was going to kiss a male disciple in front of the congregation. It would last several minutes. She had said it wouldn't be a romantic kiss, but a spiritual kiss between her and the disciple's True Self.

She wondered out loud who it would be. I hoped it would be me. Again, as if reading my mind, she looked at me and said, "But it won't be you, Marcus. You're not the one." *"Okay,"* I thought, *"I'm not the one."* And that was the end of that.

During the next part of the Retreat, Kalindi and The Lady sat in their chairs in the rear of the room. Kalindi spoke personally with different people. Everyone was tuned into her every move. Once again, without warning, she called me in front of her and asked me to sing my song. There were a couple hundred people in the room this time, so I felt more pressure.

I started strong and this time, in the middle of the second verse, my True Self emerged! Here he was – this powerful, strong, open, loving being with no fear or agenda. It was like when Gourasana entered me. I felt taken over, except this time it was all of me. This whole being felt so different from my illusory ego self. I loved him.

As I adjusted to the frequency of my True Self, I directed my gaze at KJG. She was staring at me with a startled look on her face. I kneeled in front of her and looked directly into her eyes. The energy was pouring through me in a way it never had before. The Lady was joyous. She recognized what was happening.

Kalindi came out of her chair onto the floor in front of me. She gazed deeply into my eyes. I returned her gaze without fear or hesitation. Pure love was exchanged; I felt merged into her. We were the same. I was experiencing True Realm love with her. I was swirling in this love and it was swirling in me. The love wrapped around us, and we wrapped around it, while simultaneously expanding in every direction.

Kalindi leaned in to kiss me. Ever so softly, I kissed her back. When our lips touched, I saw pillows of colored clouds and felt I was embraced in this endless fulfillment. We kissed like this for several minutes. Hundreds of people were watching. I was aware of it, and yet it had no impact on me.

Gently Kalindi drew back. As we opened our eyes and saw each other, we broke into euphoric smiles. Kalindi started snapping her fingers and energetically playing with me to keep my True Self engaged.

As we completed our rapturous experience together, I was on cloud nine. As I walked away, I felt like a different person. I lay down somewhere close, near a side wall, and cried. I cried from my depth. How joyous and full Divine Love is. Inside my True Self, I found both God and Love and nothing else. There was no separation. They were not two things. It was all one. God, Love, Ultimate Truth – it was the same and it was who I am.

After a while, I sat up and opened my eyes. I observed the room from a detached point-of-view. There was a lot of activity but I didn't care one way or the other until I felt my True Self fading and my material self re-emerging. I knew I couldn't hold onto my experience. The physical world was becoming dominant again. I began to hear sounds and sense movement. It saddened me to lose my connection and yet I was uplifted.

I closed my eyes. One year had passed since my first True Self experience. Now I'd experienced it a second time. I knew what it felt like. I was turned on and encouraged even as I realized that my True Self can only be present to the extent I have let go of my false self.

Over the years of my practice, I'd seen how my false self was manufactured from my conditioning, ego-development, and personal identification with the roles I'd created in my life: my identities, morals, beliefs, culture, status, and so on.[1]

False doesn't equate with bad. I still needed my ego-self to function in the world. False simply meant that this aspect of my personality was external, passing, and impermanent. It was a temporary persona I had created.

On the other hand, I did not create my True Self. It did not develop from my upbringing, societal choices or experiences. It was nothing I had manufactured. It was my soul and inmost, essential being. It had existed before me and would continue way after 'Marcus' was gone.

My work was to keep emptying out this vessel I inhabited – emptying out not only the negative aspects (fears, judgments, illusions, hatred, anger, laziness, righteousness, etc.) but also any and all attachment I'd created to the 'positive' aspects of my personality. All ego manifestations needed to fall away for me to breathe and flourish as my True Self.

I knew I was on track. I reveled in how God used Kalindi to give me what I needed. Truly, she came to serve others. It was through her that I experienced what I needed in order to keep going through the hard times and then receive such blessings as my True Self awakening.

A few weeks later, Kalindi told me more about the True Self. She said, "Your True Self has never lived here before. It is best served by simplicity and clarity. It cannot abide chaos and disorder. Therefore, a calm, simple, and orderly existence is most conducive. This is why it is best to live simply while minimizing confusion and chaos."

"The True Self carries a feeling of freedom without limitation. The True Self requires an awakened consciousness and grounded material existence. The material self must learn to function in ways that allow the True Self to be expressed. It takes humility for this

---

1 "This means that this concocted False Self, this manufactured identity that is who we think we are, has to go. Until that False Self dies, you don't really know who you are. Your True Self knows spiritual things, and knows God. So if you don't awaken it, you really don't know God. You can be religious, but you don't encounter God at any depth. It's just spinning the necessary prayer wheels, whatever your tradition tells you is the appropriate prayer wheel. It isn't really transformative." Robert Rohr, *Immortal Diamond: The Search for Our True Self,* 2013.

to occur. The True Self cannot control how we spend our lives. Only the material controls that role."

She looked at me and I looked at her. We fell into silence.

I remembered how, after first connecting to my True Self, I felt very light and slightly out of control. I remembered feeling like driving 100 mph and steering my car off a cliff into the ocean. It seemed like it didn't matter. I was flying. It was just for fun.

Now, as always, Kalindi guided me to obey the laws of the land. She said, "Never knowingly harm yourself. Always be respectful and caring of others."

In the years to come, Kalindi assisted me several more times to tap into my True Self, albeit in less dramatic ways. On one occasion when she was redecorating the living room at Ames, she asked me, "Marcus, does this picture look good over the couch?"

From my clueless male mind, I said, "I don't really know, Kalindi."

She responded firmly, "Marcus, your True Self knows. It can see and feel the whole room. Close your eyes and get in touch. Reclaim your connection."

I did as she asked, *"Could I connect to my True Self just like that? I trusted her, but was it actually possible?"* I went inside and felt something.

Immediately Kalindi said, "Okay, Marcus, open your eyes and tell me."

I looked at the painting. It didn't fit there. I could feel it.

Kalindi agreed, and then she asked, "Where does it fit?"

I looked around the room and, without hesitation, responded, "It belongs over by the lamp in the corner." Boom! That was it. Kalindi was pleased and I had learned a hugely valuable lesson.

We repeated this experience several times. She'd quiz me about jewelry, clothing and the like, and the answers came only when I let go of who I thought I was.

Holy Matrimony

Something else momentous happened at the Retreat. Right at the beginning, Kalindi asked if any couples wanted to be joined in Holy Matrimony – a spiritual union for men and women willing to commit to each other's freedom. Kalindi, The Lady, and Maha[1] were ordained ministers. As clergy, they could marry people, though in this situation the ceremonies were intended only to be spiritual and not legally binding.

Kalindi scheduled these weddings for the last day of the Retreat. Several couples had raised their hands and she had arranged for cakes and other celebratory accessories for these ceremonies. While preparations were being completed, Kalindi sat off to the side of the room.

Suddenly, I was overcome by this wave of desire to exchange vows with Marie. Marie had not participated in the Retreat. Kalindi had given her a personalized program of deep prayer and meditation as a way to find more opening with God.

I went to Kalindi and said, "I'd like to marry Marie."

Kalindi asked, "Does she want that with you?"

I replied, "I don't know, she's not here."

Kalindi said, "Call her."

I was elated. It felt like I had Kalindi's blessing. When I called Marie, I found her deeply immersed in the tearful prayer of "Only You, Lord, Only You."

I knew I was out of sync with her. I was too overly excited. My words poured out in a jumble. I told her what was happening and, without so much as asking how she was, blurted out, "Would you join in Holy Matrimony with me?"

After some silence, she quietly said, "No, Marcus, sorry. I can't imagine that right now. I need to stay focused on my deeper work. Marriage would only be a distraction."

---

1 Maha was Kalindi's only child. She had grown up with Gourasana and participated in the Mission from an early age. Over the years she had been groomed by Kalindi and The Lady to be their successor.

I was crushed. We talked a moment longer. It became clear she would not change her mind. When I got off the phone, I wanted to cry and hide under a rock.

Reluctantly, I went back to Kalindi and informed her about what Marie said. No doubt, I looked like a dejected puppy dog.

Without sentiment, Kalindi asked me to go and help with the rest of the preparations. Giving and service were to be my way out of this misery.

I did the best I could. For those exchanging vows, this moment was the highlight of the entire Retreat. Being near them only made me feel worse. I couldn't wait for the ceremony to end.

It did. Now it was Sunday evening and the Retreat was over. I helped to break everything down and clean up. My consciousness was in the crapper and my heart was heavy. All around me others talked about powerful and enlightening experiences they'd had. Everyone was so ebullient and all I wanted to do was go home and cry.

A couple of days later, I was still nursing my burdensome heart when I got a call from Marie. It was around 11:30 in the morning. Marie and K♪G were at the Center together. She wanted to know if I could come over right away. She wouldn't tell me why but the tone of her voice was so light and happy that I rushed into my car.

The twenty-minute drive was horrific. The whole time my mind was out of control. It kept telling me that Marie was going to break up with me. That's why she was so happy. Finally and forever, she was going to let me go. I did my best to hold my own, fighting off the negative thoughts.

Finally I arrived. When I walked in, to my surprise, there were quite a few people at the Center, including Kalindi, The Lady, and their teams.

Marie grabbed me and took me to a quiet spot. I was shaking like a leaf. She looked at me with her loving eyes and softly said, "If you still want to join together in Holy Matrimony, I'd like to have that with you."

All my fears melted away. I was like the proverbial drowning man who'd just been thrown onto shore. I hugged Marie for a long time, and then I asked, "What happened? What changed?"

Marie said, "Kalindi asked me this morning why I said No. When I responded that I didn't want to be distracted from my goal of Full Union with God, she told me that I didn't have to worry about that. There was already enough of my True Self available. Then she added that you need commitment in order to let go of your fear of losing me."

"So you're doing this for me?" I asked.

"I'm doing this for us," she responded.

I was blown away. I could not believe this was happening. I was marrying my beloved Marie! Once again, God had come through for me. Two days earlier I was crushed. Now, with God, the impossible was about to take place.

KJG knew I needed this. She was so right. My desire for Marie was great, I had no interest in other women. I was primed for commitment.

Marie and I went shopping to buy something that resembled a wedding dress. When we returned to the Center around 6pm, Kalindi had transformed the meditation room into a wedding cathedral with cakes, candles, streamers, and other accoutrements. There were some 20 people there and Kalindi told us Maha would officiate. During the brief ceremony, Maha quoted from The Prophet by Khalil Gibran, *On Love* and *On Marriage*.[1] I was in ecstasy.

The celebration was joyous and unique. It included the traditional cake-in-face action and let-go dancing, as well as Kalindi on the microphone reminding everyone that while Marie and I were joined together, she was not mine and I was not hers.

She said, "Remember, Marcus, you have no exclusive rights to Marie. She belongs to the people. She is God's Love for the people and that will never change."

---

1   Kahlil Gibran, *The Prophet,* Borzoi Books, 1923

Of course, K♪G was right. I would never own Marie. She was not mine. That was all right. Deep down I didn't want to own anybody. As long as we were together, she could do what she needed to for God.

There was no honeymoon. We had that one night together. Marie was back with Kalindi the next day. I was okay with that too. In fact, I was relieved – happy and grateful to have made this commitment. I told my family. We sent out wedding pictures.

For practical reasons we decided to get legally married. Later that week we went to City Hall. While at the courthouse, I took the opportunity to formalize my name change. And so it was that Marcus Bond officially married Marie Elaine Alire on March 30, 2000.

Married Life

Kalindi was preparing to go back to Maui. She needed to rest. Before leaving, she arranged for Marie and I to live together in the team house. We were not going with her. I was so grateful to Kalindi for giving us this time at the beginning of our marriage.

K♪G wrote me the following letter:

Dear Marcus,

You'll be on The Lady's Team and my Team. Even when you are away from me, you must make sure that I am calm. You can do that by calling me in the morning before I start my day and at the end of the day when I get ready for bed. You will help me calm down and chill out any time I call for you. The only time that is not possible is during The Intensive. You have to call me the morning The Intensive is starting and talk very sternly with me, even if I am calm and think I do not need to hear what you have to say. I have to be humble and listen. This is what you need to say to me:

"Kalindi, I am going into The Intensive with The Lady and won't be able to come help you if you get too excited or are not calm. You must use The Intensive period for complete solitude. No work. Just rest, recuperate, watch TV, exercise, play games, have some laughter with Blaise, or watch TV with Karin. If you want company, have Maha come visit you. Your secretary is available in case you want him to type something. That is all you can do until The Intensive is over, because you want me to be in that room with The Lady."

"If you don't listen to what I am saying and you start spinning around, not sleeping, working all the time, etc., then Karin is going to call me and we will talk with you and decide what we're going to do with you. Blaise will be there also and we may have to call the doctor if you won't listen."

"So, behave yourself and only do what I have said here on this list. Read this list three times per day because I'm going to manage you very tightly during The Intensive. I'll be calling you every day to check in. I'm going to be on top of you during this time. Don't forget, I am MG in a box for your safety and calm existence in this world."

KJG gave me my marching orders. I wondered if I would be able to do what she was asking. Managing and ensuring her well-being was hard enough when I was with her, let alone from 2,500 miles away. Still, I decided I would give it my best shot.

When KJG gave me guidance that pushed me beyond my comfort zone, things happened at several levels all at once. On the surface, I was given a material task – to call her and see how she was and what she was doing. On a spiritual level, I was surrendering – saying Yes to whatever she asked. On a mental level, I was pushed through my perceived limitations – forced to go deeper in order to accomplish what I thought I couldn't.

In this instance and in coordination with Karin, I managed to do quite well. KJG was able to rest and rejuvenate. During Intensives, I supported The Lady and stayed at her team house. The rest of the time, Marie and I did our service and lived together as husband and wife.

Sweet Kalindi

It was June and I was staffing The Intensive. When I was called out of The Intensive, I was surprised. The person who came to get me said, "Kalindi wants you to sing to her. She's having a hard time. She needs the comfort of hearing you sing and feeling your love."

I took a deep breath and put the phone to my ear. Kalindi was in tears. I was instantly touched and went to the deepest part of my heart.

As she cried, Kalindi said, "Please, please, Marcus, sing-sing to me. Do it now, sing-sing to me."

I started singing her name, *"Kalindi, Kalindi, Kalindi, I love you, I love you. Sweet Kalindi, I love you."* I sang it over and over, my voice soft and soothing. I started to cry.

Kalindi said, *"Please, please, Marcus, sing-sing, never not, never not. Always sing-sing to me."*

As I sang to her, I felt the energy of God lift me into a higher place. My singing became stronger. After several minutes of singing this way, Kalindi went on, asking me, *"Please Marcus, sing your love song every night on my answering machine."*

She was pleading with me, *"Please give care to Kalindi. Gourasana's Love lives in your song, great love comes from your song. Sing-sing every night by yourself to Kalindi on my answering machine. Every night, please, please. Like you sang when you were here, when K♪G had such a hard time."*
We began to sing back and forth to each other:

K♪G: *"Taking care of Kalindi, holding Kalindi. More power coming, coming, coming. Kalindi is vulnerable, Kalindi is fragile, so fragile. Kalindi withstands so much."*

Me: *"Yes, Kalindi is so fragile, fragile, fragile, so sweet, so soft, and so innocent. I hold you Kalindi in my love. I love you, I love you. Yes, Kalindi, I love to sing to you, I'm singing to you all the time. I'm singing to you every day. Holding you in my heart, in my heart is where you live. It is the greatest joy in my life to know I can do that for you every day."*

Everyone recognized that K♪G held an enormous amount of energy and power, and it was easy to forget that she was also a person and sometimes it was too much for her. Like all of us, she sometimes needed comfort and relief.

Me: *"Yes, yes, I will never stop singing to you. I am always, always, always singing to you. It is my prayer, my mantra. It is my everything, you are my everything. My love, my everything. Thank you, thank you sweet Kalindi, I love you eternally sweet Kalindi. Holding you in my heart, in my heart is where you live. Will always, always, always be singing my love for you, so you can keep going and going and going. I'll be singing to you from everywhere."*

Kalindi and I cried and sang together for another fifteen minutes on this call. Afterwards, I sang every night onto her recorder for the next six months. The devotion of singing to her every night was God's gift to me. To this day, our song and her endless love and energy lives and grows daily inside of me. ♪

Kalindi La Gourasana
Maui 2007

KALINDI LEAVES HER BODY

*"This is very different from the exoteric views of
the Spiritual Master! In the exoteric view, you merely have to
believe in Jesus (the Spiritual Master) and be a good person,
and that's enough to get you into heaven.
It is a kind of 'vicarious salvation,' where Jesus (through
his sacrifice) is presumed to have already done most of the work.
But in the esoteric view (reflected in the actual lives
of the Christian saints, rather than the churchgoers),
much more is involved.
The Spiritual Master also must be a Spiritual Transmission Master.
You need to engage in 'mystical communion' with Jesus
(by meditating on his Transmission) and take as many years or
lifetimes as is required to duplicate the Master's State –
and at long last, realize (or enter) 'Heaven'"*.

Adi Da

"None of us knew Maharaj-ji; we just knew our own projections.
But the relation with the guru is not totally our projection,
nor is it entirely created for us by the guru.
It's an interaction in the circumstances of the moment.
Your needs as a soul determine the form
of manifestation of the guru.
Of course, how the guru manifests
may not agree with your values or concept of a guru."

Ram Dass

Ten Years Later

It was Monday, April 19, 2010. I was on a world-wide conference call with hundreds of congregation members, sitting in
a large room with fifteen other disciples at a house in Colorado
Springs. Maha, Kalindi's daughter, had just told us that Kalindi La
Gourasana had left her body on Sunday, April 18. I was unable to
believe what I heard.

The week before I had been told that K♪G was not doing well, yet
there had been no hint of severity in the message I had received.
Things turned for the worse when, on Sunday, Kendra had come
to me with some disturbing news – Kalindi might have died. That
sounded absurd to me.

I called Siddhartha, her current companion. He was with her
in Maui. He assured me that Kalindi was fine. Later I learned, he
was hiding the truth.[1]

K♪G lived her life preparing for conscious departure. She
taught that spiritual life was a preparation for leaving the body
behind, and that the overall consciousness we have attained at
the time of death, determines where we go when leaving the body.

Kalindi said that spiritual life was, "About letting go and being as prepared as possible for the inevitable death of the body, which can happen at any time."

She described herself as, "God's travel agent, guiding us towards our final destination – Home." For all the years I knew Kalindi, she had lived in material and spiritual readiness to go at any time.

Kalindi spoke at length about conscious departure on a practical level. She instructed us to have our wills, healthcare directives, and all other material matters fully addressed, including instructions on what to do with our body, music to be played at our memorial service, and so on. This way, when it is time to go, we were neither held back by unfinished business, nor leaving a mess behind for our loved ones to clean up.

Like all Masters, Saints, Seers, and Mystics, she encouraged us to focus on death as a way to live fully in the ever-present now. She would say, "Focusing on death is not negative, it makes you more alive, and brings you out of denial into the present moment."

I agreed with her intellectually, though actually knowing that death could happen to me at any time was hard to realize. In fact, this truth is still difficult for me to grasp.

Kalindi La Gourasana 2008

So, as I heard Maha say, "Kalindi left her body on Sunday morning April 18, 12 hours after being admitted to the hospital on Saturday night by Dr. Tavakoli."

All I could think was, *"This can't be."*

---

1   Maha had asked that everyone who knew to not say anything about KJG's passing so she could inform the entire congregation at once on the Monday night conference call.

Our Last Time Together

Five weeks earlier, I had been walking on the beach with KJG. We were together in Maui. All was well. She was healthy and enthusiastic. There had been no real signals or warnings. I had no clue that this would be our final conversation, or the last time I would ever see her again.

I had flown with Kalindi to Maui at the end of February. Yes, KJG was in need of rest and recuperation. But then these times were normal with her. She had spent the last six months working assiduously with her spiritual and organizational leaders.

Everything was now in place for the smooth running of the Mission for her upcoming five-year seclusion. Kalindi had covered every base. She had made sure that everyone and everything was taken care of before she went into deep retreat.

KJG had been talking about going into seclusion for years. As the time approached, everyone close to her knew that letting go of everything was going to be challenging. Her plan was to retreat to an undisclosed location, and to stay there with a small crew with no contact with her disciples or the organization until 2016.

When we first arrived in Maui, the plan was for several weeks of R&R. Kalindi needed to recuperate before making final arrangements for her seclusion. She was staying at an oceanfront condo in North Kihei, with her business secretary and communicator at her side, to finalize the severing of her involvement with the organization.

I stayed at Kalindi's house in Maui Meadows with the other team members. I was scheduled to leave on a red-eye flight the night of March 13, returning to Colorado Springs at KJG's request to help update the manual used by those caring for her.

On the afternoon of my flight, KJG invited me to spend time with her. When I arrived, she looked spry and fit and immediately asked if I wanted to walk on the beach with her. I eagerly agreed.

As we walked out the sliding glass door, she turned to me and said, **"Marcus, you have to start writing the book. We are about to head into a whole new chapter."** I nodded my head, thinking the new chapter she was talking about was her upcoming seclusion.

For the past five years, KJG had been talking to me about writing a book about my experiences with her. She was right, I had seen her in virtually all of her manifestations during the years we had together.

At the same time, I didn't know how I would fulfill her request. I didn't know anything about writing a book and had never imagined undertaking such an endeavor. Not to mention that between my service work with KJG and coaching work to support myself financially, there was no space available in my psyche or in my calendar for writing a book.

As I followed KJG out to the beach, I thought, *"Well, maybe while she's in seclusion I could start it."* It was a beautiful spring day in Maui. We walked up and down the beach, turning around every 10 minutes or so. KJG was relaxed and in high spirits. She talked about how well she felt and how relieved she was to be emptying out all Mission business. She wanted nothing left inside of her.

As we turned back towards the condo, KJG stopped. I leaned in to hear her words above the ocean breeze. She looked at me emphatically and said, "Now that you have finally let go and stepped into your destiny, your transformation can really take off now."

It was gratifying to hear this affirmation. KJG did not readily lavish praise of this nature. I knew she was referring to my recent decision to walk away from my current business and return to manage her team and accompany her into seclusion for the next five years.

This was my deepest and most significant surrender yet. I was willingly choosing to give the next five years of my life to my Master, stepping away from my personal and professional life.

This time, saying Yes to KJ'G required continual letting go of the part of my ego that knows, specifically, what I thought would happen from me saying Yes to these five years. I believed I would have to give up everything. It felt so final, with no escape or back doors possible.

When I participated last November in a seminar led by The Lady, I was able to clearly see the part my ego played in all of this; and that my thoughts about the future were worthless, negative, fear-producing make-believe that I conjured out of thin air.

Where was my trust and faith? When had Kalindi ever disappointed me? How much more did God have to give me before I realized this was what there was for me to do? After the seminar, and consistently until our last time together when KJ'G would ask me if I was on-board, I would say Yes. I would gulp, take a breath, and say Yes.

This Yes was such a huge let-go and surrender for me that it propelled me forward accordingly. And, as it turned out, it wasn't what I thought anyway. It turned out that God had other plans.

Two Weeks Earlier

When I left Maui in March, KJ'G and I agreed that I would return to Maui on April 17, 2010, and that would be it. Two weeks before that, while in Colorado Springs, Siddhartha and I received a phone call from Ginny in Maui.

Ginny filled us in on what had been happening during the last couple of weeks. As KJ'G let go of her role in the organization and her spiritual leadership, more of Gourasana's full Presence and Energy had entered her.

KJ'G called The Lady, asking her to come to Maui. Once she arrived, The Lady jumped right in as KJ'G downloaded information and guidance into her.

Ginny said that, "At some level, it felt like she was handing over the reins rather than going into a five-year seclusion."

348

Ginny told us, "While Dr. T and the rest of us wanted her to rest her body, the energy was overriding anything happening on a physical level. We were concerned because, when she was containing so much energy, she might not sense when her physical systems were out of balance."

Just as I began to be concerned, Ginny told us, "No need to be too concerned. Dr. Tavakoli is onsite and monitoring her closely."

Still, all this was perplexing. We discussed it for a while and then, at the end of the call, Ginny said, "Marcus, we think you should come over. That might be comforting for her."

I don't know why but, without thinking I said, "I think Siddhartha should go." I looked at Siddhartha. He replied, "Yes, I will go."

When Siddhartha arrived a couple of days later, he reported, "When I first arrived, The Lady was still there. K♪G, out of her great love for all of us and with great intensity, was preaching and speaking non-stop to move the illusion."

"As soon as The Lady left, she went into an open-ended release from every attachment she ever had. It was a clear and purposeful surrender. It was as if she heard from God that it was her time to let go now."

He added, "Once this shift occurred, she stopped talking and interacting with anyone. When we brought her food and drink, she looked at me with an expression that asked, "Why are you bothering?""

"We don't really know or understand what is happening with her. Still, her nervous system was getting maxed out, so it is good she is resting quietly."

No one knew it but K♪G's death process had begun. Instead of recuperating, her health deteriorated. She became bed-ridden. Her organs were not doing well. Dr. T tried to handle her deteriorating health at home. He put her on IV's and personally monitored her levels. K♪G asked him not to send her to the hospital. She warned that if he did so, she would surely die.

In the week before Kalindi's death, her entire care team went into radio silence. Too many rumors could get started. It was better to say nothing at all. The team focused on being there for her as K♪G entered this quiet stillness and continued letting go into whatever was happening.

Physically, what was happening was medically alarming. Within a few days, Dr. T knew he could no longer take care of K♪G at home. Despite her warnings, he called for an ambulance to take her to the hospital. As soon as she was put in the ambulance, her vital signs plunged to dangerously low levels.

The Emergency Room doctors were at a loss. They did not know how to help her. Every major organ was shutting down and all their interventions failed. No matter the protocol used, her body was unresponsive. K♪G refused all pain medication, and spent the night in her hospital bed with one or two caregivers present.[1] Everyone present sensed she was dying and no one could help her.

For years, Kalindi had said she would choose her moment of death just as Jesus had his. That moment came in the morning. Monique was holding her hand, standing at her side.

From Monique, "That morning, I sat alone in the room with Kalindi, singing softly to her for an hour or so. At some point, I sat on the chair next to her and kissed her hand, in my mind saying, 'Goodbye.'"

"In the next moment, the warning bells went off on every machine in the room. The nurse in the room witnessed that the moment I kissed her goodbye, all of her vital signs flat-lined simultaneously."[2]

Just like that, K♪G was gone.

After Kalindi's Passing

With Kalindi, I knew I was where I was supposed to be, and that I was doing exactly what I was supposed to be doing. I was at the right place at the right time and I could relax without questioning myself.

If there was anything off, she would tell me, and I would correct it. After so many years together, it was that 'simpatico' between us. Giving to her and loving her was my entire job. From being with her, not only was I safe, I was contributing to the overall consciousness of mankind.

KJG was the focal point of my life. Now I had lost the most important person in the world to me. She was everything – Master, Guide, Teacher, champion for my soul's desire, enabler of my True Self, protector, friend, lover, and companion.

For many years, she had acted on behalf of my spiritual being more than I. She held and carried my very desire for God – not letting go until I could feel and hold it myself.

With her in the world, I knew I was safe. She was my compass of light; always beckoning me closer to the Truth. Now she was gone and I was alone. **Or maybe I wasn't?**

The next morning, while still in a fog of disbelief, Kendra came into my room. Her eyes were swollen from crying all night. I broke through my denial and fell to my knees. Kendra held me as tears of sorrow and loss poured out.

That whole week, and many times since then, I would be taken over by enormous grief, sadness, and loss as my realization of her being gone physically would sink in at ever-deepening levels. Usually this wellspring of emotion would emerge after I saw that I was holding on to who I thought KJG had been, missing the ever-changing and ever-present flow of her energy now.

---

1 Ginny, Siddhartha and Monique rotated throughout the night. Monique had been Kalindi's main caregiver since 2001 after Karin had gone to Germany to support the disciples there.

2 The ER Nurse said that she had never seen that happen before. That usually there is a sequential shutting down of organ systems.

I couldn't grasp the emptiness. How could she go so soon? K♪G had been destined for a long life. She told us this herself. Sometimes even Masters don't know.

During the next weeks, as I helped to close her personal affairs, I also became aware of being filled with both her love and energy. Somehow, even more of Kalindi was available now than when she was in a body. She had become like Gourasana. Her presence seemed to concentrate in ways it hadn't when in the body. My purely energetic connection with Gourasana now included Kalindi. It was true what I had read – that the energy of a Master does increase when no longer confined by the body.

Early on, I had gone through a transformation from personal to impersonal love for K♪G. At first, we had shared this physically intimate, emotional, romantic kind of loving that on my part included so many illusory habits, concepts, and beliefs.

Then our love became less passionate and more impersonal. God's Love is more about soul matters along with basic human love, care, and respect. It is encompassing and therefore univer- salizes even the most personal forms of love. There were times when I came to feel closer to K♪G when away from her, rather than at her side. It was like my five senses were now out of the way. The deeper joy of Divine Love would sometimes get lost inside the sensory enjoyment I found in her company.

When I was with her in the body, I experienced her on many levels. Sometimes she was so spiritually heavy, so deep, that I felt myself in free-fall depth as in some trough of the ocean. At other times she was gloriously light and loving. She could be playful and innocent like a small child one moment, moving from intense concern to indifference in an instant. Her personality was more like the weather – in constant change rather than attached to itself.

Simultaneous with whatever transpired personally, there was this palpable power: His Presence. I could see and feel it in her body. It was manifest. I came to know it as the Light and Love of God.

One time when Kalindi was off to Maui and I was staying behind, I drove her to the airport. At the curb, I whimpered in her ear, "I'm going to miss you." She pulled back and looked me in the eye asking, "Why? I'm not going anywhere."

She exposed my sentimentality, and let me know that **love based on physical proximity** was a limited concept of the mind. Like so much else, it could be transcended.

K♪G is no longer bound by time and space. She is now both in God and this world. Her energy remains as present as ever. Since her death, I have felt her very much with me. Although the physical connection is gone and only memories are left of our physical relationship, Kalindi La Gourasana is vibrantly alive in me.

Whether or not on this physical plane, K♪G is still transmuting my karma and illusions to speed up my liberation – the one caveat being that I have to continually quiet my mind and stay connected within to allow it to happen.

2000 to 2005

This book covers the three years spent with K♪G from 1997 to 2000. During this time, my mind was blown and my soul uplifted. Looking back, it was a virtually non-stop, break-free scene, especially during 1998 and 1999 when she changed from Kalindi to Kalindi La♪ to K♪G, sloughing off who she had been like clothes that no longer fit. As a newcomer, I was swept into some of the most potent spiritual work happening on the planet.

It has taken me three years and seventy-five percent of this book to share those three years with you. We will see if He plans for me to write a second book. Certainly the material is there. So much took place in her final decade of life.

The years between 2000 and 2003 were very difficult for me in my transformation. In mid-2002, during a financial squeeze, I volunteered to come off paid staff in order to help reduce costs for the organization.

The following year, as I launched a new version of a Coaching and Consulting firm with a former colleague, I reached a crucial point in my transformation. This shift manifested from an interaction with K♪G at her house in Maui.

K♪G's house had an outside gym open on three sides. The wind-blown red dirt of Kihei accumulated rapidly. My job was to clean it each day prior to Kalindi's exercise time. Never really knowing when she might wish to work out, I cleaned it several times each day.

I felt useless as I wiped down the dust-covered barbells. Then I grew alert when I heard K♪G's car coming up the driveway. I got scared and wanted to hide. I did not want her to see me. As was often the case back then, I thought she was having negative, judgmental thoughts about me.

I was relieved when K♪G and her sister got out of the car and went into the house. For a moment I thought I was in the clear. I went back to the negative thoughts spinning around in my head.

In mid-conversation with myself, K♪G's sister appeared and said, "Hi Marcus, Kalindi asked me to come tell you that **she loves you.**"

Right then, the illusion's control of my mind fell away and my heart opened!

Then she continued, "Also, she was wondering why you were hiding behind that tree?"

God Bam!

I had to laugh, not only at myself but at the whole sad, absurd, mental reality I lived with. Then it really hit me – as a deep realization – that I was the only one thinking those things. K♪G never saw me in that way. It was only me. These were my projections. This was my hell and no one else resided there. And yet, some part of me always found it hard to believe that she didn't see me that way. How crazy-making is that?

I remembered my Uncle Lew saying. "The ego is mad. It thinks everyone is thinking about you when, in truth, they are thinking about you thinking about them. Almost everyone is too self-absorbed in their own thoughts and projections to give a damn about you. We are all insane."

Man, he got that right!

Kalindi loved me completely. Regardless of my thoughts, feelings, and self-judgments, she loved me. My awareness crackled. I shifted the focus of my thoughts — from my pity-party to her exalted, unconditional love. In this state I experienced God's love for me and then, quite miraculously, my own self-love.

This experience jolted me towards knowing that God's Love is constant and unconditional. To this day, my mind will argue that I can lose love. I can build scenarios when this or that happens and make a case for being unlovable, but such thoughts no longer own me. The shackles have come off. The illusion no longer rules my house of love.

In 2003, my relationship with Marie changed as well. This change began when Kalindi arranged for us to live together. She wanted us to have more stable and consistent time together. Other than traveling with her to Munich for three months in the summer, Kalindi stopped including me in her travel plans.

I was grateful for this opportunity. Marie and I had continued to have an up-and-down relationship with one another. I still could not fully feel that Marie loved me or that she desired to stay by my side. I needed constant reassurance. My feelings of abandonment from childhood had driven me to build a case of unworthiness so deeply embedded that **I was convinced I was unlovable.**

Marie would say, "It's up to you, Marcus. I am here with all my love. Now you have to let it in."

Marcus and Marie 2003

I wasn't capable. I had begun to feel the Love of God within and therefore became less dependent on Marie as my source of love and fulfillment, yet I still couldn't let her love in … until one day when the walls simply collapsed. This occurred during a particularly powerful interaction. My heart opened all the way and I felt all of Marie's love.

She made me look at her and then whispered, "I'm here with you. You don't have to struggle or feel alone. Please let me in."

I mumbled, "But it's not safe to be vulnerable."

She purred, "That's OK, Marcus, I love you anyway."

That was it. Her pure words penetrated my heart and I started weeping. As we sat on the bedroom floor, I felt her love for me as much as my love for her. For the first time in my life, I experienced the love that came from God in meditation inside a man/woman relationship.

Marie was elated for me. Finally, I had dropped the walls around my heart. It was as if my soul could now check this box as done.

And done it was because, unexpectedly, this experience proved to be the beginning of the end of our relationship. A new door had opened within me. It was difficult to grasp, understand, or believe but my overriding need to feel loved by a woman was dissipating.

I was coming to realize that some totality of experience was all inside of me – the love I felt for and from Marie, the sexual ecstasy and pleasure, the entire man-woman experience – all of it was inside of me. The illusions I had about women were starting to dissolve and therefore my constant 'need' for a woman was fading away as my freedom of choice increased.

It took two years before Marie and I felt our relationship was complete. It had served its purpose. In mid-2005, we mutually agreed to let the relationship go. We separated in love and remain close friends today.

2006 to Early 2010

As late as 2005, when there was still the hint of a personal relationship, Kalindi would tell me I could leave her at any time. When I protested, swearing my allegiance, she would smile and say, "I've heard it all before, Marcus. You could leave both me and the Mission."

When I objected even more vehemently, she replied, "I know the power of the Illusion, Marcus. It can turn anyone away from God, away from Kalindi. There are so many who profess their undying love, devotion, and commitment, then turn away in denial, judgment, and blame."

She was right about the others. I had to acquiesce. As in all other areas, she had no illusions around loyalty or commitment. Besides, I had personally seen some of her closest and most dedicated disciples turn away from her. Even though I felt 100% sure, what did I really know?

Sometimes KᴊG would talk about the Mission dissolving and that she would carry on with the few who remained. She asked me if I was one of these. She wanted to know if I would follow her anywhere.

I always said Yes, even though I knew I would never make it Home by hanging onto her pajama pants. As time went on, I came to an ever-deeper commitment as her disciple. I wasn't going anywhere. In my heart and soul this was true for me.

From 2006 to 2010 were the years during which all my endeavor started coming to fruition. I was stronger and clearer in myself, with God, and with the world. Being less self-absorbed, I was able to become more present and felt more solidly alive.

As I cast aside any sense of abandonment, my feeling of dread dissipated. Joy took its place. God became my foundational rock. I knew I would always be okay – no matter what.

As I surrendered to Kalindi as my Master, my internal attachments and fears began to fall away. It was a natural process of seeing what kept me separate from love and therefore her, and letting it go.

These experiences helped me to learn how to have oneness with others. When not guarded, afraid or attached, I could release my separateness, let it fall, and enter into a kind of liquid merging with other beings. For me, this remains an exquisite by-product of my time with KJG.

In 2007, while living in Colorado Springs, I was with KJG in her cottage. She sat in her favorite zero-gravity chair. I knelt on the floor in my usual place on the left side of her chair. We had been in quiet conversation for some time. There was a pause in our exchange. KJG closed her eyes.

Kalindi and Marcus
outside Taco Bell

I was in this constant loop of inquiry back then. What had at first interested me had become a terrible weight. I kept asking, *"Why me? Who am I to be so close with this incredible spiritual Master? Why would God choose me?"*

I knew these questions were about unworthiness. I could not stop believing that there were so many other people more qualified and better suited, and that there was nothing special about me.

I, too, closed my eyes and tried to relax into silence while always ready to follow her next cue. In this state, a realization flashed in my head and a knowing rose from deep inside me. God chose me. I said Yes. It was as simple as that.

My heart was drawn to love Kalindi. My spiritual desire and practices allowed me to serve her with fewer and fewer reservations. She accepted me without judgment or blame. She and I shared an intimate connection. I was neither more special nor less special than anyone, but I was with her and she wanted me there. This realization felt like my essence. I had read that Self-Realization comes when we learn who we are in God. That's what was happening to me. I was realizing my True Self.

It was in this energy that Kalindi lived. She was who she was in an endless string of Now. She just kept going in the **Infinite Now.**

I remember one time, in a hotel room, while I sat on one bed, she knelt on the other. She was in the act of letting go of who she thought she was. As soon as one identity was released and another self came in, she let that one go as well. She began to let go so fast that she was unable to keep up.

She started shaking her head, making unintelligible sounds, like 'bleep, bop, boob, ha, hey, heh, etc.' She put her head down on the bed. Then I started feeling different energies in the room and began to assign names to them – Krishna, Buddha, Jesus ... I seemed to recognize the energies. They came clearly, like different tastes of the same water.

After a while, K♪G quieted. As she calmed, the energy in the room settled. When I asked if she could talk about what had happened, she said, "He was changing me so rapidly I could not keep up with the realizations and changes. After that I had to let go of realizing all together. Only the energy mattered. That's when I put my head down."

When I mentioned Krishna, Buddha, and Jesus, she said, "Yes, they are here with Gourasana. You recognize their energy because you were with each of them during their incarnations on Earth."[1]

"I was with them? I was in their company?" I liked that. I particularly resonated with Buddha and Jesus, and then recalled the depth of devotion and love I had experienced at a Hare Krishna festival in Venice Beach, California.

---

1 "... An Avatar (Perfect Being) appears on Earth every 700-1400 years and is 'brought down' into human form by the five Perfect Masters of the time to aid in the process of moving creation in its never-ending journey toward Godhood. In other ages this role was fulfilled by Rama, Krishna, Buddha, Jesus, and Muhammad. Meher Baba, *The Path of Love*, Sheriar Press, US, 2000.

Kalindi La Gourasana 2008

My soul was always open to God and Kalindi. My willingness was not about being well-trained or best-suited; it was about living from that depth of truth. From this place, I realized how God sees me and that Self-realization is indeed the same as God-realization.[1]

KJG continued to change during this period. The shape of her face and body took on more of the features and size of Gourasana. Each year there was less 'sweet Kalindi energy' and more of a masculine, father-like Presence.

My role with Kalindi also changed. I became less of a caregiver and more of a friend and companion. Whenever she needed to chill out, she would call me to join her. Sometimes we shared living quarters; at other times, I lived close by and available.

She set me up to work on personal projects such as her music and video library. I always handled travel logistics for her and her entourage. Occasionally, she would task me to spearhead an organizational project, but mostly she kept me out of the business side of things. That way she would not be tempted to talk with me about organizational matters when we were together.

What Now?

With KJG gone, it was up to me to keep going and put into practice what she had given to me. I would no longer be at her side. She would no longer point out my illusions, corral my ego, or guide me towards the light.

Even so, I would keep on. I would continue to deepen and develop my connection to God and to my beloved KJG, who had freed my heart and consciousness from so many shackles of illusion. I stayed on her path of 100% willing surrender. She was still my spiritual force of Love.

Even though my Master was gone, and I now found myself in the same boat as many others whose Masters have left their bodies, I was also aware that now it was up to me to be fully responsible for my spiritual life.

Kalindi Watching Over Me

I learned to be guided by Kalindi from within, like so many who never had a personal relationship with her, yet who had been deeply touched and guided by her from the subtle plane. I now came to trust what happened to me when I sought out her energy in meditation and life.

As new experiences presented themselves, I would ask, *"How would K♪G guide me here?"* Using the radar of my heart and seeking purity and truth, I would ask myself, *"Does it feel right?"* And then I would wait for an answer.

I was looking for an energetic stamp of approval. I would tune into the place where I found God in myself and wait to feel an energetic harmony. Then I would start to feel Kalindi's love as though she was coming closer to me. I would even be flooded with love for myself. I noticed that the more K♪G drew close to me, the more my actions came from love. I would also listen carefully, using discernment to hear the whispers. As much as I could, I stayed away from my mind with its judgments and evaluations. I was using 'Smart Faith' – faith plus intelligence. Over time, I developed greater and greater discrimination in my awareness and heart.

---

1 "Self-realization and God-realization occur simultaneously." Gourasana, 1991

In the fall of 2010, I moved to Munich, Germany, to continue my work in the Mission as organizational liaison, assistant, and communicator for Jim St James (the 3rd in line from Gourasana).

By the summer of 2012, two years after KJG passed, my heart and awareness were more connected. I had sufficient control of my mind to significantly reduce my mental suffering.

I could accept what was inevitable – the physical aches and pains, illness and disease, old age and dying. These eventualities are unavoidable and therefore must be weathered. However, the mind-fuck, along with its endless loop of ego-driven concepts and beliefs, were unnecessary. Gratefully, with each passing year, I was attaining greater control of my being – senses, emotions and thoughts – and finding the peace and depth I had always longed for. Slowly my mind was being mastered and my thoughts were becoming my friends.

Kalindi continues to act as a mirror for my soul and, at the same time, reflects back where my impurities and attachments hide out. She remains my example of what is possible in a human being. Not that I could ever become her. She was a unique phenomenon – a vast, still pool that reflected back God's Love and showed me that it is possible to find Home in this lifetime. Indeed, I am more aware of limitless possibility inside of me.

During the thousands of hours I sat in KJG's vibrational field, I rarely accessed her levels of consciousness. Even so, she always took me to the highest level of which I was capable, and at times I could at least intuit her exalted vibration.

I like to think I could be with KJG at a higher level today – closer still to where she always wanted me to be, and able to be present, to share, to give, and to exchange ever greater love with her.

During the last five years, I have also focused on tuning into The Lady. While I continue to feel Gourasana and Kalindi very strongly, being in The Lady's presence – her awareness, consciousness, love and mastery – helps hold me snugly in the Vortex of all three of their energies.

I am grateful that The Lady has weathered all the storms and continues to carry Gourasana's and Kalindi's Mission forward. I feel blessed to be on The Lady's radar. I hope I will never be foolish enough to think I can find my way all the way Home without some living guide. Her consciousness elevates mine

The Lady 2014

and clearly shows me where my gaps exist and how I am not yet awakened in entire areas. I am also thrilled to be cultivating the spiritual friendship with her that God intends us to have.

Divine Relationship

Two years after KJG passed, the desire to write this book became overpowering. I threw myself into the unknown project, feeling her presence and energy moving me forward.
I gave KJG control of the undertaking, and found yet another level of being with her. After all, I had no idea how to write a book. I certainly felt guided by her – the timing, the words, the content, and the money – even the choice of Joseph Gunnels as my writing guide came from her. She clearly brought everything I needed to complete this endeavor.

My relationship to KJG has evolved into that of the watcher and the watched. Everything I do, everything I think, and everything I feel is experienced against the backdrop of her watching over me. Her constant and powerful presence as my Master tacitly creates ongoing radical changes in my awareness which, in turn, lead me toward an ever-deepening spirituality. Her enduring presence, wisdom, and expansiveness keep me well-situated in the passing show that is my life.

When I turn to K♪G now, I immediately go right to God (which makes sense given what she said she was – a doorway or gateway to The Almighty). This is my real experience now. When I feel stuck or my faith weakens, I tune in to that place within where Kalindi and Gourasana reside in my soul. I am then flooded with love, awareness, and a sense of being held.

K♪G always reminds me to trust. She is my signal that everything is inextricably connected in a grand plan. Often, during the writing of this book when I felt unsure or disconnected, I had to stop until I reconnected to her presence. As I situated myself, she would come as a welcome intrusion into my everyday life, like a manifestation of Grace.

As I approach the end of this book, I am recalled to my first Intensive when I declared that all I wanted was to love and be loved. Declaring my desire was one thing, feeling that desire in my heart and bones was something else again. When I started my path, I wanted Real Love. I got what I came for. I have found it and my quest for more will continue until my last breath.

It is with true satisfaction that I fulfill K♪G's wish for me to write this book. Perhaps I will write another, perhaps not. Either way, I will never really finish writing or talking about her. Whatever the future holds, I remain in an eternal dialogue with her until my last breath.

Our love affair continues … ♪

Marcus Bond

Boulder, Colorado
December, 2015

AN INVITATION

Now that we've been on this intimate journey together, I'd love to hear from you. If you want to share any of your insights, aspirations, experiences, breakthroughs or realizations, feel free to contact me at marcus@miracle.org. I will read your email and respond to you.

In addition, I offer one-on-one spiritual and business coaching, mentoring, and counseling for any life changes or goals you want to accomplish. If you desire this type of assistance you can email me at marcus@miracle.org.

By your Side
with Love and Grace,

Marcus Bond, Ph.D.
Boulder, Colorado

CENTER OF THE GOLDEN ONE®
CONTACT INFORMATION

Kalindi's teachings are available through The Center of The Golden One. The Center, founded in 1991, was named after a current-day Incarnation of God, Lord Gourasana, The Golden One.

The Center has a worldwide network of centers and communities that offer meditations and spiritual programs to help people come closer to God.

Kalindi's books, lectures and talks are available through the Center's Bookstore online at:

store.centerofthegoldenone.com

You can learn more about the many offerings (Seminars, Workshops, Programs, and Meditations) available through The Center of the Golden One Worldwide at:

centerofthegoldenone.com

ACKNOWLEDGEMENTS

I would like to express my love and appreciation to my mother and father who have always whole-heartedly loved and supported me and my endeavors and desires, no matter what twists and turns came with my choices. Like my parents, my wonderful brother and sisters have always been there for me. I've been blessed by the love of friends, lovers, and wives – even when the form of our relationships changed.

I am particularly grateful for Joseph Gunnels who helped me learn how to write. He guided me and held my hand, showing me how to find my authentic voice. He encouraged and acknowledged, and then criticized and pushed, when I struggled at diving deep enough to find that bed of pearls seeded by Kalindi. His own depth and spiritual connection sprang like a river, giving me needed respite from the ever-deepening flow of this unique story.

My deep appreciation goes to the Munich community who supported and loved me during my years abroad – Marianne, Sybille, Jürgen, Siegmar, Josef, Gabriela, Carol, Christian, Jim, Beate, Barbara, Alex, Gali, Torsten, Vero, Brigitte, Hans Jo, Charlotte, Karin, Marie, Katrin, Doris, Claus, Lucas, and all the others I have not named.

Sybille Paskuda was by my side the whole time, both energetically and by providing grounded editorial support. God Bless her always!

I would like to offer my to indebtedness to Darrin Zeer, Karen Tenney, Alison Adler, Jim St James, Tristan Gribbin, David Resnick, Tara Rose, Jeff Owens, and many others who provided important feedback on the manuscript throughout the entire process.

Marlowe Kayce and Sophie Simmons generously provided all the necessary proof-reading and copy editing. It was a pleasure to be corrected by both.

My deepest, heartfelt gratitude to The Lady for her unwavering support, enthusiasm, and inspiration throughout the process; she was the wind beneath my wings.

To Michele Campbell for her weekly project management calls and encouragement; and to Sylvia Litchfield for her inspirational accounting help;

To Tara Rose for her emotional and administrative support to bring this project to completion;

To Desiree Luth for her assistance, wisdom, and understanding about what goes in to publishing and marketing a book;

To Amundi Sigurdsson for his extraordinary patience, design skills, and love of Kalindi, as witnessed by the beautiful front and back covers;

To Dirk Gräßle for his patient interior formatting help;

To Josef Schweihofer who inspired me to invite people to pre-order the book even before its completion.

My special thanks and deep gratitude go to Marilyn Bond, Alan and Judy Brostoff, Barbara and Alex Saager, Jim St James, Deborah Byers, Marianne Ten Cate, Jan Kleinlangevelsloo, Petra Bartscherer, Tara Rose, Sheryl Dvorin, and the many others who provided financial contributions.

Great appreciation goes to Darrin Zeer for his awesome Foreword, as well as The Lady, J.M. Sandlow, Joe Sugarman, and Neelama Eyres for their powerful endorsement quotes.

Much appreciation goes to Leslie McDonald, Monique Jaspers, and Minka St James for the hands-on care and assistance with all of Kalindi's photos.

Thank you to David Kramer, J.M. Sandlow, Tamara La Toto, and Center of The Golden One® for granting permission to include its many quoted teachings, materials, and photos.

Finally, I wish to thank "The Core" – those who were the first to gather around David Swanson and Carol Seidman in the Presence of The Lord.

REFERENCES

In Order of Appearance:

Sri Chinmoy, *The Wisdom of Sri Chinmoy,* Blue dove Press, 2000

Richard Rohr, *Immortal Diamond: The Search for Our True Self,* Jossey-Bass, 2013

Margery Williams, *The Velveteen Rabbit,* Doubleday, Reprint 1991

Rabindranath Tagore, *The Religion of Man,* Macmillan, 1930

Hermann Hesse, *Journey to the East,* Picador, Reprint edition, 2003

Søren Kierkegaard, *Fear and Trembling,* Princeton University Press, 1983

Colgrove, McWilliams & Bloomfield, *How to Survive the Loss of a Love,* Bantam, 1977

M. Scott Peck, *The Road Less Traveled: A New Psychology of Love, Traditional Values and Spiritual Growth,* Touchstone, 1988

Sheldon B. Kopp, *If You Meet the Buddha on the Road, Kill Him! The Pilgrimage of Psychotherapy Patients,* Bantam Books, 1976

Paul Reps, *Zen Flesh, Zen Bones,* Shambala, 1994

Shunryu Suzuki, *Zen Mind, Beginner's Mind,* Shambala, 2011

Ram Dass, *Be Here Now,* Lama Foundation, 1978

Osho, *I Am That, Both and More,* Jaico, 2009

Bhagwan Shree Rajneesh (Osho), *The Sound of One Hand Clapping,* Ma Yoga Laxmi Rajneesh Foundation, 1st edition 1981

Ram Dass and Rameshwar Das, *Polishing the Mirror: How to Live from Your Spiritual Heart,* Sounds True, 2014

Kalindi, *Introduction Talk to the Love's Awakening Seminar,* January 16, 1993

Gourasana, *Breaking the Cycle of Birth and Death* (San Diego: Miracle of Love, 2001) quotes #38, #100, #249 and #319

Adi Da Samraj, *The Knee Of Listening: The Divine Ordeal of the Avataric Incarnation of Conscious Light: The Spiritual Auto-biography,* The Dawn Horse Press; Revised edition, 2004

Swami Chinmayananda, *Narada Bhakti Sutra,* Chinmaya Mission, 1990

The Lady, *Listening for the Whispers of God in Only You: Uncompromising Truth and Love* series of talks. San Diego: Miracle of Love, 2004

Kalindi, *The Female Phenomenon,* an unpublished booklet, San Diego: Miracle of Love, 1997

Kalindi La Gourasana, *Love God, Love Yourself and Love Each Other* booklet in *Come into the Light and Stay in the Light* series, San Diego: Miracle of Love, 2008

Calm in Gourasana, a drawing by Ginny Robinson for Kalindi. San Diego: Miracle of Love, 1994

Eben Alexander, M.D., *Proof of Heaven: A Neurosurgeon's Journey into the Afterlife,* Simon & Schuster, 2012

Kalindi La Gourasana, *Ultimate Freedom: Union with God,* San Diego: Miracle of Love, 1998

Ram Dass and Rameshwar Das, *Be Love Now: The Path of the Heart,* Harper Collins, 2010

Gourasana, *The Radical Path Home to God,* San Diego: Miracle of Love, First Edition, 2008, pages 12, 344, 404

Christopher Isherwood, *Ramakrishna and His Disciples,* Vedanta Press and Bookshop, 1965

Anandamayi Ma and Joseph Fitzgerald, *The Essential Sri Anandamayi Ma: Life and Teaching of a 20th Century Indian Saint,* World Wisdom, 2007

Ken Wilber, *A Theory of Everything: An Integral Vision for Business, Politics, Science, and Spirituality,* Shambhala Publications, 2000

François Fénelon, *The Complete Fenelon,* Paraclete Press, 2008

James Steinberg, *Divine Distraction: A Guide to the Guru-Devotee Relationship,* The Dawn Horse Press, 1991

Gopi Krishna, *Kundalini: The Evolutionary Energy in Man,* Shambhala, 1997

Irina Tweedie, *Daughter of Fire: A Diary of a Spiritual Training with a Sufi Master,* The Golden Sufi Center, 1995

Raj Pruthi, *Vedic Civilization,* Discovery Publishing House, 2004

C. B. Purdom, *The God Man: The Life, Journeys and Work of Meher Baba,* Sheriar Foundation, 1971

Chogyam Trungpa, *Cutting Through Spiritual Materialism,* Shambhala Classics, 2002

Paramahansa Yogananda, *Autobiography of a Yogi,* The Philosophical Library, 1946

Ramana Maharshi, *The Spiritual Teaching of Ramana Maharshi,* Shambala, 2004

Kalindi La Gourasana, *Material Self versus True Self* in Golden Information series of talks. San Diego: Miracle of Love, 1998

Kalindi La Gourasana, *The Divine Grace of Efficient Living and the Disciplined Lifestyle for Spiritual Transformation,* San Diego: Miracle of Love, 1999

Katarina Sky, Photo Card of *The Beloved,* Katarina Fidel Inspired Photography, 1997

The Heavenly Host of Light Beings, a drawing by Ginny Robinson for Gourasana, San Diego: Miracle of Love, 1994

Berthold Madhukar Thompson, *The Odyssey of Enlightenment: Rare Interviews with Enlightened Teachers of Our Time,* Wisdom Editions, 2002

Neale Donald Walsh, *God's Message to the World: You've Got Me All Wrong,* Rainbow Ridge Books, 2014

Kalindi La Gourasana, *Illusory Love Binds You, Love of God Frees You* workbook in the *Listen, Say Yes and Act* series, San Diego: Miracle of Love, 1998

Kalindi La Gourasana, *Cry of the Soul* in Golden Information series of talks. San Diego: Miracle of Love, 1998

Meher Baba, *The Path of Love,* Sheriar Foundation, 2000

The Lady, *Quote from The Lady for Kalindi,* San Diego: Miracle of Love, 1997

Ramachandra Dattatrya Ranade, *The Constructive Survey of Upanishadic Philosophy,* Bharatiya Vidya Bhavan, 1926